# IN WHOSE
# INTERESTS

PATRICIA MARCHAK

# IN WHOSE INTERESTS

*An Essay on Multinational Corporations in a Canadian Context*

McCLELLAND AND STEWART

McClelland and Stewart Limited
*The Canadian Publishers*
25 Hollinger Road
Toronto, Ontario
M4B 3G2

Canadian Cataloguing in Publication Data

Marchak, M. Patricia, 1936-
  In whose interests?

Bibliography: p.
Includes index.
ISBN 0-7710-5488-2

1. International business enterprises.
2. Corporations, Foreign — Canada. I. Title.
HD69.I7M3  *1979*  338.8'8    C79-094066-3

60,629

The quotation from George Strauss is reprinted
from "Tactics of Lateral Relationship: The
Purchasing Agent" by George Strauss published
in *Administrative Science Quarterly*, vol. 7, no.
2 (9/62) by permission of *The Administrative
Science Quarterly*, © 1962.

Printed and bound in Canada by Webcom Ltd.

# CONTENTS

# LIST OF TABLES

# LIST OF FIGURES

# ACKNOWLEDGMENTS

I am indebted to three colleagues whose criticisms and comments on drafts of this book have gone beyond duty and friendship. They are Martin Meissner at the University of British Columbia, Wallace Clement at McMaster, and Craig McKie in Ottawa. The final manuscript, while not meeting all of their criticisms or incorporating all of their excellent suggestions, is undoubtedly a better one because of their contributions.

I am also indebted to typists who worked on early drafts, including Lorraine LeMieux, Ellena Jamal, and Maureen Skuce. Peter Saunders and Diana Swift, of McClelland and Stewart, have been both encouraging and helpful in their suggestions. Bob Stewart at UBC has prepared the index with a much appreciated concern for accuracy.

As is ever true, Bill, Geordon, Lauren, and Mom have tholed my addiction to writing and even aided and abetted the enterprise. They surely know I'm grateful.

I have yet another debt which is more diffuse and includes too many friends and colleagues to name individually. These are people who share my puzzlement with the curiosity we call Canadian society, and who have been generous in their sharing of ideas on that subject. Where I recognize the source of ideas I have provided the reference for readers, but, as is inevitable in a lively intellectual environment such as currently exists in Canadian social science, some original thoughts become unacknowledged general knowledge. I trust that colleagues will view textbooks produced in that atmosphere as collective productions, though weak arguments, errors, or omissions should, of course, be attributed entirely to the author.

P.M.
Vancouver, 1978

# INTRODUCTION

The young woman hired to guide visitors through the corporate smelter at Kitimat informs her entourage that Alcan is one of the largest aluminum companies in "the free world." The free world apparently means an economy planned and organized by privately owned corporations rather than by the state. It also means, but this is less apparent, an economy planned in the interests of private corporations rather than those ostensibly represented by the state. The interests of privately owned corporations are by definition those of its owners. The practical interests of the state are more ambiguous but in the democratic creed of the same "free world" they are those of all citizens. The tourist is left to ponder the irony.

## I

There are two puzzles in this. One is about "reality." What are the components of this system that calls itself a free world? How does it operate, what are its guiding principles, how does it create its own technologies and use these in the production of goods and services? How does it use people? What are its consequences for people in different regions and with different personal attributes? How has this system evolved? Where is it going? Who is in charge, and in whose interests is it designed?

The second one is about ideology. Why is this called a free world? What is meant by freedom? What is meant by a "free labour force" and "free enterprise" and "freedom to work?" Why does the guide not find these terms puzzling?

The reality, unfortunately, is not open to view as is that part of the Alcan smelter designated for the public tour. One is obliged to seek it out in dark corners as well as public galleries. One is hindered in the search not only by deliberately placed obstacles, information not made available, alliances not acknowledged, but by one's own immersion in the same ideology that forestalls the curiosity of the guide. What we perceive as truth, what we take to be facts, what we understand as knowledge: these are embedded in the nature of the society we inhabit. Conversely, what we perceive as problematic is that which is not explained but which is unavoidably evident on the fringes of what we take to be knowledge and fact. Much that is infinitely puzzling does not strike us as problematic because it is outside the range of puzzles that affect our livelihoods: we shelve and ignore such realms. Much else that is genuinely puzzling we explain superficially and go on unperplexed: our stock of beliefs, unexamined and untested, takes care of that. Such is the power of ideology that large segments of a population will believe explanations for their economic and social system even where it is possible to demonstrate that such explanations are unrelated to factual evidence.

One such belief in our society, for example, is that we live in a "free enterprise" economy. This means, apparently, a system in which numerous competing firms strive to sell their goods on an open and unregulated market, each having the same terms for operation as the others, and with government acting only as something of a referee in the market place. In reality, the economy is dominated by a few very large corporations which have access unavailable to smaller companies to resources, transportation, and means of marketing goods; and government acts and has always acted as a support for these corporations. There is no actual secret involved here; indeed (and the reason for this becomes another aspect of reality in need of explanation) a Canadian prime minister went out of his way to inform Canadians in 1976 that "The free market system, in the true sense of that phrase, does not exist in Canada."[1]

We are the society of large corporations. In the city our suburban homes are manufactured by the building division of one of the large "development" corporations, placed on land owned by the real estate division, with aluminum-sided outer walls, complete kitchen facilities, and wall-to-wall carpeting provided by yet other subsidiaries of the same or similar companies. The salesman informs us that we have "free choice" in where our livingrooms are situated: there are three basic plans.

Shopping is close by, as the advertisements claim, and it can be conducted at Safeway or Dominion or Loblaws: whichever has the territorial rights for the area. One shops by private car, the quintessence of the corporate economy for it combines utmost privacy and individual mobility with one of the most organized industries on earth – and does it at the expense of the public purse and public convenience. The public pays for the roads, the parking spaces, the infrastructure that permits the growth of service stations and used-car lots. The public accepts the pollution and the steadily decreasing availability of public transportation. The public can no longer remember the days when a corner grocery serviced a walking clientele, and provided free house deliveries. The cars become obsolete within a year of their purchase, but the system depends on the perpetual renewal of the consumer population. The car industry once provided much additional employment indirectly in service stations, but these have become less serviceable to the public as manned stations are replaced by self-serve mechanisms. One wonders if this is in the public interest, but one isn't consulted. In any event, paying the mortgage on the subdivision house and meeting the payments on the furniture, travelling to and from the corporate stores, to and from the corporate offices of work: these take too much time, there is little time left for pursuing problems of the public interest.

At the corporate store the convenience and sociability of the corner store is replaced by vast arrays of apparent choices between products, although on closer inspection many of the products are found to be put out by the same few companies. When the cart is full, and the consumer is convinced that this has been another experience in free enterprise, he is permitted to provide his own service once again, lifting the goods from the cart onto the moveable counter where only one cashier is required to handle hundreds of dollars' worth of business. He can even carry it all out to his car: the privacy of self-service on corporate premises is all part of the arrangement.

The city tourist observing Alcan's free world sees much that is familiar: the same shopping centres, the same stores, the same look-alike houses, the same cars. Kitimat, no longer legally constituted as a company town, won plaudits throughout the world for its neatly laid out streets and suburb-without-a-city appearance when it was planned in the 1950s. There is no unemployment in Kitimat. When there is a downturn in world demand for aluminum or pulp, workers simply have to leave the town. There is no low-cost housing for them, and the town was not designed for a mixture of workers and non-workers. This is the ultimate in the corporate society: there is nothing else in Kitimat, everyone is engaged in corporate work, the town itself is the fully corporate creation. It is not called "the town of the future" without cause.

## II

Multinational corporations, such as Alcan, are viewed by admirers as the harbingers of a new age. It is an age in which petty national conflicts are outdated along with national states, an age in which people in all societies enjoy benefits from industrial production, an age of sophisticated technology in the plant, increasing leisure time and personal wealth for all workers.

This view is under attack from critics who view the multinationals as destroyers of diverse and meaningful cultures, as imperialist oppressors, as the cause of growing poverty in resource regions and growing inequality in the world's distribution of wealth. In particular, such critics view these corporations as opponents of genuine freedom, indeed as the instruments by which a new phase of fascism is emerging throughout the world.

There is evidence to support both views. Workers in the industrial centres have benefited in some ways from corporate growth. They are affluent consumers of material goods, they are physically healthy, and their children enjoy a long adolescence free of obligatory labour. Corporate bureaucracies provide employment for women, and a declining proportion of men are employed in dangerous and physically debilitating jobs. Furthermore, large corporations, when pressed by social demands and government legislation, are better able to introduce health benefits, pollution controls, and environmental protections than small companies. In defence of Alcan, for example, one might point to the investment in a ventilation system for the fluorspar mines in Newfoundland when Alcan took over the St. Lawrence Corporation in 1960.[2]

The affluence of corporate workers, however, comes at a price. There is mounting evidence that multinational corporations not merely tolerate but actively create great poverty in underdeveloped countries from which they obtain resources and to which they sell manufactured goods. Directly or indirectly they also create poverty in resource regions of industrial countries, including the Atlantic region of Canada. Though they provide high wages to workers, their labour policies lead to increasing levels of unemployment. Their pricing methods and their systems of internal markets between parents and subsidiaries are major contributors to inflation. And though they employ large numbers of bureaucratic personnel and ever fewer unskilled workers, the cost has included decreasing community participation in decision-making about industrialization, decreasing community autonomy, and decreasing control over work by workers. A sizable proportion of their production consists of war materials, with the potential cost of war to workers when no alternative means can be devised for corporate expansion – and corporate expansion is essential to maintenance of the corporate system because high capital investments are predicated on corporate expansion for their profitability. Finally, though they have more capital with which to combat the pollution they cause, they also have more economic power to avoid government control or social pressure when pollution controls are expensive or inconvenient.

This essay adopts a critical perspective. The basic argument is that multinational corporations do not operate in the interests of society at large or in the interests of a national society such as Canada. They create and sustain a set of interests peculiar to their own well-being and growth. They are efficient organizations for which human labour and management or technical skills are resources with primarily monetary value. Such resources, along with natural materials, are managed by and for corporations so that technology, labour, and knowledge are harnessed to corporate growth rather than to social welfare. Ultimately, corporate interests are the interests of a particular class though the benefits may be distributed much more widely during periods of corporate expansion.

When we use the term "interests" we are confronted with a question of what those interests are. Ideologically, private corporations in a capitalist system are committed to profit as an end in itself: their interest, and that of their owners, is to increase profits. They boast of their capacities to create profits, they are measured and measure themselves in terms of their annual accumulation of profit. Yet one wonders if the drive to create profits in itself explains a willingness to dam rivers, flood forested valleys, ignore the claims on territory of non-industrial populations, manufacture weapons and spacecraft capable of destroying all life on earth; if it explains the intense commitment to the production of goods, any goods, for a market. Sleeping pills for pregnant women, prefabricated meals for airplane travellers, napalm, instant towns, Ski-doos, electrically operated toothbrushes, poodle-shampoo, Coca-Cola – all are produced for profit, and no moral priorities are established. "Like all material objects they have momentum but no morality,"[3] is the description of these corporations provided by one observer. Yet that is not true, for though no moral priorities are established for the products of the system, the market is run by rules, property is controlled by legal provisions backed by state force, and workers are governed by the corporate order. The apparent and "legitimate" objective of all of this is the creation of profit. The very fact that corporations are so eager to provide this explanation might induce us to examine it more closely.

It is true that the right of shareholders to earn profits is so well enshrined in social customs that it has been upheld in courts against corporations which occasionally chose, especially in the first half of this century, to spend funds on "social philanthropy" instead of dividends. In a 1916 case against Henry Ford, regarding his decision to reduce dividends while reducing prices and increasing wages, the Supreme Court of Michigan declared: "A business corporation is organized and carried on primarily for the benefit of the stockholders. . . . it is not within the lawful powers of a board of directors to shape and conduct the affairs of a corporation for the merely incidental benefit of shareholders and for the primary purpose of benefiting others."[4]

Nonetheless profit is a weak explanation. Profit is only money, and money is a means for obtaining something else or it is nothing. It can be used as a measure of something else – a euphemism for prestige, importance, strength – but measures are not goals in themselves. It can be used as a means of obtaining power, and power, at least, can be understood as an end. Power is the capacity to determine the rules of the game; the right or the ability to enforce decisions. Economic power is political power where it brings with it these capacities.

Economic power becomes more than political power in its extension to non-human nature. The conquest of nature, the transformation of the natural and material world through the application of science to any given circumstance, the production of goods irrespective of social demand for them or social good, and the imposition of a corporate and dominant class conception of progress and standards on the universe: these are the ultimate expressions of power. Says George Grant of the objective of science as it is undertaken in North American universities, "the motive of wonder becomes ever more subsidiary to the motive of power."[5] In explaining the same drive to dominate life, Lucien Karpik describes modern economic institutions as producing goods purposelessly, producing them as an end in itself, because "the capacity to impose a certain universe of merchandise appears as a legitimate project."[6] Power is exerted in the "free world" through control of technology, control of capital, and control of production. All rest on the accumulation of capital, thus the drive for profits and growth. It is exerted in the "unfree world" in much the same way, but the capital is obtained without the same utilization of consumer markets. In both systems, power is tied to large corporations and the capacity of large corporations to impose themselves on and alter the natural universe.

In the environment of the 1970s one hears many "new" voices of management declaring that profitability is no longer the only yardstick of performance. Social responsibility, good corporate citizenship, corporate "caring" are popular re-interpretations of corporate objectives. An executive annually lent to the United Way, the contribution of corporate funds to universities for purposes of research, the establishment of philanthropic foundations and the financing of public television programming: these are pointed out as transformations of the greed of an earlier era into the generosity of a modern one. One might attribute this to the profitability of Henry Ford's philanthropy, now understood in historical perspective. But one might also suspect there is a link between declining competition and increasing paternalism. In any event, there is nothing in the history of corporate development to suggest that the cause is altruism: corporations have consistently acted in the interests of corporate survival and dominance, and their shareholders and directors continue to decide how best that may be achieved. While good corporate citizenship may mean a new park or research grant, it still means for the corporations themselves the right to withdraw from a country or region if cheaper labour or more generous taxation laws are available elsewhere, and to withdraw with the accumulated profits earned in that country.

The general argument in this book, then, is that multinational corporations operate with the objective of increasing corporate power and the power of a class of corporate owners and directors; that power may be understood as the capacity to determine conditions of existence for a large segment of world society and to manipulate the natural world. This argument is carried out through a series of smaller-range arguments regarding technology, resources, the labour force, organizational structure, management, class structure, and the role of the state.

### III

The essay is divided into two parts. Part One, consisting of three chapters, is concerned with the political economy of corporate capitalism with particular reference to the Canadian situation. Chapter 1 introduces the argument that monopoly is the characteristic form of capitalism; competition is characteristic only of the labour market. It provides a discussion of the parallel development of large corporations in Eastern European countries, and considers how these corporations in both the "free" and "unfree" worlds are linked to the way in which national governments have evolved. Basic definitions and data on corporations in Canada are provided.

Chapter 2 is concerned with how technology is altered within emerging capitalist structures and how it is contained in and directed by corporations operating within highly concentrated markets. The comparatively low level of technological innovation sponsored in Canada is considered, and explanations for this are examined. The argument is advanced that large corporations have not been primary sources of technical innovation and are not essential to the innovative process, but that they have harnessed technology to their own interests by virtue of their control of capital. This control has the disadvantage not only of stifling innovation occurring within smaller enterprises, but of channelling innovative capacities toward marketable products consistent with existing market controls.

Chapter 3 is about the effects of market control by large cor-

porations on resource regions, and the role national and provincial governments in Canada have played in supporting corporate control. It is argued here that Canada is, for the most
part, a resource region; that its development has been directed
toward provision of raw materials for American manufacturing
industries; and that current development, including the oil-
extraction industry and the construction of pipelines, re-enforces
this pattern.

Part Two is concerned with the internal organization of corporations, and with the contributions of sociology to an understanding of these. Chapter 4 examines some of the systemic
aspects of these organizations, and considers how management
as a function has become ever more specialized and with what
consequences for a country of subsidiaries. The growth of
systematic organization is traced through two examples, Du-
Pont and Massey-Ferguson. This chapter advances the argument
that the much-publicized decentralization of multinational corporations refers to the establishment of production facilities on
foreign territory and not to the locus of control. Head offices
still determine priorities, establish policies, control finances, and
co-ordinate production. This discussion refers back to the
arguments in Part One where it was shown that technology,
along with policy and financial control, is harnessed to the interests of the parent firm and its home nation.

Chapter 5 is about the development of an industrial labour
force and some of the effects of changes in technology for production workers and clerical workers. It provides a brief review
of the standard literature regarding management of workers in
manufacturing plants, together with a discussion of the particular problems encountered by management and workers in
resource industries. Here the argument is advanced that an industrial labour force is one which is freely available for employment when and where needed by employers, which is paid in
wages and on the basis of an implied or explicit contract, and
which is dependent on employment for survival. In the development of such a labour force, the primary objectives of those who
own industrial production machinery and plants and of those
who manage production have been to ensure a steady supply of
labour which possesses appropriate skills, and to reduce labour
costs while increasing productivity and profits.

Chapter 6 is about workers who are managers, and about theories of organization which comfort managers. These theories describe corporations as co-operative enterprises in which members voluntarily contribute their skills in return for symbolic as well as material incomes. They thereby contribute to an ideology which ignores economic power, the structure of authority, the economic causes of social change, and the interests being served by large organizations. They also contribute to organizational inabilities to place responsibility with corporate members for action detrimental to the wider community.

Chapter 7 deals with the links between class and corporate organization. It reviews studies on ownership and directorships of organizations in the United States and Canada, and considers the differences in patterns for the two countries. It is argued here that while corporations establish and sustain interests peculiar to their organizational growth and survival, these interests are neither random nor disassociated from the chief beneficiaries of corporate growth who are owners and decision-making executives. The Canadian component of this international class has traditionally comprised the financial elite of the country. The larger part of the class is American, and its position is connected to ownership of financial and industrial assets in the United States and elsewhere in the world, including Canada.

A concluding chapter summarizes the book's arguments and examines the relationship between market expansion of the international system and the extension of benefits to industrial, urban workers in North America. It then considers the probable consequences of a decline in the rate of expansion. This involves examination of government statements on the demise of free enterprise, the introduction of wage and price controls, and advances toward a tripartite system of controls for industrial production. Because these events are current, the arguments in this final chapter are necessarily speculative.

The national focus for the book is Canada, and it is written primarily for Canadian students in undergraduate courses on organizations theory and industrial sociology. However, one of the objectives is to locate the Canadian situation within an historical framework. For this reason, several chapters contain information on the development of capitalism in Europe and the United States and on how these developments elsewhere affected

Canada. In addition, the text contains references to theories and studies which are traditional components of the "normal" literature for studies of organizations and workers, and contemporary theories and studies proposed or conducted in manufacturing areas where parent companies reside. These have been included for various reasons: some because they help students of any industrial society to study features of organization, some because they represent an ideology of management, some because they illuminate the differences between parent and subsidiary companies.

The book does not provide a description of multinational operations in the "third world," and of Canada's role in supporting these. That subject is the next logical step for students who have concerned themselves with multinational operations in Canada, and the bibliography provides several readings that deal with it. We also stop short of a full theoretical analysis of the relations between either the state, in abstract terms, or the Liberal government in Canada and multinational corporations or capitalism. The objective here is to introduce the elements of such an analysis, to link these to some of the more traditional materials in social science courses on organizations and industry, and in this way to provide undergraduate students and general readers with an entry route into the literature of political economy.

# PART ONE

# CANADIAN POLITICAL ECONOMY

# CHAPTER 1

# LEGAL FICTIONS

*A Corporation has the capacity, and subject to this Act, the rights, powers, and privileges of a natural person.*
  – Canada Business Corporations Act, 1974-75.[1]

*(a primitive society) . . . has for its units, not individuals, but groups of men united by the reality or the fiction of a blood-relationship. . . . But though the Patriarch . . . had rights thus extensive, it is impossible to doubt that he lay under an equal amplitude of obligations. If he governed the family, it was for its behoof. . . . The family, in fact, was a Corporation, and he was its representative, or we might almost say, its public officer.*
  – Sir Henry Maine[2]

It may be grammatically incorrect to use the phrase "in *whose* interests" in connection with impersonal corporate organizations, but the phrase is legally appropriate. In Canadian law a corporation is an individual entity with all the attributes of singularity and private interests even though it contains a large number of separate members who may pursue their own ends. *The Canada Business Corporations Act* spells out the similarity between "real" persons and "corporate" persons. It informs readers that individuals are "natural persons." But the generic term "persons" includes: "an individual, partnership, association, body corporate, trustee, executor, administrator or legal representative."[3] The *Act* then goes on to say that a corporation has the rights and privileges of natural persons. Canadian law in this respect is a continuation of European law dating back to the Roman period.

The legal fiction that corporations are persons permits them to do all that natural persons may do under law. Though they are biologically incapable of certain human actions – dancing, loving, giving birth, for example – they have equivalent forms; they grow, act, elevate members, and demote them; they spawn new and dependent corporations; occasionally they die. Without hindrance, they own, buy, sell, trade, work, and make momentous decisions, and they do all of these things in the name of the corporation itself, not in the name of any individuals who may be the instruments of the action at any given moment in time.

That individual members are legally but instruments is clear from the protections and requirements of the *Corporations Act*. Corporations purchase property, and such property is not held by the individuals who execute the property transfers nor are individuals held responsible for such purchases by the law. The property remains in the title of corporations after such individuals leave the corporations or die. Corporations sign contracts which likewise are binding beyond the lifetime of those who actually put pen to contract form. Members may be held accountable by the corporation at the internal level, but their actions taken on behalf of the corporation are recognized legally as corporate, not individual, actions. In addition, the corporation may appropriate the actions of members where such actions occur on corporate property: thus corporations "own" the labour of their workers, the creations of their technical personnel, the administrative innovations of their managers, the profitable undertakings of their representatives.

It is this spiritual unity, this capacity to act as if they were persons, this legal status of single entities regardless of their individual members, which distinguish corporations from any random aggregation of members acting in their purely personal capacities.

A well-known description of corporations catches the spiritual unity and transcendence. This was stated by U.S. Chief Justice Marshall in 1819 à propos of a judgment on corporate power:

A corporation is an artificial being, invisible, intangible, and existing only in the contemplation of the law. Being the mere creature of the law, it possesses only those properties which the charter of its creation confers on it, either expressly, or as incidental to its very existence. These are such as are supposed best calculated to effect the object for which it was created. Among the most important are immortality and, if the expression be allowed, individuality; properties by which a perpetual succession of many persons are considered the same, and may act as a single individual.[4]

Nonetheless, the strength of the corporate body rests on its being very different from its legal definition. Vis-à-vis the outside world, it is a unified whole. Internally, it is a complex coordination system for large numbers of individuals with highly variable and distinctive functions. The essence of the modern corporation is its division of labour, its capacity to utilize multitudes of highly specialized skills toward common ends. Quite unlike human individuals, the corporate person has all the advantages of many talents and energies: it is only legally that is like a "natural person." In yet another significant respect it differs from natural persons: while it represents its own interests, it exists because natural persons – in large degree absolved from personal responsibility by virtue of their corporate identity – use it to advance their own, as it were ulterior, interests. There are, in fact, three distinct kinds of interests being served by corporations: organizational, class, and private. One of our tasks here is to untangle the mutually supportive interests involved in the maintenance of these legal fictions.

I

The industrial corporation is the central economic unit of the capitalist society. Corporations are not peculiar to that particular type of society – they predate the emergence of capitalism and exist in societies that are not entirely or at least not ideologically within the capitalist sphere. They are, nonetheless, so central to capitalism that a standard definition of capitalistic enterprise provided by Werner Sombart in 1930 is almost identical to a definition of corporation as given in legislation:

. . . an independent economic organism is created over and above the individuals who constitute it. This entity appears then as the agent in each of these transactions and leads, as it were, a life of its own, which often exceeds in length that of its human members.[5]

Capitalism is an economic system whereby a class of persons owns and controls the predominant means of production, and labour is purchased by this class in return for a wage but no share in ownership or controlling rights; and whereby production of commodities is designed for a market, and guided by the calculated profitability of their sale.

Such a definition is useful only if we understand the terms involved, and identify in what respect they distinguish the system of capitalism from other economic systems. The word systems is itself ambiguous because both capitalism and industrialism are called systems and historically the two are intertwined, yet theoretically, at least, they are different entities.

Industrialism refers to a mode of producing subsistence. It is equivalent, logically, to hunting and gathering and agriculture, as systems by which subsistence is produced. More than one such set of activities may coexist in time and place: an industrial society also includes agricultural activities; a society which engages mainly in hunting and gathering may also cultivate the soil, and so forth. The major activities, however, characterize the system, and typically the secondary activities are organized with reference to the predominant one. A distinguishing feature of industrial production systems is that the food required by the whole population is produced by a very small proportion of its members, while the majority is engaged in producing goods and services not directly linked to subsistence needs. Other distinguishing features, but with reference to the definitions on which we are now focusing not as essential, are reliance on non-animal forms of energy and utilization of raw materials of the earth for purposes other than food and clothing.

Capitalism refers not to industrial production as such (even though we find it difficult to separate the two) but to the organization of any system of production which includes classes, private ownership, and control of the means by which goods are produced, a market for distribution, a labour market, and reliance on profitability as a guide for production rates and forms.

Theoretically it is possible to organize an industrial production system without simultaneously developing a capitalist system: that is, industrial production might be organized without the creation of an owning and controlling class together with a class of wage-labourers. It might involve a distribution arrangement which obviates the need for a market and calculations of profitability. Such a system is the objective for present-day China, Cuba, and several other "new" states in Africa and Asia. These countries have not yet developed full industrial systems: they are still predominantly agricultural societies. It is therefore too early in history to state that genuine alternatives to capitalism have been successfully developed for the maintenance of industrial production.

An earlier and still on-going experiment with a different way of organizing industrial production is the Soviet system. This is sometimes labelled "state capitalism," though its proponents argue that it is socialist in contrast to capitalist. "Mainstream" capitalism, that system which flourishes in most of Europe and North America and which dominates most economic transactions throughout the rest of the world except for China, Cuba, and the Soviet countries, is characterized by private ownership of the means of production and an ideology which gives legitimacy to the calculated profitability of goods on a controlled market. The Soviet variant is characterized by state ownership of the means of production, small-group control of these means, and an ideology which condemns profitability as the criterion of good management. In common with capitalism, the Soviet system includes a labour market and a differential wage system for payment of workers. Although the market system is not fully developed at the level of private consumers, both by accident and intentional planning, it is a feature of interaction between Soviet states and between them and the capitalist societies. Partly for this reason, though profitability is not regarded as a primary objective for state planners, in practice calculations of profit are routinely undertaken and guide a large part of industrial planning.

Though industrial production is, historically, tied to capitalism, capitalism itself is not tied to industrial production. Capitalism preceded the development of fully industrial societies. It may have existed in a number of societies which never became industrial production systems. (This point is open to debate, but the debate regarding the capitalist propensities of such civilizations as ancient Rome, or before that Mesopotamia and the Phoenician states, is outside the realm of our present discussion.) It is possible, though not demonstrably necessary, that capitalism as a means of organizing production had to precede industrialism. It is possible that the development of industrial production systems absolutely required certain conditions which only capitalism could provide, such as high concentrations of capital, a market, and wage-labour. Conditions for development of such a system should not be confused with conditions for maintenance of industrialism: once capital is available, at least theoretically other ways of organizing both distribution and labour may be feasible.

## II

Capital itself is accumulated wealth, including the means of production, which may be used for the production of yet further wealth. That is, it is not simply money used for private extravaganzas or simple commercial exchange. The capitalist, then, is one who holds capital in large amounts for utilization by industry or for investment purposes by which further capital may be obtained.

The wage-labourer is one who has no means of support other than the sale of whatever he or she possesses, such as physical strength, skills, knowledge, time, and energy, for an income which can then be used for private consumption, including (and sometimes restricted to) subsistence goods such as food and shelter. The word "proletariat" refers to such wage-labourers: it is a Roman word and originally referred to that class of persons who sold their labour for a wage in contrast to both a leisured class and slaves, or, later, serfs. As an historical aside, it may be noted that we still speak of "waging war," in reference (though no longer explicitly recognized in this way) to soldiers being paid for their work and in contrast to an army of serfs performing obligatory duty for landed estate-owners.

The basic distinction between the capitalist and wage-labourer is not wealth as such: a wage-labourer may (again, in theory) be well-to-do. The capitalist, however, by virtue of investing wealth in a production system, is accorded certain legally protected privileges. These privileges are called "rights" in the same system which describes itself as a "free world." Such rights of ownership may include determination of the rates of production, control over raw resources for a region or nation, capacity to employ others at rates, under conditions, and for times determined by owners, choice of means for disposing of goods, and establishment of prices for goods and services. The wage-labourer does not have these rights, even if he or she provides daily labour for the enterprise for the duration of a life-time. The difference then, is not measured in money, but in power. The rights of ownership provide economic power, and with that, a more persuasive political and social power since all of these means of controlling production involve as well control of resources, regions, nations, labour, peoples, and the very fabric of society itself.

A dominant class must have a basis for power. In agrarian economies, the basis is normally land or the capacity to control effectively large food supplies. In the mercantile period of early capitalism, the basis was merchant capital or the capacity effectively to control trade routes and merchant markets. In industrial capitalism, the basis is industrial capital or the capacity to control effectively the plants and technical equipment required for industrial production together with the markets for both supplies and finished products.

While these basic distinctions are crucial to our understanding of the class structure in contemporary capitalist societies, they are not the only divisions of the society. Each of these classes contains segments with somewhat peculiar circumstances and occasional differences of interest as a consequence. The basis for power may be actual instruments of production such as machines, industrial sites, plants; or may be capital needed for the purchase of such instruments. It is not always the case that a class segment controlling industrial plants also controls sufficient "fluid" capital for further investment. Two segments of an owning class may therefore have somewhat different concerns with respect to capital and its uses. In addition both an owning and a working class are distributed over the national territories of the world, and nations have different stakes in the outcomes of economic decisions. What is in the interests of one nation or region is not necessarily in the interests of any other, may even be directly contrary to the interests of others.

As well there are groups in the industrial society which are not strictly defined as classes yet which hold crucial positions, specifically small business owners, independent contractors, independent farmers, and self-employed professionals.

Finally there are groups which though contained within the industrial class structure have attributes in many respects more important to their economic positions than class membership, specifically women who are not wage-earners and certain ethnic and religious groups where ethnicity or religion are regarded as important by a society.

In order to appreciate the situation of Canada, a nation dependent on resources and with a large part of her manufacturing establishments controlled by non-national corporations which are owned by a non-national class, we are in need of knowledge about the differing interests of such groups as financiers and industrialists, corporate executives and small contractors, American and Canadian workers, workers in the manufacturing regions and workers in resource regions, male and female wage-earners and housekeepers, immigrants, and native Indians. We will return to these distinctions again when we have considered something of the history of capitalism and the nature of its present ownership structure.

### III

Modern capitalism, that is capitalism as an unbroken though changing system up to the present time, emerged possibly as early as the twelfth century in northern Italy, Flanders, and Holland, and by the thirteenth or fourteenth century in Britain. It was not a dominant economic system in Europe until well into the fifteenth or early sixteenth century, and not an emergent world system before the late seventeenth and eighteenth centuries.[6] Feudalism died slowly, submerged by many and diverse events, of which the development on a large scale of the money economy, the creation of more efficient methods of producing surplus, the growth of market towns and a pan-European market system, and the displacement and emigration of peasants from the manorial lands were the most significant. It had a

number of features which are worthy of note because they contrast sharply with fully developed capitalism.

Two such features were the reciprocity and paternalism
characterizing relations between lords and serfs or peasants.
Another was that though peasants were obliged to produce
surplus food for owners of land, they nonetheless owned their
own tools (means of production), and produced their own subsistence along with that of the owning class. A third was that the
economic unit, the manor, was relatively self-sufficient. It produced most of its own food, shelter, clothing, and other goods;
it also used most of what it produced. Not all, of course: some
surplus had to be generated so that the lord could live in a castle
and at leisure, so that some luxury items and certain other items
such as salt could be purchased from outsiders, and so that a
standing army could be maintained, ostensibly for the protection of the manorial population.

Another feature was that the prevailing ideology was not conducive to the accumulation of unlimited profits. While the accumulation of things by a lord was acceptable, the development
of money as a means of creating more money was for the most
part not possible and in any event not viewed as a reasonable
way of life. Religious strictures against usury were well ar-
ticulated, and occurred so frequently in texts and early town
legislation that a later reader must suppose the ideology of the
times prohibited such practices. That is not to say the practice
did not occur (obviously it must have occurred, why else the frequent strictures?), but simply that it was not accepted, taken for
granted, assumed to be proper as it was by the eighteenth century and certainly in our own time.[7]

These conditions gradually changed as a cash-currency slowly
replaced exchange-in-kind and trading regions increased in extent. These necessitated greater cash reserves and turned usury,
the lending of cash at interest, into a regular business. The
development of trade occurred together with the growth of
towns independent of manorial estates, and of townspeople
engaged in crafts production, money-lending, and merchant activities rather than food production. In order to trade on such a
cash market, manorial lords began seeking ways of reducing
their obligations to the peasantry and of increasing the value of
their land for purposes other than subsistence agriculture, such

as cutting of timber stands for lumber markets, or pasturing sheep for wool markets. Inevitably this meant the growth of a landless peasantry, people who were as yet neither employed workers in towns nor protected serfs on estates. In addition, serfs able to obtain more lucrative employment, sometimes in the crafts and merchant houses in towns, sometimes on the land-clearing activities of estates undergoing the change-over, emigrated illegally. With the emergence of the money economy and market, then, the entire system of feudalism, with its aristocracy and serfs tied to one another, began to break down.

That class which has since become known as the urban bourgeoisie, in contrast to the landed aristocracy, emerged within these early feudal towns. One of the persistent puzzles for economic historians has been where this class obtained its wealth in the fourteenth and fifteenth centuries, before it was able to employ a productive labour force through which it could accumulate profits. This question is raised by Maurice Dobb in his study of the rise of capitalism.[8] Plunder and monopoly, in Dobb's opinion, were the characteristic features of the early merchant guilds and of the towns which they moulded in their own interests. Monopoly, perhaps more than outright plunder (though this has never been absent), continued to be the prominent feature of emergent capitalism. Monopoly over trade was achieved through combinations of merchant traders into corporate bodies designed to achieve collective advantages.

The towns, in their stuggle for control over trade, gained the right to regulate all market transactions within their territorial limits. Such regulations were designed to ensure the advantage of townsfolk in their transactions with suppliers from the countryside and with buyers from the feudal manors, or with buyers and suppliers from distant areas. The dominant groups in the towns were the merchants, and these merchants had formed guilds whose collective power permitted them to ensure the advantage not only of townsfolk vis-à-vis outsiders, but also the advantage of merchants vis-à-vis craftsmen and other town-dwellers. These guilds provided themselves with exclusive charters for particular areas of wholesale trade.

These trading guilds, in control of the town administrations and having a monopoly on external relations, soon created an employer-employee relationship with craftsworkers.[9] The power of merchant capital, as contrasted with labour and crafts skills, continued to increase and culminated in the development of still more exclusive corporations of merchant "adventurers" in the sixteenth and seventeenth centuries.

These monopoly conditions rested ultimately on the capacity to back restrictions on competition by force. In the thirteenth and fourteenth centuries, corporate bodies themselves occasionally provided the force where these were still allied with manors, particular lords, or ecclesiastical orders, and where the occasion involved a disputed "territory" such as the location of a local market or control over a locally produced commodity. As merchant capitalism emerged throughout Europe, however, it was the control of exports and imports from more distant territories that required support, and such support could be best mustered at the level of a corporate unit larger than specific merchant guilds or their town administrations.

The Knights of St. John in Malta and the Knights Templar of the twelfth and early thirteenth centuries had been chartered by the Catholic Church under the sovereign authority of the Pope to carry on their monopoly trade in international currencies. Their demise was due largely to the growth of a conflicting set of sovereign powers in the form of national kings and nation-states. The Merchant Adventurers of England was chartered by Richard II in the fourteenth century. This corporate body included wealthy merchants from several leading towns in England and was provided with exclusive rights to the textiles trade between England and northern Europe, backed by the sovereign authority of the British monarchy. The British "Russia Company" was established in the mid-sixteenth century for purposes of trading in Russia under the protection of an agreement with the Tzar. The Africa Company, the Eastland Company, the Spanish Company, the Levant Company, and the Hudson's Bay Company were established throughout the next century, all chartered under the sovereign authority of the English crown. Similar trading companies were chartered by the kings of European states, and the charter in each case signified the intention of the "crown" to support its merchants by force if necessary.

The relationship between sovereign power and merchants was actually one of mutual support. The sovereigns depended on their merchant class for currency: as became clear in the crisis of the French monarchy in 1789, the crown and the aristocracy had no independent economic power to maintain themselves. Their political power depended on the willingness of the merchants to sustain them. In turn, the merchants required some centralized power with the capacity to summon an army into action. This mutual support system functioned well into the eighteenth century, until qualitative changes in the system of production created a need amongst the merchants for more direct political power.

Mercantile monopolies were engaged in obtaining commodities such as spices, textiles, furs, and later foodstuffs and timber, for European markets. They were not engaged in the production of new goods. The class which succeeded them in the form of a combination between merchant-financiers and craftsmen-traders was engaged in the production of new goods, the impetus for such production being a greatly expanded market in European colonies and the emergence of an industrial (landless) labour force. This class was an industrial bourgeoisie, and the era this class ushered in was one characterized by industrial, as contrasted with mercantile, capitalism. In the colonies, of which Canada and United States were prominent members, mercantilism continued: the point of establishing colonies was to obtain raw materials for industrial goods produced by mother countries. Manufactured goods were traded back to the colonies, and colonies then became both suppliers and customers for industrial products.

The market system expanded to include, and eventually became dominated by, industrial products and industrial labour. If one were to choose one aspect only of industrial capitalism as the overriding feature of that system it would be these commodity and labour markets, and if one is to understand the relationship of the democratic political system to the economy it is again the market which is the crucial element.

## IV

There has probably not been a time in European history of the past several hundred years when absolutely no market existed: the manor house of the fifth to fifteenth centuries normally engaged in the sale and purchase of some goods, cash was a common but not dominating commodity far back in history, and some small portion of all populations which were otherwise agricultural had traditionally been involved primarily in trading through the medium of money. However, the development of markets in the modern sense involved the use of money as a medium for exchange of *most* goods and services, including labour, and the erosion of alternative forms by which producers and consumers of goods might be related to one another. This system implies that all things, including people, can be given a monetary value, and that all things can be bought and sold.

It is sometimes argued that a market can exist only if there is competition. That is, goods and services are offered for a price in competition with other offers, and the consumer chooses which of several or many goods to purchase. Likewise, the employer offers a wage, the labourer is free to choose employment at the highest wage offered; or, the labourer offers services, and the employer is free to purchase labour at the lowest price offered. It might be argued by those who view the market as necessarily competitive that a system in which one or a few very large corporations control the conditions of production and sale is not a market system; similarly where one or a few unions control the conditions for sale of labour. The problem here is in the restrictive definition of market.

A market is not necessarily competitive. Markets are systems in which everything is bought and sold, under any conditions of monopoly or competition. It is in contrast to a feudal or communal exchange or exchange/redistribution system that one best understands the characteristic of the market system. In other systems, the relationships between producers and consumers is with greater intention mutually protective, normally involving reciprocal obligations for exchange of goods and services. The rich may live off the poor and require of them labour, but labour is not purchased, and the rich are, in turn, expected to provide protection, shelter, and various other conditions of livelihood to their slaves, serfs, or fellow tribesmen.

Competition does not exist where a single company or a few companies together control essential conditions for the production and sale of goods. Resources, other supplies, transportation, storage, access to consumers, technical knowledge and technical expertise, growth capital: any or all of these may be controlled so that competition is restricted or eliminated. Where this occurs we may speak of a monopoly or oligopoly situation. Technically a monopoly consists of one company (or one government agency) controlling the market, oligopoly of several companies or similar corporate groups sharing a restricted market. In many practical instances, the difference between the two is not significant in terms of effects on labour, small business, or consumers. A monopoly or oligopoly market situation need not imply that there are no other firms in an industry, simply that other firms, by virtue of the dominance of one or a few large firms, operate on conditions and in a market where they have few or no independent options. Many of these other firms, as in the case of contractors in the resource industries or sales agencies in manufacturing, are essentially a service sector for the dominant companies.

An absence of competition is evident in an industry where we find that one or a very few firms control a large proportion of the total assets, receive high proportions of the total profits, are accountable for an equally high proportion of the total sales, or control the largest share of all "value" added to raw materials and labour through manufacturing. Where these "indices" of monopoly or oligopoly are present, we may speak of an industry being "highly concentrated"; that is, control rests with very few firms. Parallel to this, ownership is usually similarly concentrated; that is, control rests not only with very few firms but the firms are owned by very few separate investors and controlled by very few directors. These two kinds of concentration, however, do not necessarily occur together: it is possible for very few firms to control a market sector but for ownership of the firms to be quite widely dispersed. In discussing market concentration, we are focusing on the number of firms and their competition or lack of it, rather than the number of owners.

As the previous section indicates, high concentration was characteristic of the earlier phases of mercantile capitalism: a few firms held monopoly control of certain trades, and competition was severely restricted. With the development of colonies and the expansion of trade both geographically and in terms of products, the capacity of merchant houses to control markets declined. Producers of industrial goods entered a period of competition marked by a drive to create new products through technical development and concern with means of creating old products on a vastly greater scale for mass consumption. Technical developments in the uses of fuel energy and in transportation radically altered the conditions of production and marketing, such that existing large companies as well as emerging new companies had to cope with a changing technological basis and could not rely on earlier political alliances or town regulations for restriction of competition. The degree of actual competition varied by industry, depending on how radical changes in that industry might be and what effects were experienced from changes in transportation, etc. However, it appears likely that in most industries some degree of genuine competition between producers of goods and services was sustained throughout initial phases of technical development. Across the industrial spectrum for Europe, competitive capitalism reached its peak in the latter half of the nineteenth century.

Up to about the middle of that century, manufacturing activity remained the prerogative of European countries, still dominated by Britain. Colonies remained as regions from which resources were extracted on an essentially mercantile basis, and as consumer populations for manufactured goods. European manufacturers expanded their plant sizes on home territory in order to create goods for these colonies, and generally established agencies abroad for the marketing of goods. They were not yet able, given transportation and communication distances, to establish manufacturing plants abroad.

Experiments in multinational production were launched in the second half of the nineteenth century, attendant on the construction of railways and canals for transportation of products. Many of these manufacturing firms were the offspring of fledgling American enterprises, established in order to compete with British manufacturers in Europe and in colonies. By the turn of the twentieth century, a few of these firms had managed to establish themselves in positions that permitted them to restrict competition from newcomers to their industrial fields, but these were still exceptions. In spite of frequent attempts at and frequent successes in obtaining restrictive legislation against competition, and in spite of manipulation of transportation and storage facilities so that competitors could not market their goods, as well as mergers, combines, and other forms of collusion, competition was still widely evident when the competing countries entered the war of 1914-18.

By the end of that war, the technical capacities of dominant firms had developed to a point at which they could monopolize certain fields of knowledge, the infrastructure of roads and railways had been constructed for easy access to foreign countries, and for a time the United States (unmarked by the ravages of the war, and economically the chief beneficiary) competed only with Britain for world dominance. American corporations grew rapidly during the 1920s and greatly expanded their manufacturing facilities at home and abroad. Canada, which up to the war had remained a British colony in fact if no longer in constitution, became the territory most favoured for American expansion. The tendency toward high concentration, which is inherent in the nature of the system, became fully evident in the post-war period. In resources, manufacturing, transportation, communications, and financial sectors, fewer but larger companies each year dominated the respective markets; simultaneously, fewer but larger companies controlled the largest subsidiaries in several fields. Corporate complexes emerged consisting of a single parent corporation holding controlling shares in numerous other companies throughout the world in every phase of industrial and financial activity. (The process by which this occurred is examined in depth in Chapter 4.)

## V

There are three kinds of markets: one dealing in commodities, one in finance and services (particularly to commodity-producers), and one in labour. The first two of these overlap: companies dealing in both markets are likely to be components of corporate complexes ultimately owned and controlled by the same groups. The first two are also highly concentrated.

A first indication of concentration in Canadian industry is provided in statistics on financial data for companies operating in Canada for the Canadian government under the *Corporations and Labour Unions Returns Act*. This information includes industrial and service (utilities) companies, but does not include financial institutions. Table 1 summarizes this information. In the mid-1970s, there are almost 216,000 industrial and service corporations in Canada with assets of $250,000 or more (the minimum size for reporting financial data to the Canadian government). Of these, 941 control 64 per cent of all assets. Of the 941, 502 are foreign-owned companies. Concentration is particularly high in petroleum and coal manufacturing, where 18 corporations, 16 foreign-owned, control 99 per cent of all assets; in rubber manufacturing, where 8 firms, again all foreign-owned, control 84 per cent of all assets; in tobacco, where 6 foreign-owned firms control 95 per cent of all assets, and in primary metals, where 19 firms control 91 per cent of all assets. The mining industry, and most of the high-technology, capital-intensive manufacturing industries are both highly concentrated and extensively foreign-owned.

The degree of concentration is very much understated in these figures as given in Table 1.[10] Each corporation falling within the inclusion rules of federal legislation is counted, but the largest corporations are not in fact separate in their industrial activity, ownership links, trading arrangements, or financial activities. Thus Cominco is counted as a large mining corporation, but Cominco is actually part of the vertically integrated corporation, Canadian Pacific. Cominco, in turn, owns wholly or in part numerous other mining, transportation, and engineering companies. Figure 1 provides a listing of the major companies which are included in the Canadian Pacific complex in order to illustrate this typical feature of contemporary capitalism; Figure 2 shows the structure of another Canadian company, Noranda.

Likewise, Imperial Oil is counted, but so are the great many separate subsidiaries of Imperial as listed in Figure 3. It may be noted that several of these companies are under consortium ownership, especially the major pipelines and Syncrude, with Imperial as one or the leading shareholder along with other oil companies and sometimes governments. Given these extensive sharing arrangements between very large corporate parents, it is impossible to provide an absolutely precise figure for the degree of influence exerted by a company such as Imperial on the total economy. What becomes apparent is that when it is in their interest the major oil companies combine their capital costs in order to pipe oil and gas to their manufacturing customers: so much for competition.

Because these gross figures overestimate the number of corporations with extensive control over resources and manufactur-

## TABLE 1

### Proportion of Total Assets in Industrial Sectors Held by Largest Corporations and Percentage of Foreign Ownership, 1975

| Industrial Sector | Total Number Firms | Number with Assets $25 Million and Over | Percentage all Assets Owned by Firms in $25 M + class | Number Foreign-Owned Firms in $25 M + class | Overall Percentage Firms Foreign-Controlled |
|---|---|---|---|---|---|
| *Agriculture, Forestry, Fishing* | 10,839 | 2 | * | 1 | 9 |
| *Mining* | | | | | |
| metal | 218 | 51 | 95 | 28 | 44 |
| mineral fuels | 875 | 61 | 83 | 42 | 71 |
| others | 2,818 | 24 | 45 | 16 | 55 |
| *Total: Mining* | 3,911 | 136 | 82 | 41 | 57 |
| *Construction* | 33,353 | 57 | 24 | 22 | 74 |
| *Public Utilities* | 12,666 | 136 | 91 | 27 | 8 |
| *Wholesale Trade* | 31,727 | 86 | 31 | 42 | 28 |
| *Retail Trade* | 46,882 | 50 | 33 | 18 | 21 |
| *Services* | 48,789 | 51 | * | 27 | 23 |
| *Manufacturing* | | | | | |
| food | 2,887 | 52 | 55 | 34 | 50 |
| beverages | 391 | 18 | 72 | 9 | 30 |
| tobacco | 19 | 6 | 95 | 6 | 100 |

| | | | | | |
|---|---|---|---|---|---|
| rubber | 122 | 8 | 84 | 8 | 93 |
| leather | 377 | 1 | * | 0 | 23 |
| textiles | 802 | 14 | 54 | 10 | 59 |
| knitting | 289 | 0 | * | 0 | 24 |
| clothing | 1,894 | 0 | * | 0 | 16 |
| wood | 2,330 | 10 | 33 | 6 | 29 |
| furniture | 1,345 | 2 | * | 2 | 23 |
| paper | 525 | 71 | 91 | 35 | 41 |
| printing, publishing | 3,420 | 10 | 33 | 1 | 12 |
| primary metals | 506 | 19 | 91 | 6 | 14 |
| metal fabricating | 4,260 | 23 | 36 | 16 | 43 |
| machinery | 1,192 | 23 | 50 | 19 | 67 |
| transport equipment | 1,047 | 38 | 78 | 28 | 78 |
| electrical products | 880 | 33 | 71 | 25 | 66 |
| non-metallic minerals | 1,215 | 24 | 66 | 19 | 66 |
| petroleum and coal | 53 | 18 | 99 | 16 | 92 |
| chemicals | 970 | 41 | 70 | 33 | 75 |
| miscellaneous manufacturing | 2,949 | 12 | 26 | 6 | 50 |
| *Total: Manufacturing* | 27,473 | 423 | 69 | 279 | 56 |
| *Total: Non-Financial Industries* | 215,640 | 941 | 64 | 502 | 33 |

* Assets not divulged where small number of companies in bracket or other reasons which might permit identification of individual companies.

SOURCE: Tables 2, 3, and 5, CALURA, Part I, 1978 (61-210). Computations in col. 3 are mine.

# Figure 1: Canadian Pacific Limited, Canadian Holdings

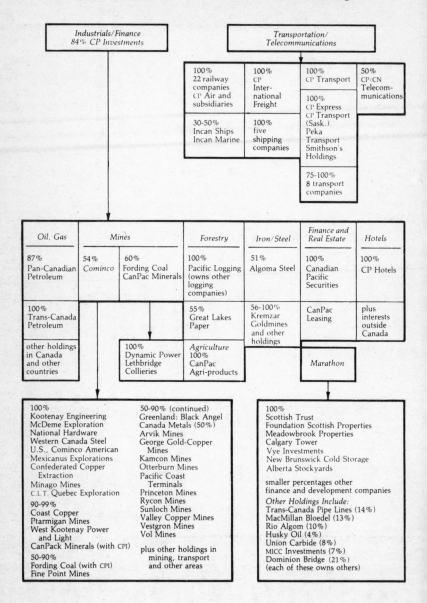

SOURCES: Statistics Canada, *Inter-Corporate Ownership, 1975*, based on Chart 20.

## Figure 2: Noranda Mines, Canadian Holdings

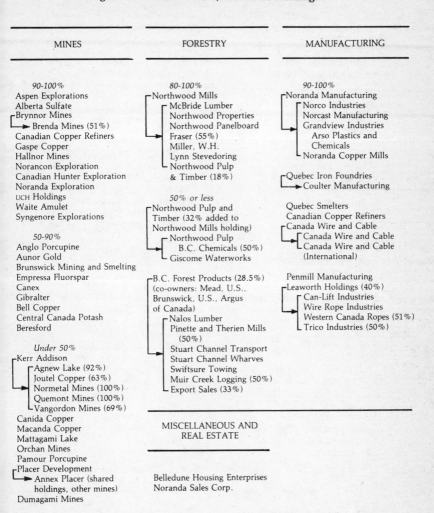

MINES | FORESTRY | MANUFACTURING

**MINES**

*90-100%*
Aspen Explorations
Alberta Sulfate
Brynnor Mines
└─► Brenda Mines (51%)
Canadian Copper Refiners
Gaspe Copper
Hallnor Mines
Norancon Exploration
Canadian Hunter Exploration
Noranda Exploration
UCH Holdings
Waite Amulet
Syngenore Explorations

*50-90%*
Anglo Porcupine
Aunor Gold
Brunswick Mining and Smelting
Empressa Fluorspar
Canex
Gibralter
Bell Copper
Central Canada Potash
Beresford

*Under 50%*
Kerr Addison
┌─ Agnew Lake (92%)
│  Joutel Copper (63%)
├─► Normetal Mines (100%)
│  Quemont Mines (100%)
└─ Vangordon Mines (69%)
Canida Copper
Macanda Copper
Mattagami Lake
Orchan Mines
Pamour Porcupine
Placer Development
└─► Annex Placer (shared
    holdings, other mines)
Dumagami Mines

**FORESTRY**

*80-100%*
Northwood Mills
┌─ McBride Lumber
│  Northwood Properties
│  Northwood Panelboard
├─► Fraser (55%)
│  Miller, W.H.
│  Lynn Stevedoring
└─ Northwood Pulp
   & Timber (18%)

*50% or less*
Northwood Pulp and
Timber (32% added to
Northwood Mills holding)
┌─ Northwood Pulp
└─► B.C. Chemicals (50%)
   Giscome Waterworks

B.C. Forest Products (28.5%)
(co-owners: Mead, U.S.,
Brunswick, U.S., Argus
of Canada)
┌─ Nalos Lumber
│  Pinette and Therien Mills
│  (50%)
└─ Stuart Channel Transport
   Stuart Channel Wharves
   Swiftsure Towing
   Muir Creek Logging (50%)
   Export Sales (33%)

**MANUFACTURING**

*90-100%*
Noranda Manufacturing
┌─ Norco Industries
│  Norcast Manufacturing
├─► Grandview Industries
│     Arso Plastics and
│     Chemicals
└─ Noranda Copper Mills

Quebec Iron Foundries
└─► Coulter Manufacturing

Quebec Smelters
Canadian Copper Refiners
Canada Wire and Cable
┌─ Canada Wire and Cable
└─ Canada Wire and Cable
   (International)

Penmill Manufacturing
Leaworth Holdings (40%)
┌─ Can-Lift Industries
│  Wire Rope Industries
├  Western Canada Ropes (51%)
└─ Trico Industries (50%)

## MISCELLANEOUS AND REAL ESTATE

Belledune Housing Enterprises
Noranda Sales Corp.

SOURCE: Statistics Canada, *Inter-Corporate Ownership Directory*, Ottawa: Queen's Printer, 1975, based on chart 16. Subsidiary holdings are 100% if not otherwise specified.

## Figure 3: Imperial Oil, Holdings in Canada

| Exxon | Other Shareholders | |
|---|---|---|
| | *Foreign* | *Canadian* |
| 69.7% | 10.5% | 19.8% |

### Imperial

| Subsidiaries listed in Annual Report, 1976[1] | Principal investments and co-owners[2] |
|---|---|
| W.H. Adam | Alberta Products Pipeline (30%) |
| Albury Company | (Gulf, Shell, Texaco) |
| Allied Heat and Fuel | Interprovincial Pipeline (32.8%) |
| Archibald Fuels | (Gulf) |
| Atlas Supply Company | Montreal Pipeline (32%) |
| Bourque Brothers | (BP, Gulf, Petrofina, Shell, |
| Building Products | Texaco) |
| Centres Citadelle | Nottingham Gas (35%) |
| Champlain Oil Products | (Mobile, Union) |
| Delta Roe and Twine | Rainbow Pipe Line (33%) |
| Devon Etates | (Aquitaine, Mobil) |
| ESF | Redwater Water Disposal (45%) |
| Esso of Canada | (Gulf) |
| Donat Grandmaître | St. Laurence Tankers (50%) |
| Hall Fuel (1965) | (Canadian Fuel Markets) |
| Hi-way Petroleum | Syncrude (31%) |
| Home Oil Distributors | (Cities Service, Gulf, |
| Imperial Oil Developments | Governments of Canada, |
| Imperial Oil Enterprises | Alberta, Ontario) |
| Imperial Oil of Canada Shipping Company | Tecumseh Gas Storage (50%) |
| The Imperial Pipe Line Company | (Consumers' Gas) |
| Ioco Townsite | Canadian Arctic Gas |
| Lou's Service (Sault) | (15 companies in consortium) |
| Maple Leaf Petroleum | Trans-Mountain Pipeline (8.6%) |
| Midwest Fibreboard | (Gulf, Shell) |
| Mongeau et Robert Cie | |
| James Murphy Fuel Oil | |
| Nisku Products Pipe Line | |
| Northwest Company | |
| J.P. Papineau | |
| Poli-Twine Corp. | |
| Polybottle | |
| Renown Building Materials | |
| Les Restaurants Le Voyageur | |
| Robbins Floor Products | |
| Seaway Bunkers | |
| Servacar | |
| Stanmount Pipe Line | |
| Transit Company | |
| Western Oil and Trading | |
| Winnipeg Pipe Line | |

[1] *Annual Report*, 1976 and *Financial Post* updating to March 1978.
[2] *Financial Post* listing, March 1978.
NOTE: Properties not listed. This includes service stations.

ing in Canada, analysts concerned with concentration examine a smaller number of corporations which in each industrial sector control the larger proportion of all assets, sales, profits, or value-added to products. These, too, interlock in their ownership structures. For Canada, the *Financial Post* annual listing of companies ranked by sales, based on government statistics gathered under the *Corporations and Labour Unions Returns Act*, provides an indication of which corporations are dominant. In 1977, the first thirty were ranked in this order: General Motors, Ford Motor, Imperial Oil, Canadian Pacific, Bell Canada, Chrysler, Massey-Ferguson, Alcan Aluminum, Inco, Gulf Oil, Canada Packers, MacMillan-Bloedel, TransCanada Pipelines, Steel Company of Canada, Brascan, Noranda, Seagram, Moore, Texaco, Dominion Foundries and Steel, Genstar, Domtar, Abitibi, Canadian General Electric, IBM, Canadian International Paper, Consolidated-Bathurst, Burns Foods, Imasco.[11]

*The Financial Post* listing does not separately include major subsidiaries where their assets and sales are consolidated with those of parent companies already listed; but since some subsidiaries are not consolidated for purposes of financial reporting there is some inconsistency in the listing. Alcan Aluminum, for example, is ranked 8th in terms of sales. The Aluminum Company of Canada would rank between the 12th and 13th companies if it were separately listed. Likewise Cominco and Algoma Steel: both subsidiaries of Canadian Pacific Investments, itself a subsidiary of Canadian Pacific Limited as shown in Figure 1. Cominco would rank about 29th, and Algoma about 46th if they were separately listed. Other major companies, also listed separately, are linked to such major complexes as Canadian Pacific by smaller shareholdings. One of these is MacMillan-Bloedel, for which the 13.5 per cent of shares held by Canadian Pacific constitutes the largest single publicly listed holding.

The listing also does not identify the links between companies which are owned by financial corporations. Argus is such a corporation, and Argus holds controlling or significant shares in Massey-Ferguson, Domtar, Dominion Stores, Hollinger Mines, Standard Broadcasting, and many others on the majors list; as well it is connected through holdings with Cominco, Noranda, the Mead Corporation, U.S., and many others. Power Corporation likewise owns vital shares in many of the majors, as shown in Figure 4. A takeover bid by Power for Argus was the original spark for the establishment of a Royal Commission on Corporate Concentration in the early 1970s. The merger did not take place, though eventually the Commission produced a report (1978) which argued that such concentration of holdings should not be interfered with by government legislation.

We may note from this list that many of the dominant companies in Canada are foreign-owned. In 1977, the *Financial Post* identified 68 wholly owned subsidiaries of foreign corporations among the top 200 corporations as measured by sales, within the manufacturing, resources, and utilities industries. The *Post* identified another 47 which were 50 per cent or more owned by non-residents, and another 20 in which foreign shares represented significant and possibly controlling interests. Altogether that is 135 out of the largest 200 corporations in these industries. Nor are discrete numbers the best indication of foreign ownership: as Table 1 indicates and more detailed studies have demonstrated, foreign-owned firms are, on average, four times larger in terms of assets than their Canadian counterparts. Foreign-owned firms, moreover, are dominant in the high-value and capital-intensive industries. Canadian firms predominate in such industries as leather goods and furniture, where higher degrees of competition are evident and lower profits generated overall.

American ownership of plants and equipment is not unique to Canada, but Canada has a higher degree of such ownership than any other industrial country. The overlap between lists of the dominant firms in Canada and United Nations lists of dominant firms in the world is significant: the same companies which control the Canadian economy also control a large share of the world manufacturing and resource sectors. The United Nations 1973 ranking of the largest 60 companies in the world ranked by sales identified 34 as being American by nationality, and of the total 60, American firms held 8 of the top 10 positions, and 14 of the top 20. These companies are all familiar to Canadians and may be compared to the *Financial Post* list: General Motors, Standard Oil of New Jersey (now Exxon), Ford Motors, General Electric, International Business Machines, Mobil Oil, Chrysler, Texaco, International Telephone and Telegraph, Western Elec-

## Figure 4: Power Corporation, Holdings in Canada

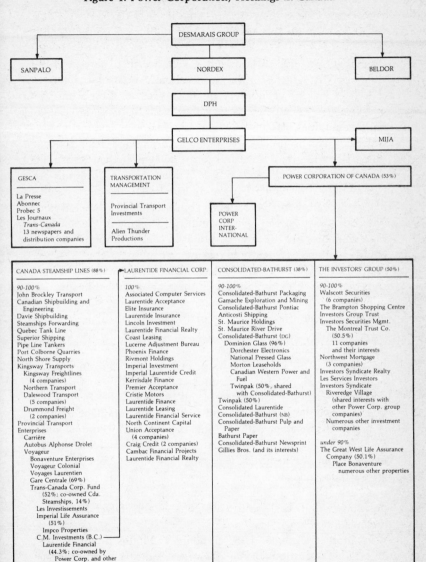

SOURCE: Statistics Canada, *Inter-Corporate Ownership Directory, 1975*, Ottawa: Queen's Printer, based on Chart 19. Holdings by subsidiaries are 90 per cent or more unless otherwise stipulated.

tric, and Gulf Oil. Altogether, of the 650 largest industrial corporations in the world, 358 are American; of the very top 211
corporations with sales in 1973 of $1 billion or more, 127 are
American.[12]

Several Canadian scholars have examined these data in order
to determine which corporations actually control the larger
share of Canada's economy. The most recent of these studies is
by Wallace Clement, who argues that in all there are 113 dominant companies.[13] These include the financial institutions in
Canada, which, unlike the manufacturing and resource industries, are largely owned and controlled within the country. In
Clement's judgment there are 196 dominant corporations in
United States, of which 131 are multinational, defined as companies operating in five or more countries and/or having over
one-fifth of deposits in foreign countries.[14] Some of the remaining companies are not multinational in that definition, but are
continental, in that their holdings include subsidiaries in Canada
and Mexico. Of the total 196 American corporations, 146 have
subsidiaries in Canada, and 31 of these are included in the 113
dominant corporations in Canada.

Clement identifies the degree of ownership of total assets in
each industrial sector held by corporations in the list of 113
dominant firms in Canada for 1971. In finance, five banks control 90 per cent of all assets and 91 per cent of all income for all
banks, and similarly few institutions control between 80 and 90
per cent of other financial assets and revenue in life insurance,
sales financing, mortgaging, and trusts. Four dominant mining
corporations together with their major subsidiaries control a little over 56 per cent of all assets and 64 per cent of all sales in the
metal mining industry.[15] The sectors of high concentration
follow those indicated in the CALURA table shown above, but the
numbers of independent firms actually involved in controlling
positions within each sector are considerably fewer than that
table can indicate.

In another study of U.S. companies, Phillip Blumberg examines the operations of the 100 largest industrial corporations
in 1972, and concludes that these firms control 47 per cent of all
assets, 41 per cent of all sales, and 51.5 per cent of net income in
all industries in that country. They employ between them 43 per
cent of all workers.[16]

Non-industrial companies, and particularly banking and other financial institutions, are similarly concentrated. These companies are particularly crucial to our understanding of concentration, because they, in turn, own significant shares in industrial corporations listed as dominant in the United States. For the top ten industrial corporations ranked by market value, financial institutions were found in a 1969 study to hold percentages of stock ranging from 10 to 53 per cent. Xerox and Gulf Oil, for example, had shareholdings of 53 and 50 per cent respectively by institutions; International Business Machines, 43 per cent; General Motors, 20 per cent; Exxon, 30 per cent; and American Telephone and Telegraph, 10 per cent.[17] Institutional ownership shares of such dimensions do not characterize all industrial corporations: a fair number of these are still owned entirely by private families, a larger number are controlled by shares held by identifiable private groups in combination with institutional holdings of less than 10 per cent. However, the proportion of shares held by such institutions increases with the size of corporations, and at the same time the number of institutions involved in shareholding decreases. The 13 major U.S. banks in 1973, according to another study, held 5 per cent or more of 9 out of the 10 largest, 47 out of the 100 largest, and 80 out of the 200 largest industrial corporations. They held 10 per cent or more shares in a total of 30 out of the 100 largest industrials.[18] The increasing presence of American financial institutions in industrial corporation ownership has accompanied the growth and increasing concentration of industrial corporations. In order to expand, such corporations have sought outside sources of funds, and banks or other financial companies have been the major source of these. In Canada, however, banks have been restricted mainly to portfolio investments, that is, investments carrying no ownership shares, in the multinationals.

As is evident in the international comparisons, concentration has a regional as well as industrial dimension. In 1970, 67 per cent of all manufacturing establishments in Canada were located in Quebec and Ontario. In spite of the expansion of the country in the interim, this is not a significantly different proportion than in 1920 when 72 per cent of manufacturing establishments were located there.[19] In Northern Canada, on both East and West Coasts, and throughout the Prairies, industries consist mainly of forestry and mineral or oil extraction processes. Few areas support refining, smelting, or manufacturing of the resources. The Atlantic, a flourishing region of early industrial activity, was eclipsed by Central Canada when the demise of British imperial preferences coincided with the growth of American industry and the gaining of control of the export-import trade by Central Canadian financiers. It has never been able to regain its strength, and the consequences are implied in the very low incomes of a high proportion of its population, a high unemployment rate, dependence on resource industries, and a small range of available occupations for its young people many of whom migrate out to Central Canada in search of employment.

By way of providing an illustration of the effects of differential growth in manufacturing, a comparison may be made between two cities of roughly equal size in terms of their occupations by industry (Table 2). Hamilton is in the heart of the industrial belt. Calgary has recently become a regional financial centre in connection with oil, but in 1970 it still lacked manufacturing of substantial size. The situation of Calgary could change with a shift in economic interests for the major corporations. Current struggles between the Ontario-based federal government and the Alberta provincial government over oil royalties presage such a shift, but the impact of this on the occupational structure of Calgary would be years away. Meanwhile Calgary, more affluent but otherwise like other Western cities, has a very limited occupational range.

The heart of an industrial economy is its manufacturing industries: resources are extracted for these, and the capacity of a region to be self-sustaining (where it is unable to avoid the surrounding industrial societies as is true for the whole of Canada) is dependent on its ability to manufacture industrial products. As these data indicate, and as the following chapters consider further, Canada is not self-sustaining, the larger part of Canada is not included in the manufacturing economy, and Canada has traditionally played the role of resource supplier to the industries first of Britain and now of the United States.

Very similar forms of concentration have been occurring in the Soviet countries. Russia and East Germany have become industrialized in part at the expense of the Central European small countries. These satellites have roles similar to that of Canada as suppliers of raw materials for industry, agricultural produce, and parts for the manufactured products of the Soviet Union. Within each of the nation-states in the Soviet sphere, internal variation is apparent, and uneven industrial development is a cause of considerable regional disparity.

By way of providing a comparison, recent data collected in Poland indicate the tendency toward concentration of industry in that country. The corresponding large corporations are known as WOGs. WOGs are virtual monopolists of their internal markets. In 1976, 102 WOGs accounted for 71.5 per cent of the sales of all goods and services in Poland, a rise of 20.3 per cent since 1973.[20] Corresponding decreases in the number of independent enterprises and independent sources of employment (still formally permissible in Poland) occurred in the same period.

The process of integration is very similar to that in private capitalist economies: first enterprises within the same general industry merge; secondly, local and regional enterprises that formerly served a small area are taken over by the larger central WOG; third, enterprises in supply and marketing industries are brought under the same central control. In the case of the Soviet countries, these mergers and umbrella industries result from decisions within the overtly political arena by "state planners," whereas in the private enterprise economies they are made by boards of directors in the private sector. The reasons for such decisions, from the point of view of the decision-makers are similar: large-size units reap economies of scale; there are organizational advantages; and control over the total industry and market is more effective. From the point of view of the outlying hinterlands and their population, there are the same disadvantages: relatively low employment opportunities in professional and technical jobs, which are concentrated at the centre, regional disparities in the distribution of income and other things, and, in particular, very little regional autonomy.

According to Polish sociologists, the interests of the WOGs are dominant at the level of political decision-making. Less industrialized regions have become more backward over the past decade, and ever more subject to the domination of the monopolies as resource hinterlands. Workers in the central sectors obtain higher wages, better health care, vacation facilities

## TABLE 2

Comparison of Manufacturing Statistics for Hamilton, Ontario, and Calgary, Alberta[1]

| Industrial Groups (Selected) and City | Establishments N | Total Employees N | Production Workers N | Office and Support Staff N | Total Wages and Salaries $000 | Total Value Added (by Manufacturer) $000 |
|---|---|---|---|---|---|---|
| *Food and Beverages* | | | | | | |
| Hamilton | 102 | 4,620 | 4,620 | 1,251 | 26,737 | 53,999 |
| Calgary | 84 | 4,527 | 2,247 | 1,280 | 24,185 | 54,417 |
| *Primary Metals* | | | | | | |
| Hamilton | 26 | 24,022 | 20,315 | 3,707 | 208,499 | 505,131 |
| Calgary | 12 | 667 | 571 | 95 | 5,224 | 10,477 |
| *Metal Fabricating* | | | | | | |
| Hamilton | 155 | 8,230 | 6,047 | 2,183 | 63,207 | 115,871 |
| Calgary | 77 | 2,321 | 1,811 | 510 | 17,864 | 29,295 |
| *Machinery* | | | | | | |
| Hamilton | 31 | 5,685 | 4,297 | 1,388 | 48,514 | 70,786 |
| Calgary | 13 | 557 | 420 | 137 | 4,246 | 8,356 |
| *Transportation and Equipment* | | | | | | |
| Hamilton | 15 | 1,708 | 1,303 | 405 | 12,209 | 22,489 |
| Calgary | 21 | 931 | 721 | 210 | 6,075 | 9,328 |
| *Electrical Products* | | | | | | |
| Hamilton | 21 | 6,334 | 3,871 | 2,463 | 49,253 | 80,808 |
| Calgary | 10 | 265 | 208 | 57 | 1,631 | 5,025 |

| | | | | | | |
|---|---|---|---|---|---|---|
| *Non-Metallic Minerals* | | | | | | |
| Hamilton | 37 | 2,783 | 2,170 | 8,154 | 20,000 | 39,320 |
| Calgary | 20 | 612 | 490 | 122 | 4,438 | 12,429 |
| *Chemical and Chemical Products* | | | | | | |
| Hamilton | 32 | 2,232 | 1,285 | 11,468 | 20,539 | 80,173 |
| Calgary | 15 | 734 | 516 | 218 | 5,957 | 13,789 |
| *Total: All Industries* | | | | | | |
| Hamilton | 681 | 66,807 | 51,447 | 14,703 | 518,771 | 1,103,487 |
| Calgary | 510 | 14,838 | 10,742 | 4,096 | 104,744 | 211,870 |

[1] Population: Hamilton: 498,510 (metropolitan region); Calgary: 403,330 (1971 Census).

SOURCE: Statistics Canada, *Manufacturing Industry of Canada: Geographical Distribution, 1970*, Table 8.

and other privileges than workers in the small enterprises (even though many of the small enterprises are also under state control). One sociologist has pointed out the comparison between Poland and Canada in these terms: ". . . one can argue that it matters little whether the decisions in a given region are private or public as long as the inhabitants of the region have not their say in the decisions concerning their region. In both cases industrialization is externally induced."[21]

## VI

The role of the state in Eastern European countries is more clearly defined than in the Western democracies. The objective of the Soviet system has been to create a system of government which has control of the economy and which can thereby overcome the problem of parallel structures with more power than the state. Ostensibly the central planning committees of the Communist parties direct the economy in the interests of the "working class," which, since private owners of capital no longer exist, includes everyone. As suggested in the previous section, the central planners have actually moved in directions very similar to those of the liberal democracies with respect to their economic institutions. These, like Western corporations, are highly concentrated structures with a managerial class and considerable control over technological development. The interests of the managerial class and of corporate employees generally appear to take precedence over the interests of labourers and workers in lesser state agencies and what remains of private (not free) enterprise. The similarity between the two systems is not accidental: the role of the state in both includes three functions which may be served by either direct state control or a combination of state and private enterprise. These functions are: (i) to maintain a monopoly on the "legitimate" use of force, to be used against internal dissidents as well as external societies if necessary; (ii) to legitimate the power of the dominant classes and the legal/institutional framework which facilitates the exercise of that power; and (iii) to provide the means by which capital may be accumulated and invested in industrial development.

Theoretically capitalism could flourish within any political system, but it is the case that historically it has flourished primarily in combination with a system known as "liberal democracy." Democratic institutions are not direct extensions of corporate businesses, whether or not they function in the interest of such businesses. Indeed, their condition for being is that they provide the sovereign power which guarantees stability to the society so that the economy may function. They do this ultimately through their monopoly of legitimate force. In theory the state is supplied with this capacity because it is the living embodiment of the general will, the instrument by which "the social good" is to be determined and achieved. It is supposed to be the instrument by which all individuals living within the territorial borders of the nation express their collective interests. Those who act on behalf of democratic nation-states, that is, national governments, are expected to act with reference to collective sentiments and interests, and to be accountable for their actions. Such expectations, ultimately rooted in theories of democracy as far removed from the reality of liberal democracies as that of Rousseau's "Social Contract," justify the actions of democratic governments in capitalist countries.[22]

Yet capitalism itself is not primarily concerned with "the social good" nor is it expected to be so. The ideologically accepted objective is to produce profits for investors. That is, the population at large views profits for investors as legitimate, and accepts the rightness of a system designed with such profits as its objective. The underlying rationale for this, already provided in the eighteenth century by Adam Smith, is that when all persons pursue their private ends, the net result is the social good.[23] Thus corporations are viewed as entities *sui generis*, that is, organizations which are independent of their private members at any time: they are not assumed to act specifically on behalf of society, nor believed to embody the "general will" of their employees, and not held accountable to their members for decisions taken in the interests of the corporate body by those whose own interests dominate corporate action.

This division of spheres, and the acceptance of it by the population rests on the assumption that the state is the paramount institution. Yet the state in liberal democracies, unlike private corporations, has limited control over economic behaviour: it can tax its citizens and apply public money to industry or welfare, it can enact legislation pertaining to the economy and can back this up with force, but it does not control markets, technology, or major investment decisions. These areas of control unequivocally rest with private corporations. These areas of decision-making permit corporate leaders to invest in or withdraw investment from a region according to their own interests, to employ or not to employ workers in need of jobs, to develop technology for whatever purposes will provide the greatest profits. This is economic power, and a state could use its ultimate sanction of force against those with economic power only by way of self-destruction.

Rousseau recognized the dilemma before corporations had become multinational entities, indeed before industrial corporations had emerged. He argued that democracy involved a citizenry which was entirely equal, had equal access to all relevant information, and would therefore be equally subordinate to all collective decisions. Such a population would then act in the interests of all equally. This is not a theory of "majority will." The majority is not universal. The majority in current liberal democracies is not part of an equal constituency, with equal access to information and equal penalties for insubordination to any law. Given Rousseau's definition, the state of such a nation does not have the conditions necessary for expression of a "general will," and therefore cannot be coincident with "society." It can only represent some interests, and it is of necessity subject to the interests of its most powerful units.

The theory of liberal democracy, that is, democracy within a capitalist system, developed together with a theory of competitive markets.[24] Entirely within the theory the rationale is that a free market economy – what is called "free enterprise" – could operate equally well in the political sphere: that is, the population of consumers could "buy" or "not buy" political platforms in "free elections." It further held that such a political institution as freely elected government backed by a permanent but subordinate civil service would be the most appropriate means of providing the infrastructure for the market economy without simultaneously providing strong government controls on individuals. This framework was especially desirable for individuals who happened to be investors in corporations that by their nature operate in a self-controlled economy. Liberal democracy has not been destroyed by large corporations; no more has the free market system. Both were from their inception theories – or ideologies – more than living organisms, and theories attendant on the growth of corporate organizations. As a consequence of the disparity between the real structure of nation-state societies and the ideological premises which support that structure, governments are caught in a paradoxical situation. At the real level, their power is limited by the unequal constituents on which they depend. At the ideological level, their power is limited only by territory and accountability to equal constituents. They are obliged to defend the interests of their powerful members; equally obliged to defend the interests of others against the powerful.

Historically, in fact, the liberal democratic state has seldom pitted itself against private capital. It has provided the security for the growth of corporations through its monopoly of force, force which has been applied in the not infrequent suppression of workers and dissidents and in occasional wars for which private corporations have produced highly profitable armaments. It has extended far into the society with institutional and ideological means for legitimation of the status quo. Instruments of legitimation include public schooling which trains workers and socializes the population; welfare provisions which reduce the harsher effects of the cycles of expansion and structural employment; a legal system which protects private property and individual rather than collective civil rights. Finally, and in many ways most importantly, it has provided the appropriate conditions for the accumulation of investment capital.

The final function has been served in Canada through legislation which protects the rights of banking institutions to invest domestic capital in foreign corporations and the rights of foreign resource and manufacturing corporations to own production property in Canada; through direct state subsidies to private enterprise; and through state "ownership" or partnership with private business in transportation, utilities such as hydro-electricity, and other unprofitable but (for corporate growth) essential industries. We will consider in later chapters why and how this has been the Canadian pattern.

By virtue of its structural dependency on private capital, and of its historical development, the question reasonably occurs, is the state in liberal democracies an autonomous actor?[25] We will return to this question in the concluding chapter, but here we might note two features of the state which obstruct its complete subservience to private interests. One is the sheer size of the population directly employed by the state in its many institutional arenas of education, judiciary, social services, civil service, and defence.[26] Such workers have a vested interest in the survival of the nation-state, and this can and occasionally does conflict with the interests of ruling groups. The second is the fragmentation of the state. In Canada, there is no single and monolithic state: there is a federal state with its institutional bureaucracies, civil service, and government, and there are provincial and municipal "sub-states" with their institutional bureaucracies, civil services, and governments. The interests of these various groups are not always or necessarily coincident, with the result that various governments are obliged to recognize divergent pressure groups and regional demands. In general, these regional demands are still representative of the interests of private capital, but are translated through the interests of regional groups who struggle for greater political and economic power vis-à-vis the Central Canadian elites.

Although the multilevel system of government encourages the expression of some divergent interests, ultimately such "balkanization" operates in the interests of foreign corporations. In both Quebec and Alberta strong multinational and foreign-owned corporations dominate the economy, having arrived at that position through the support of a federal government. As the locus of economic interest shifts, from the manufacturing areas of southern Ontario and Quebec toward the oil reserves of the West, regional financiers and provincial governments struggle to gain ascendency over Central Canadian financiers and the federal government. Their objective is to gain the intermediary role historically held by these groups. Like the federal government, provincial governments co-operate with corporate capital which transcends them both in economic power.

## VII

In consideration of the market economy, we have examined the commodity and finance sectors and the role of government. Markets also exist for labour, because in the market system people as well as things are bought and sold for cash.

The vast majority of wage-labourers sell their labour on an open and competitive market. This means that where they are offered choices, they sell to the highest bidder. Their price is determined by the relative scarcity of their particular skills or knowledge, the alternative sources of employment in any given region, and the relative cost of substitutes for their labour. Since there are not as many employments available as there are workers, a certain proportion of all workers compete unsuccessfully for jobs; their availability is one of the factors that determines the wage structure for those who compete successfully.

While all of these workers compete for jobs, direct competition for any group during an expansionary phase of capitalism is confined to those with equivalent "marketable skills." Among the criteria for marketable skills are years of formal education, vocational training, length of time previously employed, and particular kinds of knowledge. In addition to these ways of grouping potential workers, sex, age, ethnicity, and marital status are used by employers to differentiate between job applicants. Women are frequently obliged to compete with women for jobs defined as "women's work," so that competition for jobs is not between all potential workers or even between all workers with similar skills, but between workers with similar skills who all fit some further requirement such as being male, young, white, or single. Some of the reasons for this are discussed in Chapter 5; these reasons have to do with employer's needs (or their perception of them), not with the needs of workers. In addition, workers become differentiated by previous work histories: for instance, employment in the corporate sector brings with it an edge in marketability over employment in the marginal or small business sector. Workers who suffer highest unemployment tend to be those most frequently attached, when employed, to the least profitable businesses or the service industries.[27]

Competition also exists between a group of workers who are more often classified as "owners," these being actually owners of small businesses or merely machinery. A large number of these small business and machinery owners exist on the fringes of the corporate economy as service workers for, particularly, resource companies. Contractors compete with one another for large corporation contracts covering specific phases of resource extraction (e.g., logging, trucking, fishing, and various aspects of oil extraction described in a later chapter). Resource companies maintain these contracts because the arrangements permit them to obtain a labour force without permanent obligations, and shift many of the "risk" costs of resource extraction onto the shoulders of the small contractor. The effect of this competition is that corporate consumers have choices in the traditional competitive market sense: this constitutes a "free enterprise" economy for their benefit.

All workers compete for jobs. However, some workers obtain job security once employed through collective associations and bargaining. In Canada, one-quarter of all wage-labourers and one-third of non-agricultural workers are organized into labour unions, the prime purpose of which is to engage in collective bargaining with the potential use of strikes. While still not having the rights of ownership available to employers, those workers who have banded together to monopolize labour supplies for any given industrial production process have the means to bargain effectively for greater incomes, more job security, or other conditions for the continued sale of their labour.

In 1974 there were 178 national and international unions in Canada. Of these 81 were international unions, that is, unions with membership in more than one country. Every one of these internationals, as listed in 1974, had its head offices in the United States. In total, these international unions have over 4,000 locals in Canada, and close to two million Canadian members out of a total of over 17 million. Canadian workers represent 8.6 per cent of the total membership.[28] Of the remaining unions, 63 are national in scope and represent just under 800,000 members; another 34 come under special legislation for federal and provincial government employees and represent just under 400,000 members.[29] International unions are predominant in industries characterized by multinational corporate employers, which is to say the major manufacturing and resource sectors of the economy. National unions serve sectors under the control of national and provincial governments and, for the most part, national and smaller businesses.

The capacity of these different unions to represent their

members differs greatly; also differing are the internal arrangements of the unions for representation. Since the majority of members in international unions are American workers in parent companies or U.S.-based subsidiaries, their primary focus of protection is these workers. They normally (but not always) bargain on behalf of their Canadian workers through negotiations with parent-company employers in the United States. Having an international base, these unions may be very strong in their capacity to monopolize labour in any given industry, but this does not always mean – and some would argue does not normally mean – adequate representation of their minority groups, of which Canadian workers are the major entity.[30]

Historically, American unionism took over a nascent Canadian union movement and British-linked Canadian unions while American business was initially expanding into Canada. A major reason for this extension was the need to protect American workers against competing cheap labour in American subsidiaries in Canada. The American labour movement has not acted as a militant class-conscious organization, in large part because it has succeeded in creating an affluent segment of the working class in North America. It has not gained ownership rights or control of industrial production, but it has gained a significant share of profits in the form of high wages by co-operating with employers in the establishment of monopoly and oligopoly market conditions for manufactured goods. Much more militant and class-conscious movements have arisen in the resource regions of Canada in the form of industrial, as contrasted with trades-based, unionism, but these have been outflanked by the internationals.[31]

With this general introduction to the terms of our debate and the historical context of corporate capitalism, we encounter some of the issues that need greater consideration. These will be examined in turn as we proceed through the text. One of them is, did the corporations which became dominant succeed because of product superiority and technical expertise, and if so are they then the most socially beneficial organizations for industrial production? What has been the nature of technological development and why is it tied to corporate concentration? This is the subject of the next chapter.

# CHAPTER 2

# "TECHNOLOGY AND EMPIRE"

*We can hold in our minds the enormous benefits of technological society, but we cannot so easily hold the ways it may have deprived us, because technique is ourselves.*

– George Grant[1]

*Who owns and understands this doesn't want you around. All this technology has somehow made you a stranger in your own land.*

– Robert M. Pirsig[2]

Widespread is the sentiment that technology has its own momentum. Things are invented and more things automatically follow. The process needs only original minds, individuals who "happen" to invent technical means of doing things that no one else had ever thought of.

A divergent interpretation needs consideration when one reviews the history not of technical invention as such, but of the launching of technical invention into the public realm – the utilization and application of techniques which may well have been known and available centuries earlier. Historian Henri Pirenne observed that the Vikings lost America as soon as they discovered it, because it was of no use to Europe at that time. In repeating Pirenne's observation, historian Fernand Braudel adds such examples as the steam engine "invented a long time before it launched the industrial revolution – or should we say before being launched by it?"[3]

The word "technology" is itself revealing. Contrary to its popular use, it does not mean only the series of technical inventions which immediately spring to mind when it is introduced. It means the organization of people and ideas and things which collectively produce given modes of subsistence. To invent an automated bobbin, there had first to be an organization designed explicitly and rationally for the purpose of producing textiles; there had to be an export market for textiles; there had to be a money economy and wage-labourers; there had to be an incentive to produce textiles at a faster pace and at a lower cost in labour; there had to be the notion in many heads that the rational calculation of materials in motion could culminate in a new and useful thing; and there had to be a prior and similar process which culminated in the application of non-human forms of energy to the industrial production process. It is this totality of organized rational planning toward a specific goal, together with the more general goal of profit accumulation, that we now call the industrial revolution.

The question is not who invented this or that, but why and for whose benefit? Technical invention which is not random, not dependent on simply the bounty of nature for providing gifted spirits, is invention channelled in specific ways for specific reasons. It is invention intended to achieve some purpose. At the level of pure science, it is intended and said to be intended to advance a system of ideas, increase an understanding of natural processes. Pure science, however, exists in a social context, and here as elsewhere the context plays its part in determining or at least influencing what the scientist perceives as a problem of understanding. The scientist is puzzled in the same way as the pre-industrial hunter by what is not obvious or already explained within the existing system of ideas; for both this area of ignorance is defined by that realm recognized as knowledge. Where knowledge is defined within a specific economic context and that context is taken for granted or not itself seen to be puzzling, pure science must be conducted relative to that knowledge. The same is even more true of applications of science, or what is popularly known as technology.

Puzzles and problems are presented to the technician as given:

the need to develop a medicine that does not have a particular side-effect, the desirability of creating machinery that saves labour, the demand for additional computer hardware that can be integrated into an on-going computer system. Inventions are then but extensions of knowledge, they require no radical rethinking about the nature of the world "out there."

It is the task, in a highly specialized world, of the social scientist rather than the scientist or technician engaged in technological invention to enquire into the nature of the technical process itself. Since technology is embedded in an economic context, the first obvious "puzzle" is what the nature of that linkage is. In an industrial society, is techological innovation a function of market demands, of labour availability, of institutionalized science? Is it either dependent on, or the determining base for, concentration in industry? In what respects does the control of technological innovation by large institutions, both universities or government laboratories and private corporations, preclude the development of alternative techniques for society? In what respects, on the contrary, does such control speed up such developments? In this chapter we will consider both some examples of technological change, and some theories about the process.

I

The export of staples and import of finished products is as advantageous to a merchant-capitalist as the export of manufactured products. The objective is merely the creation of profit for the trader. Partly for this reason, and partly because the craft-guilds so quickly became self-protective corporate groups, there was neither capital nor incentive to develop new technical means of production in the fourteenth and fifteenth centuries. With the vast expansion of trading opportunities, and the development of supply colonies in the new territories, the incentive was created.

During the sixteenth and seventeenth centuries, however, it was not so much new physical plants or equipment which provided new techniques for production as it was increasing integration and rationalization of production processes. The predominant mode of industrial production was cottage or "putting-out" work, whereby a merchant employer purchased raw materials and distributed these to independent artisans who worked on their own premises. The capitalist paid the workers and then had control of the final product for markets, but did not have the means of supervising or controlling the workers themselves. Coincident with this system and emerging as a preferred system by those merchants who could afford the initial outlay was the factory.

The factory was a central establishment owned by the capitalist together with an entire production plant, such as looms for the textile industry or all tools necessary for iron-mongering. Workers could be supervised in such a system, did not have control of the means of production, and could be organized in such a fashion that each worked on components of total products rather than an entire product, thus increasing the speed and productivity of the system without increasing the number of workers required. Clearly the factory was advantageous for the employer, but it required considerable capital investment. Furthermore, as long as workers had choices, they were inclined to resist factory employment. Historian A.P. Usher argues that such factories did not succeed on a large scale until mechanization of the production processes virtually eliminated independent production opportunities:

> These new conditions of work (and therefore of living) were so distasteful to the workers that they were accepted only when mechanization had proceeded so far that decentralized production could no longer compete in the market place. The introduction of power machinery into the textile industry on a comprehensive scale was the underlying factor in the change.[4]

Some centralized industries were operating before the introduction of power machinery or extensive mechanization. This was less true of the textiles industry, in which the means of production were still relatively simple and the nature of the work suitable for all members of families, than of certain other industries in which a division of labour and organization of workers at a single location could be undertaken. In a history of the period, Clough and Cole list mines, shipyards, brewing and sugar refining as among these industries. In addition they note that centralized factories were encouraged by the granting of monopolies by government in such products as tapestries, "glass, salt, starch, soap, saltpeter, alum, and other products."[5]

In particular, coal-mines, which had been independent production units on a small scale, became centralized and large-scale organizations owned and operated by groups of capitalists. Here, as in factories, large numbers of workers were employed on a wage system, none of them owning the means of production.

Under both the independent craftsmen system of the late feudal period and the putting-out system of the early industrial period, workers normally lived and produced their goods in their own homes or small adjacent shops. Not infrequently, they were engaged as well in some family agricultural production, especially during the early putting-out phase where rural producers were less costly in wages than town-workers, thus attracting the preference of merchant-employers. But as centralized production became a more common mode, employees were obliged to work, and sometimes to live, in places owned by the capitalist-employer. Dobb mentions the ironmonger, Ambrose Crowley, who organized a village of workers by establishing not only a factory for the production of nails, locks, bolts, and various tools, but also houses which he rented to employees.[6] By bringing together all of the workmen associated with the total production of these allied products, Crowley was able to control rates of production, to integrate the productive process, to control the costs of production to a much greater degree than would have been possible had the various producers been independent craftsmen in diverse locations, and to maintain a steady supply of easily accessible labour. Similar "company towns" were established for other manufactories, and for coal-mines. The towns created for miners were notorious for their squalid conditions.

The division of labour and rational calculation of component tasks was the first stage in the mechanization of production. A great deal of machinery replicates human action, and the invention of such machinery followed from a prior rationalization of those actions. It was under the early industrial organizations that scientific management actually began, though the term and the growth of a body of experts on the subject did not occur until the opening decades of the twentieth century. An increasing division of labour provided for an enormously increased productivity rate. The division of labour was first experienced by direct producers of goods. Their jobs were broken down into smaller components, and each producer became a unit in a chain for the creation of total products rather than the craftsman of a total product individually created. The same principle was subsequently applied to "indirect" producers, those who serviced industrial production plants through personnel management, accounting, development of markets, clerical work, and interaction with customers.

The technical inventions with which we usually associate the industrial revolution may be dated to about the 1770s, with the introduction of the Hargreaves spinning-jenny followed by other significant inventions for the textiles industry, and the Watt steam-engine which, when applied to cotton manufacture, dramatically increased production rates. By the second half of the nineteenth century, virtually every industry had been affected by the harnessing of production to steam power and the mechanization of production processes. The process was uneven, both between industries and within any one industry, but gradually mechanization became the dominant feature of industrial production.

Mechanization itself means simply the use of tools of any kind either to reduce reliance on human and animal energy or to enhance human productivity. The devices which take the place of human energy for these purposes include locomotives, derricks, hoists, conveyors, portable loaders, and similar machines. These pick up goods, load them, drop them, move them from one place to another, and unload them. Some industries are primarily concerned with these operations: transportation industries, for example, or wholesale and retail outlets for such items as lumber and coal. Much of the construction industry is concerned with moving goods for subsequent use in building. The extraction of raw materials such as coal or metals also involves a great deal of hauling and handling activity both inside the mine or other site, and from the mine site to subsequent operation sites. In the manufacturing industries, the processing of materials at all stages depends on a prior hauling and handling and on a subsequent lifting away and allocating of finished products.

While the major component of mechanization is the elimination of hauling and handling jobs by human agents, some aspects of actual manufacturing processes can also be altered through mechanization. Indeed, there are many forms of mechanization which apply equally to the two stages and one has difficulty distinguishing clearly between them. For example, the development of automatic looms in the manufacture of textiles, or the automatic feeders in the manufacture of pulp provided both the energy for moving goods from one place to another and for increasing the speed and allowing for continuous operation of the processing stage. Bobbins and shuttles which were inserted and threaded automatically by machines no longer required human agents for threading and resetting; and the continuous operation of the textile machines thereby facilitated dramatically altered the entire process of manufacture.

Mechanization increased the capacities of capitalists to create integrated, rationalized production systems. This rationalization effectively destroyed what remained of crafts-guild control over production, and brought under control and into wage-labour conditions the vast majority of the population. The labour force, which is what these wage-workers came to be called (a term we now take for granted, as if it were a fact of human nature rather than a recent human creation), became at one and the same time less capable of controlling the quality or quantity of its own products and more specialized in the performance of component tasks in the production process.

The combination of mechanization and rationalization of labour gave rise to enormously increased productivity. A labour force which might produce X quantity of goods where the chief source of energy was human or animal and where tools remained merely extensions of the human hand could produce X-plus-10 or very much more where it was tied to machines activated by steam. If the wages for these workers remained the same at both periods, the rise in productivity meant profits entirely for the owner-merchants, that is, the capitalists. These profits could be, and were, ploughed back into industries in the form of increased investment in machinery and purchase of further industrial property.

As mechanization became more important, the cost of establishing an industrial enterprise became prohibitive. One required an enormous capital investment in machinery in order to compete effectively with established producers. In addition, those who were most successful early in the stage of mechanizing any particular system had an initial advantage in accumulating large capital surplus for further industrial development. Inevitably, then, there was a built-in tendency in the unregulated industrial system toward concentration of ownership.

Within two centuries, mechanization combined with capital generated through concentration provided the base for automated systems of production. Where mechanization reduces reliance on human energy, automation actually substitutes machines for humans in controlling and operating a production process. That is, it eliminates humans from a range of decision-making, not simply manual, tasks.

Automated production may include processes already highly mechanized onto which a series of information and information "feed-back" mechanisms have been superimposed. These built-in control devices regulate production. Machine-tenders may be retained for some aspects of the task, and for the tending of the "brain-unit" computer machines, but in general automation eliminates these jobs while at the same time allowing for still greater production, and particularly much greater and more systematic control, at lower costs.

For some industries, and particularly those dealing with liquids, gases, and chemicals, relatively little mechanization preceded automatic controls in the development of the production processes. For other industries which flourished through the mechanization of many processes, automation may never occur because it would not provide a technical advantage. This may be true, for example, of the manufacturing processes in automobile production and other discrete and hard-material products. Still other industries retained fairly simple forms of mechanization until the post-war era, when automated processes became applicable to their production. Banks and other offices, for example, have shifted rapidly from labour-intensive operations to computerized accounting systems within the past decade.

Different types of automatic systems for controlling production are designed for different kinds of production operations. The manufacture of such substances as plastics, metals, and wood or other hard and separate items will involve automatic "transfer devices" for different stages of their manufacture which are little more than advanced forms of mechanization. The more revolutionary type of automatic system is found in the chemical and oil-refining industries, the pulp-mill, and in the electric and gas utilities. The flow of materials, mixtures of ingredients, control of quality, total information and feedback, and self-correcting mechanisms are all built-in automatic procedures.

Mechanization and automation were and remain essential components of the total industrial complex, but they are not the whole of it. Equally important to the growth of industrial society were transformations in agriculture which were only partly connected to machines, and changes in both the nature of raw materials deemed essential to human survival and in the methods of utilizing these materials. None of these developments can be understood apart from the coincident development of corporate organizations for both agricultural and industrial production. Techniques for increasing production were consequences first of previous economic changes, then additional causes of further changes. The changes were consistently in the direction of concentration, centralization, and control of the technological process by the dominant companies.

## II

The most essential raw material for any civilization is food. The manorial system was relatively self-sufficient in its production of food, and before the erosion of that system food markets were not significant units of the society though they were present and served small-town populations. With the demise of feudalism and the rise of a landless proletariat, a pressing need arose to feed workers not themselves employed in agricultural production. The "agricultural revolution" of the seventeenth and eighteenth centuries was a response to this problem. This consisted of the development of new crops on open fields, improvements in livestock, and new implements.[7]

The development of crops which were not specifically designed for the subsistence of the producers and which included cultivated grasses and roots for livestock fodder occurred *after* the manorial estates had forcibly evicted their peasant tenants: that is, after the money economy had become widespread and the development of a wage-labour force had been created. Further enclosures occurred, spurred in Britain by the *Enclosures*

*Act* in the late seventeenth century, but the process was well underway before this legislation.

The production of new crops both permitted growth of more and larger cattle for food and increased the quality of the land in good part because the better-fed cattle provided richer manure. The increased production of grain crops thereby made possible, however, was hampered by inadequate methods of transportation to cities: thus one of the first outcomes of this improvement was an impetus to "invent" better means of transportation and more systematic transportation routes and schedules. In addition, there was opportunity for entrepreneurial organizations to organize food distribution systems.

Improvements in crop-rotation systems and in such implements as plows and hoes followed. The independent development of iron (for which there were other uses, such as arms for war, and trains and rails) provided new material for more effective plows. Harvesting machines followed. All of these machines increased productivity of the soil without increasing, indeed often decreasing, the need for labour. All depended on the existence of efficient marketing organizations and initial capital. Agriculture, as a consequence, became the domain of fewer owners and workers, ever more linked to capitalist organizations, as it underwent technological change.

The same is true of industrial production of agricultural implements and machines. These two sectors, the actual production of food and the production of technical means for improving agriculture, not surprisingly affected one another: a change in other aspects of agriculture would create a market for new implements; new implements would alter the means of producing food and renew the cycle of both interdependence and increasing concentration.

The manufacture of farm implements is one of the very few industries in which Canadian companies enjoy significant shares of world markets. This is due to a combination of large agricultural markets in North America during the early period of industrial growth, and the direction of Canadian capital into this particular industry. It is not due to technological invention. The largest American companies have similar reasons for their success. There is no evidence that the largest producers were the most innovative in technology, and there is considerable evidence that their success is allied to capital investment rather than superior products. A brief sketch of their histories provides evidence for these conclusions.

Close to sixty known harvesters were invented in the half-century preceding 1830 when the McCormick and Hussey harvesters were introduced.[8] These were invented by individual farmer-entrepreneurs in the United States. At this point, the combination of genuinely new markets (new lands being settled, new demands for grain by Europeans engaged in war, the increasingly dense city populations throughout both Europe and America) and a product that was still undergoing transformation created conditions suitable to competition. The remainder of the nineteenth century is replete with patent pools as well as disputes and temporary monopolies where patents were successfully held by one or another company, but there were numerous companies involved in production nonetheless. McCormick grew much more rapidly than competitors, and eventually gained a large share of the American market. The reasons for this do not lie with technology: McCormick was apparently a ruthless, aggressive salesman. His rise to dominance was marked by frequent court cases, partnerships entered into until the advantage disappeared, and then dissolved, and ingenious business decisions. He was aided by the timing of the construction of the Erie Canal and railroads. These reduced transportation costs of cereals grown farther west for the large populations in eastern industrial cities, and McCormick was quick to recognize these possibilities.

Toward the end of the century, McCormick, and other major producers such as Deering and John Deere in United States, Massey and Harris in Canada, entered into mergers and combinations and began to integrate vertically their enterprises. Deering, for example, purchased controlling shares in a blast furnace, coal and iron-ore properties, and hard-wood forests. Small "fringe" producers who had manufactured implements on contract to the holders of key patents were eliminated. With reference to the United States, Phillips notes:

> This fringe group served a purpose as long as inadequate transportation led buyers to prefer local producers over distant ones. With improved transportation and a stable market,

the usefulness of such arrangements diminished and implement manufacturing came to be carried on by the leading firms in their own plants. Largely as a result of this, there was a marked reduction in the number of firms between 1880 and 1890, from 1943 to 910 firms.[9]

At the retail level, independent selling agents engaged in a trade war through the 1890s, but the terms of competition – genuinely different product companies – were already being undermined by the movement toward concentration which culminated in a merger of major companies in America in 1902. The International Harvester Company (McCormick and others) replaced eight of the largest producers together with their subsidiaries in supply and related fields.

Parallel development characterized the production of plows and other tillage implements. The Deere Company became the largest single manufacturer before its merger with and take-over of other companies including some in other farm implement industries such as corn shellers, farm elevators, haying machinery, and wagons. By 1915, the list of mergers had increased, and Deere and Company had become the second largest farm implements manufacturer in the United States (second to International Harvester). Both companies were now fully integrated operations with considerable control over their supplies, transportation, storage, and retail outlets as well as investments in complete lines of farm equipment.

Steam-powered tractors were possible, and had been used in the Western states, during the nineteenth century. However, the existing manufacturers of farm implements did not proceed with development of means for adapting these engines to their implements. The internal-combustion tractor, developed apparently by companies other than the big farm implements combines, began to make inroads in the first decade of the twentieth century. It is reported that there were hundreds of small factories producing tractors, none of them with sufficient capital and control over retail outlets to overcome the movement, in the second decade, of acquisitions by larger combines. International Harvester did research and produced its own tractor by 1910, selling this to its customers for other farm implements through its control of many retail outlets, in spite of the machine's clumsy size and limited capacities.[10]

The entry of the Ford Company into the tractor business had a significant impact. Ford had already established a successful automobile business by utilizing principles of rationalization which were more advanced (in terms of plant efficiency) than any previously undertaken, and by creating a business system which allowed small farmers as well as city dwellers to purchase these goods at relatively cheap prices. These organizational and commercial capacities, more than the actual advantages of the machinery produced, made Ford a formidable competitor in any field he entered. Though he had no control over other farm implements, he successfully dominated the tractor market for a few years before 1920. Other large companies were temporarily eclipsed and some adjusted to the situation by adapting their own products for use with Ford tractors. In order to capitalize further on his market, Ford linked up with Irish inventor Harry Ferguson for development of farm implements that would become integral parts of tractors. (At a later period, Ferguson sued Ford for some nine million dollars, and subsequently [1953] amalgamated his holdings in Britain and the United States with those of Massey-Harris in Canada).

Ford's success, so much dependent on financing methods and advertising, spurred International Harvester into experimenting with innovative techniques. The experiments involved a complete retooling of their main plant in Chicago with "modern labour-saving manufacturing equipment," but it paid off in increased sales of tractors. Capitalizing on its extensive retail empire and its capacity to produce quickly a range of other farm implements along with its new tractors, Harvester outdistanced Ford by 1918. Ford's contribution along the way had been significant: he had obliged the producers to come up with better machines at lower customer costs and had a profound and lasting impact on the internal organization of factories for farm implements production. As far as the actual machinery was concerned, it was Ford who had initiated development of light-weight tractors with integrated implements (through his financial capacity to buy Ferguson's talent). The development of these products subsequent to Ford's experiments was due to the competition he provided, rather than to inititive and research in existing giant companies.

The development of tractors with integrated implements in the United States brought about the eclipse of many Canadian farm implements companies. Though the Canadian market had been almost entirely served by Canadian companies between the 1860s and 1900, protected by tariffs and aided for a while by inadequate transportation capacities for south-north trade, Canadian firms were unsuccessful – or too late – in creating competitive tractors. Relatively specialized firms very early became dependent on innovations in the United States.

Phillips, in his study of the Canadian industry in 1956, notes that none of the Canadian producers sponsored invention. They depended entirely on American designs and patents.[11] He illustrates this case with reference to the Massey Company which advanced only after an 1851 purchase of patent rights for the Ketchum Mower and Burrall Reaper from an American manufacturer, and the 1855 purchase of patent rights to the Manny Combined Hand Rake Reaper Mower. Other firms were similarly reliant on American patent purchases. Phillips compares Canadian firms to the "fringe group" in United States which produced under licence from larger companies. Canadian firms enjoyed protected markets and lower costs than American competitors, but American firms gained from the arrangement by deriving revenue in the form of royalties from purchase of patents by Canadians.

With tariffs and the completion of a trans-Canada railway, two firms emerged as dominant manufacturers: the Massey and the Harris companies. Neither company, according to Phillips' study, was innovative in techniques of manufacture, but both were expansive in innovative sales techniques. Eventually, in order to avoid further expensive competition at the retail level, the two merged. Throughout the period of high domestic protection, they became involved in extensive export sales businesses, but did not move into new manufacturing lines until American products, especially new tractors, jumped tariff walls and provided genuine competition in the Western wheat regions of Canada.

With reference to the pre-Confederation period, historian Tom Naylor observes that the pattern of Canadian patent legislation was largely determined by the interest of Canadian agricultural implements firms in promoting the importation of American technology.[12] The legislation provided no protection for Canadian inventors. With neither legislative protection nor the support of Canadian capital, Canadian inventors were effectively dissuaded from producing for a Canadian market.

By the 1930s there were three dominant firms in Canadian farm implements: Massey-Harris, International Harvester, and Cockshutt Plow Company, each of these the result of many mergers and take-overs. Massey-Harris had by this time acquired an American tractor-production firm (having decided not to risk capital in developing its own line of tractors), and Cockshutt followed suit with its purchase of Canadian rights to American-invented manufacturing processes. Massey-Harris is reported to have developed some of its own technology for combine production during the 1920s and Cockshutt developed a disc seeder, but whether these represented a "fast-growing independence on matters of implement design in the 1920s" as recorded by Phillips is open to debate, given the vast range of other implements still dependent on American technology and the continuing presence of America's largest producer in Canada as one of the three big firms.

What is now called "the second agricultural revolution" was a direct result of the second complete European war (known to the Western world as World War II, signifying both ethnocentricity in our view of the world and covert recognition that the economic system of Europe by the twentieth century had become a world system in its consequences if not its production methods). This consisted of further mechanization, new feeding methods for cattle, and development of chemicals for weed-killers, defoliants, and control of disease and insect infestations.[13] It also consisted of highly concentrated and multinational businesses taking over agriculture in every phase from food production through canning, preserving, and packaging, to marketing.

As in other businesses, improved technology and reduction of reliance on human labour involve high capitalization. Few families can afford to mechanize their production methods or purchase the chemicals and scientifically bred cattle that make the farm a viable market enterprise. Nor can the poorly equipped farmer on a small family holding compete with agribusiness.

Agribusiness is agriculture carried on through production methods similar to industry, on very large acreages and with extensive mechanization, linked to processing, transportation, and marketing of agricultural produce through common ownership and vertical integration. As family farms became incapable of providing sustenance, individual families sold their land. Sometimes this land was purchased by large companies for continued agricultural production; sometimes it was purchased by real estate developers and non-agricultural industries. Among the effects of these developments, then, was a steady reduction in both numbers of independent farms and total acreage available for food production.

Agribusiness developed in Canada much as it did elsewhere. Food processing plants were numerous throughout agricultural regions prior to the first world war. These were generally owned by farmers or combinations of farmers where they could produce surplus food for external or local markets. These included canneries, cheese factories, small creameries, abattoirs, and grist mills.[14] In addition, individual farmers marketed their own dairy products, fruit, vegetables, and meat, and combinations of farmers marketed grains.[15] By the 1920s, large firms, mainly Canadian in ownership, began to take over these small family enterprises. Mergers were followed by increasing concentration here as in other industries. In the 1950s, multinational agribusinesses were taking over national businesses, adding a further increase in concentration levels. With each decade, these large firms moved further toward total integration, so that retail stores such as Canada Safeway (American) or Loblaws (Canadian), and meat packers such as Burns Foods (Canadian) and Swift Canadian (American) are engaged in the entire production and servicing of the agricultural industry.

One of the effects of this concentration has been a net reduction in employment in the agricultural industry as a whole.[16] Another has been an increase in food imports, especially from United States. Parent companies with processing facilities in Canada, such as Del Monte, have been responsible for closure of local canneries and loss of markets for local fruit producers as they import substantial portions of their product from the United States.[17] Large retail chains with farms in the United States or elsewhere and their own transportation companies also import food that can be grown in Canada. Yet another effect is that food prices reflect decisions within the oligopolistic industrial structure and not the actual cost of food production or labour returns to farmers and farm workers.[18] Yet there is no evidence that these various developments are connected to the technological superiority of the successful companies. Weston, Del Monte, Safeway, Robin Hood Multifoods, Ogilvie, Cargill Grain, and Kraft Foods are beneficiaries of technological change in basic food production and in transportation and storage facilities, but their success is due to their access to capital for expansion and subsequent market control.[19]

Canadian farmers, farm workers, food-processing industries, and retail food outlets have lost autonomy and control of the food industry, but Canadians are nonetheless able to consume adequate quantities of nutritional foods. Much more serious are the consequences of this process for countries with no separate industrial production to counterbalance declining food supplies. Land taken out of subsistence production and turned over to cash crops or to non-agricultural industry may produce more, but it does not produce basic food for peasant tenants. As labour-saving machinery displaces peasants, these populations move to urban centres in search of industrial employment just as Europeans did two centuries earlier. However, industry is not developing on a labour-intensive base as it did in Europe, and it is, besides, controlled elsewhere and in the interests of external corporations. Where there is no industrial work, no room for labour on corporate farms which produce crops for export, and no basic food from these cash crops, there is hunger. The agricultural revolutions made it possible to feed the world's population, but the economic structure of agricultural production and distribution instead maintains a world system in which hunger afflicts some two-thirds of all people.

## III

Food is a basic requirement for subsistence at any time. Fuels and metals, however, are requirements of relatively recent date, and as requirements depend on the development and maintenance of industrial production systems. This is not to say that fuels and metals had no previous use, but that their previous uses were relatively frivolous, even if highly valued.

The "discovery" of new fuels was tightly connected to the demand for metals, especially iron: that, in turn, was created by wars (both the American and French revolutions of the eighteenth century and the Napoleonic wars of the nineteenth century), the creation of rationalized industrial production systems, and the demand for improved means of transportation, especially for agricultural produce.

Coal was finally introduced into the smelting process by the early eighteenth century in Europe (though the process was understood much earlier), and its successful introduction quickly transformed the iron industry from a dispersed undertaking by small groups or individuals with access to ore, to centralized organizations close to coal resources. What we now call vertical integration was early evident in the iron industry, where capitalists able to purchase expensive machinery for the smelting process also purchased large tracts of land where coal and iron ore were known to exist: eventually they sponsored "scientific" explorations for finding such valuable resources. Small prospectors and independent ironmongers were forced out of business if not by their inability to compete with mechanized production systems then by their inability to obtain resources.[20]

One notes here the mutual re-enforcement of technological changes in apparently different industries. The need for iron was partly dependent on the technical development of machinery and the demand for railways; these in turn were dependent on an earlier rationalization of labour and the creation of more productive agricultural systems; demand for iron in its turn spawned demand for coal, and the development of coal mining on a large scale fuelled industries in each of the other sectors. One notes as well that all of these technical developments were preceded and not merely accompanied by profound social changes, and that many such developments were entirely possible but not "useful" in earlier social contexts. Another factor involved in this process was depletion of existing resources: one of the reasons for the rise of coal as the main source of fuel in iron smelting as in other industries was the exhaustion of forests throughout Europe. Previous firing for ironmongering had been based on wood fuel.

No sooner was coal established as a major ingredient in the industrial process than efforts to reduce its dependence on labour were sought and introduced. Where labour was tunnelling with pick and shovel in underground mines of 1900, by 1910 machines combined with blasting were doing much of this work. Electric hauling, loading, and drilling machines were in general use by 1925.[21] Mechanical pacing and full integration of operations were implemented by the close of World War II with development of the "continuous-mining" machine which "chews its way along the coal seam, at the same time passing coal back to a conveyor belt or shuttle car behind it."[22] This development presaged another: that of enormous automatic shovels capable of continuously digging out high cliffs and moving large quantities of coal out of open strip mines. Whatever coal is left after strip mining is removed by "large, self-contained auger machines" which drill into the coal seam and convey coal to the surface. With each of these developments, the productivity of coal mines in terms of tons per man day sharply increased: from an average reported for 1900 of three to one of between thirty and forty tons per day in the mid-1960s.[23]

The development of oil, gas, and electrical sources of power depended more than did coal and steam on prior development of the theoretical sciences. These sciences did not accidently come into existence and subsequently become useful, of course: they were the direct result of earlier lessons to the effect that productivity could be increased through concentration, planning, rationalization, specialization, and controlled experimentation. The applications of science for the discovery of oil deposits involved geology, seismology, gravimetry, magnetrometry – and great quantities of capital. While the flowering of scientific search methods was crucial to the growth (and frequent overproduction) of the industry, capital was the much more important factor in determining which companies secured scientific knowledge and reaped its benefits.

Standard Oil was formally established in 1870 with a capital of a million dollars, 27 per cent owned by John D. Rockefeller.[24] Rockefeller made his money on an early refinery in Cleveland and through manipulation of railroad stock and railroad companies responsible for planning both rail-routes (which would carry oil from Cleveland to the heartland industries of America) and rail-rates. Rockefeller, otherwise known as secretive about his business arrangements, boasted about his capacity to exploit the railroad rebates system.[25] Likewise he boasted about his control, complete by 1875, of the refining and distribution for a large share of the American industry. He gained this edge by organizing the refiners and effectively controlling the transportation facilities, so that other refiners were obliged to sell to Standard. He observed in this connection that had the producers been willing (able?) to restrict their production and thus avoid gluts to which the industry was prone, he would not have been able to corner the market. The elimination of competition was, in his view, the fault of weak (less well-capitalized?) producers. Anthony Sampson in his study of the oil industry quotes Rockefeller: "No combination in the world could have prevented that (competition), if they had produced less oil than the world required."[26] By 1883, Rockefeller had established his own system of pipelines, thus reducing his reliance on railways, and had formed a trust, through which he bought shares in most other companies though these remained ostensibly independent. His comment: "The day of combination is here to stay. Individualism has gone never to return."[27]

The Rockefeller corporation became one of the world's largest owners of oilfields, refineries, pipelines, and distributors of oil, and major investors in transportation companies and banks.

It is within the context of the Rockefeller empire, the subsequent empires of Gulf, Texaco, and Shell, and then the separate sub-empires of Standard's subsidiaries following anti-trust legislation in the United States, that one appreciates the developing technology of the oil industry. The technology is no doubt stunning: from cable tools for drilling wells arbitrarily into the earth, to hydraulic rotary drilling in locations determined through computer processing of scientific data on all relevant factors of oil formation. "Reservoir engineering" became a speciality, and since World War II techniques have been created for recovery of oil from previously impossible sites such as the Alberta tar sands (discussed further in a later chapter).

Refining of oil has undergone a similar technical transformation. Where oil was used principally for kerosene and domestic use in 1900, the demand for power by owners of potentially high-speed machines in industry created a stimulus for refined lubricating oils. These could be most efficiently produced on a continuous rather than batch operation process. A passage by a specialist in energy resource technology and consultant to the U.S. government is interesting in this connection:

> . . . the first momentous advance occurred with the commercial introduction of thermal "cracking" in 1913. In this process, selected straight-run distillating fractions were further heated under pressure of 75 pounds to "crack" heavy molecules into the lighter molecules of gasoline components. The result not only greatly increased the yield of gasoline but lowered its cost at the very time that the age of the automobile arrived in earnest.[28]

Thus took place the wedding of two of the largest industries in the world, both of them requiring enormous capital investment, a long prior history of mechanization, and the knowledge provided by institutionalized science. By 1920 the second wave of industrialization was underway, signalled by the demise of coal and the rise of oil and gas as fuels, the eclipse of railroads, and the domination of automobiles for transportation. These changes in turn produced changes in demands for other products: steel, nickel, asbestos, aluminum, copper, molybdenum – there appeared to be no end to new demands by new industries, and most of these industries were very rapidly concentrated in the same fashion as their energy and transportation suppliers.

## IV

The United States has been hailed as the giant of innovative technique. Explanations for this have been provided in terms of its shortage of labour and high costs for skilled workers, its high capital investment capacities, and the historical development of markets along with population changes in the nineteenth century.

A theory attributing U.S. leadership to indigenous labour conditions in the crucial industrializing period goes back at least to Thomas Jefferson. He observed, in reference to the need for agricultural machinery: "In Europe the object is to make the most of their land, labour being abundant; here it is to make the most of our labour, land being abundant."[29]

In a study of differences between U.S. and European corporate innovation, Raymond Vernon has noted that Europeans have tended to innovate in the development of synthetic materials such as rayon, fertilizers, and dyestuffs.[30] U.S. corporations have tended rather to concentrate on innovations in machinery. He suggests that the reasons lie in the higher labour costs and a shortage of skilled labour in the U.S., which early gave impetus to developments that side-stepped labour as a factor of production; and to the relative scarcity of capital and raw materials in Europe during the first half of the twentieth century. Vernon observes that this initial tendency had profound consequences: European inventions, failing to conserve on labour and materials, did not command a market in the U.S. equivalent to the market created in Europe for machinery.

Labour shortages in the United States were one of the domestic factors leading to growth of national companies which found means of reducing labour input into manufactured goods. One of these was the Colt Patent Fire Arms Manufacturing Company in Hartford, Connecticut.[31] In a country hungry for fire-arms, with a shortage of skilled gunsmiths, Colt invented a mass-production system which manufactured guns with interchangeable parts. Europeans, who had plenty of gunsmiths to service their needs, had not felt the pressure to mass-produce these instruments prior to the Colt invention, though the underlying technology had long been available. In order to prevent Europeans from copying his invention, he established a branch-plant in Britain in 1853. This was not successful, perhaps because labour costs in Europe were not so high at that point that customers would avoid custom-made products.

Similar labour shortages led to the creation of manufacturing subsidiaries in Britain for Singer sewing machines. In this case, agencies had been established for sale of the machines in the 1860s with varying success and problems. Impetus for moving the actual production process abroad appears to have lain with the high labour costs in United States which were reducing the export saleability of the product.[32] The first plant in Glasgow did not manufacture the entire machine, but completed parts sent from America. The factory succeeded, and by the 1870s Singer established a full manufacturing assembly plant in Glasgow, and began to extend its marketing programme to other European countries. Says historian Wilkins of the 1870s period:

"Singer was gradually forming what would become its famous international business network. . . . It began after the company awoke to the realization that foreign business made a crucial contribution to its profits."[33] By the mid-1870s, half of Singer's sewing machines were being sold outside the United States. At a later stage, it bought out its main competitor, Wheeler & Wilson.

At a much more general level and with reference to a much earlier period of industrialization, Braudel argues that:

> The precondition for progress was probably a reasonable balance between human labour and other sources of power. The advantage was illusory when man competed with machines inordinately, as in the ancient world and China where mechanisation was ultimately blocked by cheap labour. There were slaves in Greece and Rome, and too many highly efficient coolies in China. . . .[34]

Labour is clearly one of the essential ingredients in a production process, and a shortage of the skills provided by specialized labour no doubt was a contributing factor in such advances as those in American agricultural machinery. However, labour shortages in themselves fail to explain the international differences in technological innovation records. Indeed, none of the factors most frequently cited by way of explanation appears to "hold" across the board. Canada is a particularly difficult society to deal with in this respect because, like the States, it had shortages of skilled labour, high capital reserves at a crucial period of history, and access to markets in its own Prairies, the States, and Britain. True, it did not have the population density of the States at an early period (nor since), and its natural geography inhibited the rapid growth of transportation and communication facilities. These conditions, indeed, are frequently cited by way of explaining its relative failure to be innovative in techniques.

There is yet one further aspect to American growth which appears to be significant, independent of labour shortages and capital itself though not of the way in which capital is invested. This is the growth of institutionalized science, both in universities or government-supported laboratories, and in industrial research.

In such industries as chemicals, electronics, heavy machinery, and manufacturing associated with either petroleum or other minerals extraction, U.S. companies clearly dominate world production. These industries share certain characteristics: they depend on high investment in continuing research and the employment of large numbers of well-qualified scientists; they lend themselves to a wide span of both industrial and private consumer uses; and they benefit from economies of scale in production. Estimates by the OECD for the late 1960s showed U.S. research and development expenditures to be about four times greater than those in the whole of Western Europe, and the gap was about twice as great in proportion to gross national products of individual countries. Receipts for technological royalties were nearly five times as great in the United States as in four major manufacturing countries of Europe (the United Kingdom, Germany, France, Italy).[35]

The presence of research and development laboratories does not in itself guarantee that technical innovations will come about. In fact, many of the most remarkable product developments, some of them attempted in such laboratories but without success, were marketed by these corporations because they could afford to buy out successful inventors or small companies with an innovative edge rather than because their vast facilities were productive.

W.F. Mueller studied the technical innovations of DuPont between the 1920s and late 1940s.[36] He identified twenty-five products which he deemed to have had a major economic value for the company. The list he provides suggests that DuPont's role in developing many of these was entrepreneurial rather than technical.

For example, DuPont, long associated in reputation with the development of viscose rayon, did not invent or cause to be invented this substitute for silk. Having tried and failed to perfect the process, and having decided that purchase of the only American company already in business was too costly, DuPont bought the controlling shares in Comtoir des Textiles Artificiels in Europe, thereby obtaining exclusive American patents to the new product. All DuPont added was capital. The same European company provided the option to DuPont to manufacture cellophane in North America.

The bromide process for production of tetraethyl lead was developed by an employee of General Motors. At that time (1923) a DuPont brother was GM president while also chairman of the DuPont board of directors. General Motors and DuPont had no difficulty reaching a mutually beneficial agreement whereby DuPont built a tetraethyl lead plant, the cost of which would be amortized within a year through the purchase of lead on exclusive terms by General Motors. Yet another arrangement between giants was part of this process. An employee of Standard Oil of New Jersey discovered a better manufacturing process for lead within a year of the establishment of DuPont's plant (the ethyl chloride process, 1924). DuPont, recognizing that the Standard process would be cheaper for both construction and operating costs than the bromide process, managed to reach an agreement with Standard giving DuPont the proprietary rights to the new process. These three products, rayon, cellophane, and tetraethyl lead together provided over 20 per cent of the total sales of the DuPont company in 1958 according to Mueller's report.

Overall, Mueller reviews the history of twenty-five products manufactured by DuPont, a considerable number of which were exclusively produced by that company in North America between the 1920s and 1940s. Of these, only ten were actually developed in the DuPont laboratories. And of these ten, five were considered by the researcher to be genuinely new products. It was capital to market the product rather than the technical capacity to invent it which promoted corporate success.

Nonetheless, a company which has the facilities and can employ scientists sufficient to create even five new products is in a much stronger position than one without such capital-investment capacities. The generalization is true as well of countries. Given the structure of Canadian industry (with the clear majority of its manufacturing and resource industries owned outside the country), it need not cause surprise that Canada ranks very low in technological development amongst industrial nations.

In 1969, the OECD published an analytical report on technology, based on 1963-65 data, which indicated that of the 110 significant innovations since the second war, none was produced in Canada (thus putting it at the bottom of a list of ten countries). Of all patents taken out in foreign countries, Canada again ranks low, just above Belgium (on a per capita basis, of course, that means that Canada is well below Belgium); in export performance for science-based products, Canada ranks ninth, again ahead of Belgium. In short, Canada is pretty well at the bottom of the list of countries engaged in manufacturing of science-based products, on all of the measures used in this study.[37]

Not only in technical innovation is Canada far behind other industrial countries, but as well in most measures of performance in secondary industry. The country has always provided raw materials to more advanced manufacturing economies (Britain first, then the United States), but with such an abundance of these one might expect Canada to have found ways of reducing its reliance on exports and increasing its capacities for manufacturing. In fact, even when no allowances are made for the "internal trade" between subsidiaries in Canada and their U.S. parents, by way of obtaining a more accurate picture of Canadian development, Canada is not a significant trader of manufactured products.

Pierre Bourgault, commissioned to study these data and other relevant data for the Science Council of Canada, reported in 1972 that the rate of increase in exports for science-based products was not increasing: it was, in fact, declining relative to other developing countries (and there is little doubt that this description is more apt than any signifying a genuinely advanced industrial society).[38] Canada has the least favourable balance of trade in plastics, an almost equally low position in pharmaceutical products, scientific instruments, and other electronic components. Particularly noticeable is Canada's position as a net importer of manufactured products made from nickel though Canada is the world's largest producer of that mineral; and of petrochemicals though again Canada exports natural gas and petroleum in great quantity. The only industry which appears healthy in the OECD study and Bougault's examination is iron and steel.[39]

Parallelling these data is the information that Canada is one of the few countries with less than 50 per cent of all research and development expenditures being made by and in the industrial sector.[40] Table 3 shows the comparisons.

## TABLE 3

### Percentage of Research and Development Expenditures in OECD Member Countries, by Sector of Performance, 1963 and 1967

| Country | Business Enterprise | | Government | | PNP* | | Higher Education | | TOTAL % |
|---|---|---|---|---|---|---|---|---|---|
| | 1967 | 1963 | 1967 | 1963 | 1967 | 1963 | 1967 | 1963 | |
| Austria | 63.4 | 63.5 | 9.0 | 9.5 | 0.1 | 1.0 | 27.5 | 26.0 | 100.0 |
| Belgium | 66.8 | 69.0 | 10.4 | 9.8 | 1.3 | 1.3 | 21.4 | 19.9 | 100.0 |
| France[a] | 53.1 | 48.9 | 31.8 | 35.9 | 1.0 | 0.5 | 14.1 | 14.7 | 100.0 |
| Germany[b] | 58.2 | 66.0 | 5.1 | 3.4 | 10.4 | 11.0 | 16.3 | 19.6 | 100.0 |
| Greece[b,c] | 33.5 | 15.8 | 44.4 | 74.1 | 1.3 | 0.9 | 20.7 | 9.4 | 100.0 |
| Ireland | 35.4 | 29.1 | 48.9 | 56.7 | 1.1 | 3.6 | 14.6 | 10.6 | 100.0 |
| Italy | 60.6 | 62.1 | 28.2 | 23.5 | 0.0 | 0.0 | 11.2 | 14.4 | 100.0 |
| Japan[a] | 54.0 | 56.3 | 10.3 | 11.0 | 3.1 | 3.6 | 32.7 | 22.1 | 100.0 |
| Netherlands[b] | 58.1 | 59.5 | 2.7 | 2.8 | 17.7 | 21.1 | 21.5 | 20.6 | 100.0 |
| Norway | 50.0 | 51.2 | 16.1 | 21.0 | 1.1 | 2.3 | 32.8 | 24.9 | 100.0 |
| Portugal[b] | 16.1 | 22.1 | 69.4 | 66.3 | 7.1 | 5.3 | 7.4 | 6.3 | 100.0 |
| Spain[b] | 44.6 | 25.2 | 52.8 | 68.4 | — | — | 2.7 | 16.4 | 100.0 |
| Sweden[b] | 69.9 | 69.2 | 14.2 | 16.1 | 0.4 | 0.4 | 15.5 | 14.3 | 100.0 |
| United Kingdom[b] | 64.9 | 65.3 | 24.8 | 24.9 | 2.5 | 2.5 | 7.8 | 7.3 | 100.0 |
| United States[a] | 69.5 | 70.3 | 13.8 | 14.8 | 3.6 | 3.3 | 13.1 | 11.6 | 100.0 |
| Canada | 37.7 | 39.7 | 35.6 | 40.4 | 0.0 | 0.0 | 26.7 | 19.9 | 100.0 |

* PNP = Private non profit.
[a] Including the Social Sciences and Humanities in France and Japan, and the Social Sciences in the U.S.
[b] For 1963 read 1964.
[c] For 1967 read 1966.
[d] For 1969 read 1968 or 1968/69.

SOURCE: Pierre L. Bourgault, *Innovation and the Structure of Canadian Industry*, Ottawa: Science Council of Canada, Ottawa, 1972, Table III.22. "GERD in OECD Member Countries, by Sector of Performance, 1963 and 1967", based on OECD Report, SP (71), 10, 1971.

These data reflect Canada's position as a branch-plant and resource-extraction economy, in spite of very considerable government aid and incentives for investment in industrial research and development. According to Bourgault, 1970 and 1971 were years of retrenchment for well-established companies. Chemcell, Gulf Oil, and Consolidated-Bathurst closed laboratories, while Polymer, DuPont, and MacMillan Bloedel made large-scale cutbacks.[41] They closed when government, having encouraged their establishment at very small incremental cost to the companies, did not also pay for maintenance of existing operations: in other words, these were but extensions of government programmes, and not growths of industrially sponsored research. The reason for this, as for the general lack of innovation and science-based industry, is, in Bourgault's opinion, a lack of profit-incentive for firms in Canada.

Profit incentives are created when companies anticipate an increase in profits from investments in research: without such a likelihood, they will not undertake the risk of investment. Bourgault points out that companies resident in Canada do not have such an incentive for two reasons: the vast majority of Canadian-owned companies are engaged in resource extraction and export of relatively unprocessed materials; remaining companies incorporated in Canada are not Canadian-owned and their research and development investments are made in the country (mainly the United States) of their parent company. There is no reason for a parent company to invest in duplicative research in Canada, the more so when part of a company's capacity to maintain subsidiaries without creating competition is dependent on its monopoly of innovative techniques and know-how.

In connection with this argument, Bourgault observes that of the ninety-six companies incorporated in Canada and among the "most popular" one hundred at the Toronto Stock Exchange (in terms of dollar value of sales), none is science-intensive, and only three are moderately science-intensive. Of these three, two, Moore and Massey-Ferguson, do over 90 per cent of their business outside Canada; the third is Ford Motor Company, linked to its parent through the Autopact agreements and specializing in the Canadian "allowed" range of products. According to Bourgault, both Moore and Massey-Ferguson do

*Lack of R & D in Canada*

almost all of their research, development, and engineering out-side Canada; and Ford gets its technology from the American Ford Motor Company. The remaining ninety-three companies are in resource or service industries.[42]

Bourgault advances yet another argument, and it is most significant for our study of multinational corporations. He suggests that: ". . . there is considerable evidence to suggest that Canadian manufacturing industry has been permitted to evolve into a state that indirectly discriminates against the indigenous manufacturer."[43]

The Canadian manufacturer is obliged to compete on his own domestic market with foreign corporations which are linked to their parent firms in both technology and capital reserves. They cannot compete successfully, particularly where they must depend entirely on the small Canadian market.

But this is still not all there is to it. Economies of scale are important factors, the capacity to provide large capital reserves is another factor, genuine market demand is a third, but still others have been examined and found to be important. Among these is "learning" by companies and the investment in knowledge over time which effectively obstructs entry by newcomers. Another is the existence of on-going scientific research outside industries and the effect of that research on research investments and market structures. Finally, there is the "systems" effect of self-serving technology.

With respect to the "learning" hypothesis, Bourgault has argued that companies which have been involved with a basic technology over time have accumulated the experience to recognize important developments as they occur and can build these into their existing technologies. Outsiders lack this accumulated knowledge. He cites the field of electronic computers as an example. No computers are designed in Canada, though there is a large market for them. Consequently the level of sophistication about design and parts manufacture is not high. A Canadian manufacturer, if one were to enter the field, would have to conform to specifications of the computer manufacturer and the original component manufacturers. In Bourgault's opinion:

. . . options open to the Canadian manufacturer will be to copy or not to supply: to innovate will not be an option.

Moreover, before the market is truly existent in Canada, the foreign competitor will have time to move well down on his learning curve, making even copying a doubtful proposition.[44]

If innovation is tied to size and demand of markets, capital, and a "learning curve," then one might conclude that it is also tied to corporate concentration; that is that technical development requires a monopoly or oligopolistic market structure and very large firms able to support research. This argument has been advanced by Joseph Schumpeter[45] and J. K. Galbraith.[46] One of the propositions of this argument is that only large firms are able to finance innovation; another that only large firms can afford to take the risks of failure since their successes can be so well marketed.

Neither Schumpeter nor Galbraith investigated empirical evidence to test their arguments. But others have tested these and have come up with negative results. One group of researchers conducted a study of sixty-one major inventions over the past half-century and concluded that only twelve of these had been developed in large corporations.[47] Two other studies indicated that small firms engage in as much as or more research than larger firms.[48] A leading scholar in the field of technological change economics studied the petroleum refining, coal, and steel industries from 1918 to 1958, and concluded that there was no clear and systematic relationship between firm size and innovative activity. Edwin Mansfield, reporting the results of his study, summarized the evidence:

Contrary to the allegations of Galbraith, Schumpeter and others, there is little evidence that industrial giants are needed in all or even most industries to insure rapid technological change and rapid utilization of new techniques.[49]

Another economist, studying the same material, points out that such industries as tobacco and steel are highly concentrated and not very innovative.[50] Almarin Phillips, in an introduction to a detailed study of innovation in the aircraft industry, adds to this list "distilled liquors, shipbuilding, meat packing, glass containers, plate glass, newspapers, lead and copper," all of which are highly concentrated but slow in technological development.[51] The Galbraithian argument, by contrast, which consists of a theory placing technological impetus on an oligopolistic structure, depends on the aerospace, computer, chemical, and electrical machinery industries for its evidence. These are all highly concentrated, and highly productive of innovative techniques.

Our earlier review of the harvesting business suggests that in that industry concentration was not conducive to invention. Innovation came about in the industry when a genuine competitor emerged to threaten International Harvester's monopoly. Innovation in the American automobile industry at a much later date came about because Japanese and European car makers tapped the American market for small and safer vehicles. Innovations in rayon were not introduced by DuPont, though DuPont reaped the benefits. It might be argued that oligopoly rather than monopoly – some balance between concentration and competition – is the ideal environment for technological development: but that, too, would be contradicted by the evidence. Small firms have produced innovative techniques even where they couldn't market them, and large firms even in competitive markets have been shown to be frequently stagnant as far as innovative research is concerned. In addition, several writers have pointed out specific instances, such as Bell Telephone's and General Electric's refusal to become involved in the early stages of radio-communications research, where established large firms have actively prevented the creation of superior or different products which might compete with their existing range.

When we find examples of both innovative and non-innovative industries within the oligopolistic market structure then we are obliged to seek another explanation for difference in technological developments. Mansfield, in the study cited above, suggested that the differences might have to do with the relative cost of particular technological processes in different industries. However, Mansfield pointed out that when all factors were taken into consideration, even in highly concentrated industries with high-cost technologies, medium-sized firms produced about as much in the way of innovative techniques relative to their size as did the largest companies, especially in the steel industry.

Another possibility is that it is not size as such which makes a difference but the pressure within any given industry for innovation, and this will vary with the degree of real competition and the amount of research being conducted in external locations. By external locations is meant universities and government research laboratories, independent inventor's and new, small firm laboratories.

The effects of external sources are noted in a study by A.D. Little of three "mature" industries: textiles, machine tools, and construction. Little discovered that very few innovations had occurred which had any economic impact over the past thirty years in these industries. Of the few that had occurred, most originated outside the industry with foreign technology, smaller new firms, and independent inventors. The single most important source of new inventions in these industries turned out to be firms in other industries, where these infringed on the existing monopolies. These other industries came with ideas from other kinds of applications, and with component parts that had originally been developed for other applications. The existing giants, like International Harvester, were obliged to adapt themselves to externally introduced change.[52]

Schumpeter, in *The Theory of Economic Development*, argued that the typical capitalist would engage in innovation only if probable profits were the result: consequently research would be utilitarian, and external research would be consulted only where it had clear relevance to the on-going entrepreneurial activities of the firm. Galbraith, though arriving at the same conclusion about large firms, envisioned a somewhat different process. He argued that technological development is a fairly random procedure carried on by companies having the financial and market capacities, in order to retain their competitive lead. In his opinion oligopoly creates the environment for technical research. Almarin Phillips suggests that Schumpeter is right to a point, and that Galbraith may be right in other ways but not for the reasons he gives. Phillips argues that firms will engage in and utilize existing research only where it is perceived as clearly relevant to on-going production and potentially profitable (Schumpeter). In part they will do this because they need to eliminate risk: that is, they cannot afford not to do so

(Galbraith). But there is a point of diminishing returns, where the cost of research exceeds its potential returns. Since one of the potential risks presumed to be eliminated by funding research is competition, the amount of research likely to be undertaken is directly related to the potentiality of competition.

New firms are prevented from making use of technical developments exogenous to industrial research laboratories (universities, etc.) by "entry barriers" such as very high capital outlays required for the tooling of factories, patents held by larger firms, reliance of some innovations on economies of scale for their practical applications at a market level, customer allegiance to established names, and the cost of advertising. Where these are successful barriers, the risk of competition is reduced and the pressure either to maintain a search of external sources or to create internal research activities is reduced.

This situation might lead to the expectation that monopoly or low-competition oligopoly would discourage innovation, and for some industries that appears to be the case. The difference between these industries and the research-intensive but also oligopolistic industries is this: in the latter, the very nature of the products sold in the first instance changes the nature of the market and determines its subsequent needs; continuing research and development is a direct response to market demands created in the first instance by innovative technology. Phillips places a heavy burden on external science as the prime factor in this innovation process. He argues that where no exogenous scientific endeavour which is related and potentially profitable is being carried on, the impetus to innovate within any industry is low. This would follow from the general principle that the objective is to reduce risks: if there is no outside information being produced, all firms in the industry are equally secure and the cost of internal research is higher than anticipated returns.

Phillips' final hypothesis follows from this general argument: that concentration in the market is a function of technical progress, including specifically progress in exogenous science. Those firms which take advantage of such progress must themselves engage in further research on direct applications of general science principles, and then must cope with the retooling and other expenses involved in making use of the results. This leads to a tendency to seek further ways of eliminating competition, reducing investment risks, and increasing capital reserves – all reasons for combining with competitors to exploit a new technology.

The distinction needs to be made between "basic research" that "pure" science undertakes, in contrast to empirical applications typical of industrial research laboratories. In effect Phillips is arguing that this basic research is what provides the systematic theory out of which new technologies are conceived. It is possible that this argument should be combined with that proposed by Bourgault along the lines suggested (for quite other purposes) by Thomas Kuhn,[53] by way of making the links between technology and vested interests clear.

Kuhn developed the theory that science operates on a series of paradigms. A paradigm consists of a systematic body of theory together with a methodology for discovery, a set of problems or questions which grow naturally out of existing theory and which can be approached with existing methodology, potential applications of the theory, and various norms for the conduct of research. The same paradigm may continue unchallenged for any length of time, until there is an accumulation of contrary evidence or questions and problems that somehow lie outside its domain. At this point it becomes apparent to some scientists that the basic problem is not that they cannot discover answers to their questions or solutions for the contrary evidence, but that the basic paradigm is inappropriate, faulty, inadequate. So ensues a period of search for a more comprehensive theory, and one of several or many proposed challengers will finally succeed as the new dominant paradigm in the field.

If Kuhn's historical argument is true of science, then it may be equally applicable to the fruits of science. A basic theory generates a technical breakthrough. The company or companies that make or first appropriate that breakthrough are able to create their own technological "system" or "paradigm." The system they create brings with it its own market demands, but outsiders cannot enter the system without accepting its basic rules. The development of computers, for example, involved several companies in competition at one point, but when one of these succeeded in having its hardware installed in a number of heavy-use locations that in itself determined which other implements and which "software" could be purchased or used by

these customers. The demand for integrated hardware and programmes, a function of the original successful implants, became
the impetus for continuing research by the dominant company
but as well by competitors – real and potential. There is no
market value to be realized by research on entirely different
systems until the full potentiality of the existing hardware has
been exhausted, since customers rather literally have a built-in
investment in existing technology.

The same pattern exists in the manufacturing of office and
duplicating machines, of photographic, or stereophonic equipment, and, as Phillip's study would suggest, in airplane
manufacturing. The company best situated for meeting market
demands, because it can quickly anticipate them, is the
originator of the most successful model. To the degree that it is
successful, it creates a technology which is never a once-only innovation but a continuing process. Outsiders are obliged to
enter the field on terms dictated by the first company because
this is the only way of serving the market.

Another example of this is in the Ford/International
Harvester situation. Ford developed a product that then created
a demand for parts that could fit it, be integrated with it. Had he
been able to produce all of the non-motor parts with the speed at
which he produced the harvester, he would have continued as
the major producer in the field. He had not developed his company to a sufficient degree of integration to carry out the early
advance – but other companies which had this advantage were
thereafter obliged to enter the field on Ford's terms, as far as
technology was concerned.

This would coincide with Phillip's interpretation: the development of a basic scientific theory or paradigm gives rise to the
possibility for technical innovation; successful innovation
creates its own market system and this, even in the absence of
pressures for capital, increases an industry's tendency toward
concentration. Few writers besides Phillips have undertaken
detailed studies of any one industry, let alone a sufficient
number to test the thesis he advances, and the rephrasing of it in
Kuhnsian terms is still very tentative. If it were generally valid,
then we could say with some conviction that oligopoly or
monopoly are not, as has sometimes been asserted in their
defence, preconditions to technical development. They may

inhibit development through failure to innovate on their own initiative or through control of capital, patents, and other conditions of the market. But much more seriously, in creating their
own internal systems or paradigms for technical development,
they may so control technology that alternative possibilities
more suitable to human survival may never emerge.

# CHAPTER 3

# RESOURCES, MARKETS, AND THE STATE

*. . . If we are seriously interested in adapting our economic system to our present and future needs, it would be helpful if we could agree on the nature of the system we have now. The free market system, in the true sense of that phrase, does not exist in Canada.*

– Prime Minister P.E. Trudeau, 1976[1]

*I resigned partly out of frustration at the lack of Canadian control of projects built in this country. One of the things that bothered me was that in certain areas of technical expertise foreign-owned engineering companies predominated. Some of Bechtel's clients were to a considerable degree interested in the further exportation of Canada's resources. I was concerned that Canada didn't have sufficient reserves to justify these further exports. The power of U.S. controlled corporations to obtain government approvals was very substantial and I didn't want to go along with this. I found conflict between my duties as an officer of Bechtel and my feelings as a Canadian nationalist.*

– Bruce Willson, former president,
Canadian Bechtel, 1969[2]

In the Slocan Valley in British Columbia a group of residents refuse to believe in the virtues of big corporations. Knowledgeable about forestry practices and alternative means of utilizing the products of forests, they obtained a "make-work" grant from the Federal government in the early 1970s, and researched their situation. Their review of what has happened to their only industry over the past quarter-century might stand as a review of what has happened in almost every industry, and the consequences they note for their valley are equally true for other regions dependent on resources: "From 34 local, independent logging operators and 19 sawmills in 1952, we now have one foreign-owned mill and only one major employer in the Valley."³

At the time of the report, the only sawmill in the Slocan Valley shipped its lumber to a parent firm to be used in the construction of houses and other buildings. The population of Slocan was not engaged in manufacturing the product. Jobs here were mainly unskilled: there was no need for a range of skilled, professional, managerial workers in a sawmill owned and directed by another company elsewhere. The writers of this report argued that they could utilize more of the forest's wood at less environmental cost if they were able to establish locally owned and much smaller mills. The benefits they anticipated if such a change were implemented included local control of local resources, a much greater range of jobs, and more jobs altogether for local residents. What they could not demonstrate, and it is for this reason that their report went unheeded, was that they could break the control of markets held by large firms or obtain any financial capital for original establishment and technical development. They could not set up their own mills in order to translate their beliefs into hard evidence because, in addition to a lack of capital and market access, they could not obtain tree-farm licences for their wood supplies. The forest in which they live was and still is controlled by large corporations, under lease from the provincial government.

The forestry industry in British Columbia has less foreign ownership than any other vital industry in Canada. The process described by these researchers is of relatively recent origin: the period after World War II. What they describe are the early phases of a process of concentration in ownership and increasing foreign control which the mining industry underwent throughout the previous half-century. Manufacturing industries in Canada were more frequently still-born. As we have noted, those which dominate the economy today are highly concentrated and foreign-owned with the exception of very few which have located themselves in the American market and carry on most of their research and production in the United States.

Manufacturing industries must have resource supplies, of which wood is one. Wood is not, however, a main one and besides there are metal and synthetic substitutes for wood as a consequence of technological developments in the mid-twentieth century. More essential to American manufacturing are water, minerals, oil, and gas. These Canada has in abundance. Had the possession of natural resources been the primary factor in creating industrial wealth, Canada would have emerged as the twentieth-century giant. We know that Canada did not grow, that on the contrary she used these resources as simple market products rather than as fuel for her own industries. The question is why. The explanations that have been offered are these:

1. Canada lacked either sufficient capital or sufficient population, or both, at the critical stage of entry into industrial society, and thus was obliged to seek industry on available terms from its nearest industrial neighbour.

2. The United States was simply so well developed and so endowed with excess industrial capacity prior to Canadian development that inevitably a smaller country on its borders, especially one with an essentially similar economic system and culture, became part of its economic territory. Propinquity rather than deliberate imperialism is the basis of this explanation.

3. Canadian governments erred. Between establishing tariffs at the wrong times and on the wrong commodities, failing to provide adequate supports to developing industries, and misfiring on countless economic issues, they have through stupidity rather than cupidity lost their territory.

4. A mercantile elite gained an early stranglehold on the economy and Canadian capital, and directed this toward investment in American industries which provided a higher and more immediate return profit than development of Canadian industry would have done.

5. United States governments as well as American corporations have engaged in deliberate imperialism. Although this imperialism has been mainly economic in thrust, it has always been backed by the political and military strength of the United States.

The first three of these explanations have long histories, so long as to merit the term "traditional" even in the relatively youthful culture of Canada. While all three have some evidence to support them, none provides explanations which account for all of what is known about Canadian development. There is considerable evidence to the contrary, such as that investment wealth existed within Canada in sufficient quantity to encourage industry before the turn of the century. More problematic than contrary evidence are the remaining questions – if these explanations are held to be true – such as why a growing immigrant population on the Prairies was considered an important market for American manufacturers but insufficient by Canadians, why Canada lost population consistently throughout the period 1861-1901 and the 1930s, or why Canadian governments persisted in making decisions contrary to the interests of Canadian manufacturers. It is in response to these questions that the fourth and fifth explanations have been proposed.

At the level of sociological and political theory, the first three explanations are either part of or not inconsistent with a theory of linear or progressive development. According to proponents of this theory,[4] which was particularly popular following World War II and remains the explicit base for American foreign policy, a country or region will "take off" into industrial development once it has accumulated sufficient capital for investment and constructed adequate infrastructure in the form of transportation, communications, education, and social welfare. During the phase of creating these preconditions to industrialization it may require outside aid in the form of foreign investment. Foreign corporations, however, need not pose any threat to national development: on the contrary, they should provide a base around which secondary industries and service sectors are built.

This approach rests on two assumptions, both of which lack support in the Canadian case. The first is that surplus or profit from development will be retained and controlled by local populations, so that it will be reinvested in further development of industry within the same nation or region. It implies that foreign investors do not receive benefits in excess of their investment, particularly in the form of extensive ownership privileges, and also that the financial elite of the host nation has the same interests as other members of that population. The second assumption is that national industries are able to enter a "free market" in the world economy. Our review of data and case studies in this chapter will underline the fallaciousness of these assumptions.

The last two explanations, constituting part of a general theory of imperialism, lead to conclusions opposite those of the linear theories. They rest on the assumption that surplus is extracted from resource and low-labour-cost regions by manufacturing and financial centres. Economic imperialism means deliberate exploitation of one country's resources for the benefit of nationals in another country, ultimately backed by the potential use of force. The "centre" or "metropolitan" region exploits resources on the "periphery" or in the "hinterland" region for its own benefit, and such exploitation eventually culminates not only in underdevelopment of the hinterland but in a reversal of such development as has already taken place. The hinterland becomes incapable of reversing the exploitation, and inevitably becomes poorer and less powerful.[5]

The centre has two aspects. It is a corporate organization with subsidiaries and branch plants, the periphery of which consists of small businesses, contractors, service stations, and marginal workers who do not have the skills or the regional location to find employment in the central organization. It is also a metropolitan, industrial region where numerous corporations have their head offices and central manufacturing plants, the hinterland for which consists of resource regions. The two are not perfectly overlapping, and in that lies much of the strength of corporate organization in metropolitan regions. The corporation establishes its subsidiaries and resource extraction operations on hinterland soil, thus providing employment for local workers. The region remains a hinterland. It does not become an industrial area with a full range of occupations and power over its own resources, but these employees develop some stake in corporate survival since their income depends on it.[6]

The regional structure is linked to a class structure at both the international and national levels. The larger part of an owning and directing class has its territorial base in the metropolitan or imperial centre. This class is related to a financial class in the host or resource countries through a system of mutual supports: the financial class provides funds for imperial expansion in return for an intermediary role providing it with national power. The argument of proponents of the theory of imperialism in Canada is that American capitalism did not force itself on Canada through military penetration, on the contrary, it was invited, welcomed, and financed by Canadian bankers and politicians. This is in accord with arguments advanced by Galtung, Frank, and others whose work has been mainly in Latin America, to the effect that an indigenous elite, pursuing its own wealth and personal power, has typically provided the in-route and support for imperialism.[7] To put the matter bluntly, it is more profitable to invest in already successful businesses than to risk venture money on national companies which will then have to struggle in a non-competitive world market.

The non-competitive world market posited in a theory of im-perialism exists in the form of enormous corporate complexes which produce and sell goods in many countries through in-tegrated subsidiaries ultimately controlled and financially managed by an imperial centre. Because such complexes can manipulate capital in the form of both currency and technology, and because they own or control supplies and raw materials, transportation facilities, and manufacturing enterprises, they can effectively control market conditions. New firms from other nations are unable to enter the market on competitive terms. With respect to Canadian terms of entry into world markets, a concession to alternative explanations may be noted. Canadian companies would normally expand, all other factors being equal, into the United States. This is the largest single existing market in the world. Since it is American companies with which they would have to compete, their "natural" expansion route was blocked by the early development of large American firms. What needs further explanation with respect to markets, however, is the failure of Canadian firms to expand even in Canada, and their inability to gain strength outside North America. There have been exceptions, of course. Massey-Ferguson, for example, managed to expand into the world market and to become a shareholder in the American market. But the exceptions were rare, and the much more common pat-tern has been the demise of a Canadian competitor when it reached a size capable of sustaining expansion abroad. A case in point is Imperial Oil. This company was founded in 1880 by Canadians, but sold out to Standard of New Jersey when it en-countered barriers to entering the world market on its own. Standard controlled that market. In a later section of this chapter we will consider some of the consequences of that event.

An inability to break into world markets will have consequences for a company even within the national market if it is competing at home with a world-dominant foreign company. A subsidiary may be run at a loss, even deliberately obliged to run at a loss, while waiting for the demise of domestic competitors. A parent company may choose to absorb such losses since in the long run its control of the product area will only increase. In addition, parent companies may run a subsidiary at a "book loss" in order to reduce taxation in foreign countries while moving its capital about from one country to another at the highest rates of return or in order to ensure markets for parent-company products. For example, a company producing a given manufactured item may require its resource subsidiaries to sell their product to the manufacturing parent at prices below the market level (while competitors have difficulty obtaining supplies and pay market-level prices), and to purchase products from the parent at prices higher than the market level. The last of these policies may put the subsidiary at an apparent disadvantage, but it is only apparent since the overall policy is to the advantage of the parent company which increases its capital and capacity to influence if not control world markets. Specific examples of this are considered in the next chapter.

Since the theory of imperialism refers to the vital roles of national elites and the national government as well as to the imperial power and its control of external markets, we will review very briefly something of the history of commercial development in Canada before examining a case study of a particular and current industry in which foreign ownership is dominant.

## I

A mercantile elite developed in Canada in connection with the early timber trade, the fur trade, land development, and banking. Before and well after Confederation, this elite was closely allied with the public purse. Economic historian Hugh Aitken has pointed out that in the United States as well as Canada:

> We find close identification between political and economic elites. . . . Leadership groups, seeking their own advancement and that of their regions, acted both through the state and through business, regarding them as complementary instruments of the attainment of their goals. The state was the

source of non-market power and the dispenser of public revenues, an instrument too powerful to be neglected in the struggle for economic advancement.[8]

Nonetheless, the formal separation between leading businessmen and governors commenced earlier in the United States than in Canada. In reference to the granting of bank charters, Gustavus Myers observed:

here it may be remarked that the politicians of the United States have long since so well appraised the value of bank charters that as early as the years 1799, 1805, 1811 and 1824 bribery had been used to wrest from the legislators charters for the Manhattan, Mercantile, Merchants' and other New York City Banks. But in Canada, with many of the bank incorporators themselves leaders in legislative councils, bribery was, in general, superfluous.[9]

The demise of the fur trade, the successful negotiation of the Reciprocity Treaty, the pressing need to build railways in order to facilitate the interior export trade: all increased the pressure on the mercantile class to create a strong central government. While the advantages of union were certainly not equal for the Nova Scotia and Ontario merchants, the disadvantages of remaining colonies within a diminishing empire and without imperial protections were well understood by all. The public purse could not be fully tapped unless there was a central government with taxing powers, and borrowing powers as well were contingent on the development of a stable government.

The linking of private railroad companies, already linked to the export trades and banks, to the public government and its treasury, was nicely accomplished by promoters who later acquired the respectable title "Fathers of Confederation." They included Sir Allen MacNab, chairman of the Legislative Assembly Standing Committee on Railroads, also head of the London and Gore Railroad Company, later president of the Great Western Railway, promotor of the Canada, New Brunswick, and Nova Scotia Railway; Peter McGill, President of the Bank of Montreal, member of the Legislative Council of Canada, founder of the St. Lawrence and Atlantic Railroad Company, partner of the Grand Trunk Railway; A. T. Galt, member of the Legislative Council of Canada, promoter of the St. Lawrence and Atlantic Railroad Company, another partner of the Grand Trunk; and many others such as George E. Cartier, John A. Macdonald, John Young, and Sir Francis Hincks, all of whom managed to hold down railroad company executive posts while voting themselves contracts in Parliament and either manipulating the finances directly through their bank posts or leaning on relatives and close associates who managed the banks.[10]

For the hinterland regions within Canada, the congruence between private interests and government was absolute: the Hudson's Bay Company, after 1821 the only remaining fur trading company, was legally endowed with the rights of government, judiciary, merchant, and employer, while it had monopoly rights to the furs and was rapidly moving into land ownership and other kinds of commercial activity. Its chief factor, Donald Smith, become one of the major investors and directors of the Bank of Montreal, later became a member of parliament, and, in fashion true to the times, was among the parliamentarians who provided such largesse to the Canadian Pacific company – of which he became the president.

Summing up the Macdonald government and its "National Policy" historian Frank Underhill observed:

> What Macdonald did was to attach to the national government the interests of the ambitious, dynamic, speculative or entrepreneurial business groups, who aimed to make money out of the new national community or to install themselves in the strategic positions of power within it – the railway promoters, banks, manufacturers, land companies, contractors and such people. They provided the drive behind his so called National Policy, and they stood to reap the greatest benefits from it. They also required the fostering care of a Hamiltonian government and the lavish expenditure of taxpayers' money in public capital investment if their ambitions were to be realized.[11]

This mercantile and railroading elite (the descriptive term's double meaning having an obvious origin) did not choose to place its money in Canadian industry. Except for the supply businesses directly attached to transportation facilities, their capital was used primarily for investments in American manufacturing and resource companies. These were already established, they carried lower risks than new businesses in

Canada, and they had a greater likelihood of paying high dividends immediately. Arriving late into the industrial era, but more importantly arriving with a fully developed mercantile class with vested interests in maintaining this pattern of exports, Canada became a safe and profitable investment location for American corporations. Canadian money provided much of the initial expansion capital, Canadian democratic institutions provided the security for growth, and Canadian workers provided cheaper labour than that available in the United States. The trade that became firmly established in the late nineteenth century was therefore one by which Canada exported timber, wheat, minerals, and other raw materials in return for the manufactured products of American companies. The commercial elite maintained its domestic strength by retaining control of the financial and transportation sectors through which American industries were serviced and domestic competitors obstructed.

## II

The commercial elite in Canada, however significant its role in sustaining Canadian underdevelopment, cannot be shouldered with responsibility for United States growth on world markets. United States, by contrast with Canada, emerged from colonial status in the eighteenth century. With dense population concentrations and ice-free ports on the Atlantic coast, Americans had, at the time of the War of Independence, already embarked on merchant trading activities with countries other than Britain. Indeed, the war was occasioned because the colonies became competitive with British shipping and the sugar and rum trade. By 1867, the United States was becoming an industrial economy. Its native businesses were expanding nationally, and were establishing merchant agents abroad.

The impetus for moving abroad included both domestic conditions, such as a demand for certain raw materials unavailable or more expensive because of higher labour costs at home, and conditions abroad such as a ready market, high tariffs against imported manufactured goods, or patent laws favouring the establishment of foreign manufacturing firms.[12] The impetus was all the greater when it became apparent that growth abroad could be undertaken at low initial investment, through the backing of portfolio investments (carrying with them no ownership shares) generated in the prospective host countries together with international portfolio investment. Examples of American expansion abroad include the first Cuban Railroad (1837) built by American William Wheelright with British portfolio backing, and the Southern Railway in Chile (1858) built by American Henry Meiggs also on British funds. In addition to railroads, Wheelright constructed or established lighthouses, port facilities, gas and water works, steam lines, and coal mines throughout Cuba, most of these on British backing.[13] Americans attempted to obtain Canadian charters for railroads, but in this were thwarted by organized interests in Canada. They succeeded in other Canadian ventures at a very early stage of Canadian development. These included nickel and copper mines, pulp mills and sawmills, oil and gas wells in addition to utilities, and many manufacturing establishments for which the initial venture capital was obtained in Canada through Canadian investment houses and private investors or from British investors. In all of these cases, the American companies which borrowed such money retained ownership rights over the property purchased or constructed.[14]

Prior to the first war there were over 200 American branch plants manufacturing everything from automobile parts and the cars themselves to rubber and electrical goods. Ford, General Motors, Goodyear, DuPont, International Harvester, and Westinghouse were already firmly settled in the industrial belt from Windsor to Montreal near the American border.[15] In a pattern that was to be maintained to the 1970s, Canada had more American-controlled manufacturing plants than any other nation outside the United States itself.

Another reason for growth of American industries was the excess capacity of American technology. Mass production and mass consumption were American characteristics before Canadian industries became established, and Canadian tastes for American products were developed well before the major influxes of American capital and technology. With industries that could produce more than the American population could consume, it was perhaps inevitable that they should spill over the border in search of more consumers and raw materials to expand even further.

The First World War spurred industrial development and technology. In resources, new techniques for exploration and location of minerals, and new techniques for their rapid extraction caused an extensive development of industries in the "new" staples trades. Wheat was supplanted by aluminum and newsprint as central staples.[16] Manufacturing associated with such staples tended to be minimal in Canada; the more extensive processes and those which required a more skilled labour force were undertaken in the United States. Direct investment (ownership, as contrasted with portfolio investment or loans) increased in the resource as well as manufacturing industries after 1920.

The second war increased the demand for manufactured products, especially in such areas as steel, electronic materials, engines, synthetic rubber, and antibiotics.[17] These are industries of the "second revolution" and were already American-controlled. The growth in these industries was further increased by the Korean War. This war also generated growth in the major resource sectors: iron ore, oil and natural gas, and aluminum. Between 1949 and 1955, output of the resource industries altogether increased by some 70 per cent.[18] The Viet Nam War had similar effects on Canada, where American subsidiaries produced war materials and mineral resources for American defence production industries.

Government expenditures accounted for an increasing share of Canada's economic growth between World War II and the Viet Nam War. Defence expenditures stimulated the development of the aircraft industry, the construction industry, and the electronics industry; affected the production of such minerals as nickel, uranium, and aluminum. A large part of these resource products was exported to the United States for military uses. According to the Royal Commission on Canada's Economic Prospects, 1957, contracts with the United States government proved to be the most significant factor in nickel production, and guaranteed sales to the Atomic Energy Commission in the United States were the determining factor in uranium production. Likewise, the exploration for oil and natural gas in Western Canada has been influenced by resource depletions in the United States, by political uncertainties in other oil-producing areas serving the United States, and by American control of Canadian resource industries.[19]

This integration of industries connected with the production of war materials was increased by the Defence Production Sharing Agreements, 1959. These agreements were ostensibly intended to increase the competitive opportunities for Canadian companies and American subsidiaries in Canada to produce war materials for "North American" defence, that is, to sell goods to the U.S. Defense Department and armed forces.

> The program provides Canadian manufacturers with the opportunity to supply a wide range of defence supplies and services purchased by the United States armed forces in competition with U.S. industry. A Canadian firm offering competitive price, delivery, and quality can obtain substantial U.S. defence business and will not generally encounter discriminatory legislative or regulatory restrictions.[20]

The implementation of these agreements involved the waiving of U.S. customs duties on Canadian goods intended for U.S. defence programmes. However, the actual effect here is to strengthen American control of the armament, aircraft, and electronics industries and of essential mining industries such as aluminum, nickel, lead, copper, and zinc. In spite of massive expenditures of public funds by Canadian governments, Canadian-owned companies found it impossible to compete against U.S. firms selling to the U.S. government.[21] They were frequently obliged to buy their equipment and other supplies from the United States, and could not manufacture on a sufficient scale to reduce costs of production. As subsidiaries, which most were by the mid-1960s, they produced component parts rather than complete products. The waiving of customs restrictions at the U.S. border, then, became a facilitating mechanism for U.S. subsidiaries to supply parts to their parent firms.

In similar fashion, the Canadian-U.S. automotive agreements of 1965 were intended to bring about the liberalization of United States and Canadian automotive trade in respect of tariff barriers and other factors tending to impede it, with a view to enabling the industries of both countries to participate on a fair and equitable basis in the expanding total market of the two countries.[22] Yet again the effects of the agreement were to strengthen U.S. control over automobile manufacturing in Canada. A small range of cars is produced in Canada exclusively for the North

American market. Parent companies produce the remainder and have control of markets external to North America.[23]

Materials manufactured in subsidiaries under both the Defence Production Sharing Agreements and the Auto-Pact are effectively integrated on a continental basis. That is, the decisions are made in central headquarters of parent firms about total production, raw materials extraction, markets, and marketing of the products. This is true as well of the vital petroleum industry. Between 80 and 100 per cent of oil and gas wells, oil refining, and primary metal smelting and refining industries are owned by U.S. parent firms. These resources are essential to the growth of U.S. manufacturing establishments and also to the defence industries and military organizations of the United States. This is baldly stated in several reports on oil to U.S. governmental bodies, such as the "Schultz Report" quoted in the next section of this chapter.

Another natural resource essential to the manufacturing corporations of United States is hydro-electricity. This is abundant in Canada, and was originally one of the attractions in Ontario and Quebec for U.S. subsidiaries. Provision of the benefits of this resource depends on massive dam construction, the flooding of valleys and rivers, extensive alteration of natural environments, and displacement of farmers, trappers, or other populations in the affected areas of Canada. These effects were anticipated in the construction of the James Bay project in Quebec. The premier of that province, in announcing Quebec's intention to erect dikes, dams, and generating stations in James Bay in Northern Quebec, justified the action with reference to U.S. needs for fuel. The Quebec government and its public agency Hydro Quebec would build sixty miles of dikes, ten dams, and eleven generating stations on the James Bay area, Premier Bourassa said, because: "With the shortage of fuel, coal, oil and gas, Quebec feels it can have a major role to play in solving the Northeast United States' energy problem".[24] The 3,000 to 5,000 Cree Indians who fished, hunted, and trapped in that territory, and who had not signed away any property rights, were not consulted before this announcement. It is undoubtedly true that in moving in this direction, the Quebec government was concerned with the voting public in Quebec. Its public announcement stressed the fact that the construction would provide employment, though it did not mention that the construction would be carried on by one of the largest U.S. multinational construction companies, Bechtel. The government had to be concerned with employment of its own citizens, but it would be a mistake to suppose that the construction was planned for that purpose. The announcement was disarmingly honest about the purpose: it was to aid in the development and maintenance of Northeastern U.S. industry.

Given the context within which governments are obliged to operate, this support for the status quo is not surprising. Governments, both provincial and federal, have seldom challenged the rules of the game. When Noranda initially established itself in Quebec and sought government aid for the construction of roads and other infrastructure a Quebec government spokesman stated the prevalent defence for government aid:

> The duty of the government was apparent. In a country such as Canada the government which does not lend every possible assistance to those who seek to open the way to natural resources does not deserve the name government. We decided from the beginning that we were dealing with responsible people who were spending their own money, the least we could do would be to provide them with, or assist them to obtain, every facility for opening up the country as development progressed: with roads, then railways and all the other essentials of modern industry it lies within a government's power to give.[25]

It becomes irrelevant from the perspective of government with such a primary directive, whose money is behind the enterprise. A government will co-operate with any agency able to create expansion and expansion is interpreted as utilization of resources for an immediate market. Where a government is dependent on an indigenous financial elite with vested interests in utilities, its most "rational" action will always be to support the growth of resource and manufacturing companies which will keep the indigenous interests in business. A wealthy member of the financial establishment and a former cabinet minister in a Liberal government in Canada stated the case bluntly in the early 1970s:

Governments do not work against – they work with the vested, the established, the giants in place. The two sectors have exactly the same interest, increase the pace of economic activity and growth of assets. . . .

The level of concentration that presently exists in Canada is a direct consequence of government policy. Despite the lip service paid to laissez-faire capitalism, competition and the virtues of individual enterprise and initiative, no Canadian government has ever believed in, to the extent of practising, these principles.[26]

The assumption built in to the Quebec government's position and spelled out in Eric Kierans' description of Liberal government activities is that an increase in economic activity and growth of assets are both necessary and desirable. This same assumption is covered by such statements as "progress is inevitable" and "change is characteristic of modern society." The opposite may more aptly be the case: steadily increasing production is a means of maintaining the status quo and resisting fundamental change. If fundamental change is essential to human progress then persistent increases in economic activity are impediments.

### III

The American economy has depended on constant expansion of markets for its viability. Canada has provided a major but not the only one of these markets. Europe has provided the second most important market and underdeveloped countries have provided markets along with resources. The only areas which have not been exploited in the past are the Soviet countries and China. In the late 1960s, early 1970s, impediments have emerged to further expansion of U.S. industries in customary markets. One of the impediments is simply over-production. American companies are producing an excess of goods for present markets and are, simultaneously, losing markets to the emerging industrial competitor, Japan (which has never permitted majority ownership of industries by foreigners though its own nationals wholly own subsidiaries elsewhere), and to a rejuvenated Europe now operating through the European Common Market.

In addition, oil-producing Third World countries have found new ways of pressing their own demands, and they are beginning to create their own markets.

In response to these pressures, U.S. companies have begun to explore Soviet and Chinese markets. In 1972, for example, The World Patent Development Corporation placed an advertisement in the New York Times advertising its ability to "maintain close technological contacts with the proper governmental agencies in all East European countries." The advertisement called for American business participation:

> . . . if you own the patented or proprietary technology that East European countries need, you could work out some highly profitable arrangements. Sell technology to the communists? Can it even be done? The answer is that today it finally can be done. And is being done. In fact, over the past couple of years, major American corporations have been doing it with increasing frequency. . . .[27]

In the same year the U.S. government, Boeing Company, Occidental Petroleum Corporation, International Telephone and Telegraph, Hertz Rent-A-Car, Pan American Air/Hotel, all of United States, were among the entrants to the Soviet market.[28] Fiat Corporation headquartered in Italy is one of the more celebrated entrants. Massey-Ferguson has completed a contract with the Polish government as this chapter is being written. These manufacturing and service organizations are developing new basic rules for their production abroad. Their return on investment consists of pre-determined percentage rates on sales or set prices for managerial services. Their incentive includes the utilization of excess capacity, a relatively stable labour force which has already been disciplined and trained by Soviet state organizations, and a guaranteed market. From the viewpoint of the Soviet states the attraction is Western technology imported more rapidly than it can be duplicated, limited control over its applications, and hopefully some reduction in popular pressure for consumer goods. In addition, there appears to be some incentive to create international competition: Roumanian tractors will now, presumably, compete with Massey-Ferguson for Soviet bloc markets.

A second means by which American industry might increase its market control in the face of present pressures is to shift more of its production establishments to underdeveloped countries. While, as in the Soviet states, this might now involve stronger government control than was the case in Canada, there are off-setting advantages. One of these is supplies of cheaper labour and labour less prone to striking for better conditions. Another is simply that production would occur closer to those markets most likely to expand, thus reducing transportation costs. This is particularly the case in resource industries where equally high-grade ores or other resources can be obtained in Third World as compared to Canadian sources; such resources as nickel, copper, lead, zinc, and possibly wood suitable for newsprint. The closure of mines at Sudbury, Thompson, and Stewart appears to be linked to these developments since the owning companies (both American and Canadian) have increased their production rates and capacities in Latin America.

## IV

The most critical resource for American manufacturing industry in the 1970s is oil. However far-flung the empire, America's capacity to retain its leading position depends on its steady supply of fuel, and until oil has been replaced – as it surely will be in due course – that fuel comes from Canada, Venezuela, and the Middle East. This is not because domestic sources have been exhausted. During the first half of the twentieth century, the United States was actually a net exporter of oil. However, given increasing labour costs in that country and increasing disparities between the amount of capital required to establish drilling sites there rather than in underdeveloped countries, U.S. oil companies moved abroad. The "seven sisters" as they are frequently called are three offshoots of the original Rockefeller empire – Standard Oil of New Jersey now called Exxon of New York, Standard Oil of California also known as Socal, and Mobil; two additional American companies, Gulf and Texaco; a British state-controlled firm, British Petroleum; and the Anglo-Dutch firm, Shell. Between them, these companies controlled the world's oil supplies, refining, and marketing up to the formation of OPEC in 1960. Even as late as 1968, the majors produced 75 per cent of crude oil outside North America, the Soviet bloc, and China, down from 92 per cent in 1952 but still sufficient to enable them to exert international pressure throughout the "oil crisis" of the 1970s.[29] Between them they also controlled, and still control, most of the world's gas and oil pipelines. They split up the costs for these, several having equal shares as in the case of the Trans-Canada and Trans-Mountain pipelines in Canada. Given this context for ownership and control of oil together with U.S. demands for the fuel from producing countries, we may learn a good deal about the nature of market dominance through examination of studies of Alberta's oil industry.

The Mackenzie Delta region in the Northwest Territories and Northern Alberta contains some of the world's richest oil and gas deposits. Oil was recorded as "oozing from the ground" by Alexander Mackenzie in 1789, and geological surveys had established its existence in the Mackenzie Basin by the late 1880s. In 1888 a Senate committee appointed to enquire into the resources reported:

> The evidence submitted to your Committee points to the existence in the Athabasca and Mackenzie Valleys of the most extensive petroleum field in America, if not in the world. The uses of petroleum and consequently the demand for it by all nations are increasing at such a rapid ratio, that it is probable that this great petroleum field will assume an enormous value in the near future and will rank among the chief assets comprised in the Crown domain of the Dominion."[30]

In 1918, Imperial began drilling near Fort McMurray, at Norman Wells, at the west end of Great Slave Lake, and near the Peace River. Oil was struck at Norman Wells in 1920. Oil and gas fields were discovered in the Turner Valley of southern Alberta as well. This was exploited by a Calgary firm which was subsequently taken over by Imperial. Further major discoveries occurred throughout the region over the next thirty years.[31]

It is not incidental that the discovery at Norman Wells was followed immediately by offers of treaty-settlement with native inhabitants of the region. These same Indians had begged for help from federal authorities for many years prior to this and had been rejected: up to that time their land did not appear to have any value for southern Canada or the United States. The reason these Indians required help was that their food supplies had drastically diminished with the fur trade.[32] James Wah-Shee, an Indian resident in the Northwest Territories while Treaty 11 was being negotiated, summed up the situation in a telling phrase that Canadians may begin to appreciate: "The Treaty was signed when it was discovered that our land was more valuable than our friendship."[33]

With the much publicized "crisis" of the 1970s, actually a fight for control between some of the producing countries in the Middle East and the multinational corporations, Canadian oil and gas became much more important to United States. Canada was still a stable political entity, its investment class and government had always co-operated with American business, and its reserves were still considerable – even if somewhat more expensive than those of the Middle East before the challenge. The Alberta Tar Sands development was already underway, and proposals to build pipelines through the Mackenzie Delta where Treaty 11 had once been signed to ensure Imperial's oil supplies were energetically advanced. United States companies and government had already expressed their designs on Canadian reserves in the Paley (1952) and Schultz (1970) Reports. In both, the strategic importance to U.S. manufacturing firms of Canadian raw materials in general and Canadian oil in particular is discussed at length, and the policies of continental integration are advanced. The main report in 1970 notes that "the economic infrastructure of the United States is and can be far more integrated with that of Canada than with the economy of any other country in the western hemisphere," and the minority report, which is in general more concerned with ensuring U.S. security, argues strongly that U.S. leadership in the world depends on a secure supply of oil to its companies and its armed forces. The secure supply should involve the United States and Canada in negotiations to ensure the "orderly growth of imports of oil and natural gas from Canada."[34]

One of the earlier prospectors on the Tar Sands, Robert G. Fitzsimmons, had argued in 1953 that the international oil cartel would prevent Alberta sands from being utilized until exploitation was in the interests of their members. That meant when their alternative supplies became restricted.[35] Fitzsimmons' business was taken over by a Montreal financier, and the company, later called Great Canadian Oil Sands, was subsequently taken over by Sun Oil Company of Philadelphia. In line with Fitzsimmons' predictions, most of the prime regions had been taken over by the major oil companies by the early 1960s, yet these companies did not proceed with development. The Great Canadian Oil Sands company was the first to move: by 1967 it went into production. But this was a time of overproduction, and markets were glutted, and it fared not too well (though reasons for low returns included internal arrangements between the parent and its subsidiary, among others).[36]

In September 1960, Iraq, Kuwait, Saudi Arabia, Iran, and Venezuela founded the Organization of Petroleum-Exporting Countries (OPEC) for the purposes of bargaining with oil-consuming countries but even more with the major oil corporations on prices and oil-export revenues. Cuba expropriated the major oil refineries on its soil, and Venezuela appeared a potential follower in such actions if OPEC failed. Russian oil began to take on more significance as a source for Western Europe and some Third World countries. Several Middle Eastern countries took initial moves toward expropriation. In 1971, the oil companies jointly issued an appeal to OPEC for "stability in the financial arrangements with producing governments," a stability to be achieved through negotiation between their combined group and the OPEC countries. In exchange for stability, the resulting Teheran agreement provided the oil-producing countries with larger revenues.[37] But by 1973, the agreement had broken down.

This international drama is the context for the development of Alberta's oil sands. While OPEC negotiators had overcome obstacles of ludicrous proportions (even to begin their own negotiations, they had to operate cloak-and-dagger style, and their meetings were not infrequently sabotaged, according to the negotiators),[38] Canadian government officials happily agreed that the oil of Canada should be owned and controlled by U.S. oil companies. In Minister Joe Green's telling phrase: "irrespective of where the imaginary border goes,"[39] the United States was invited to "participate" in Canada's wealth. By the early 1970s, that was precisely what American oil companies and U.S. government officials had in mind. The Schultz Report on energy cited above made U.S. interests entirely clear.

An "outside" consultant to the oil companies and the

American government, subsequently employed by the Lougheed government in Alberta, made the continentalist position on the Tar Sands in this proposal evident:

> For the United States, early development of the tar sands could contribute to the availability of secure North American oil supplies over the critical period before its own long-run efforts to develop conventional and synthetic oil might begin to pay off. For Canada, the establishment of early and substantial volumes of tar sands production could be essential to maintenance of Canada's export potential, providing an offset to Canada's rising volumes of oil imports.[40]

Syncrude was a consortium of four oil companies operating together. The original partners were Imperial Oil (30 per cent), Gulf Oil (10 per cent), Atlantic Richfield (30 per cent) and Canada Cities Service (30 per cent). Syncrude itself owned nothing: it was merely the name under which the subsidiaries of big oil companies were joined in a monopoly with restrictions on internal competition and an agreement to split the profits. This kind of monopoly arrangement had worked before and with the same participants (though through other subsidiaries in different countries). One of the earlier such ventures was the Iraq Petroleum Company, a consortium of four oil companies headed by Exxon. Iraq Petroleum drew oil from one of the richest deposits in the world for many years without showing a book profit; its parent companies avoided taxes in Britain and the United States, put their profits into other ventures, and managed throughout to prevent Iraq from gaining any ownership shares in the operation.[41] The Arabian-American Company (ARAMCO) of Saudi Arabia was another consortium with a similar tacky history. The Iraqui experience is particularly relevant to Canada, in view of the fact that the Great Canadian Oil Sands, operating from 1967, had still reported no profit as of 1974, and the Syncrude project which subsequently set up operations demanded a royalty arrangement by which they would pay no royalties during years of loss and yet be guaranteed an annual rate of return on their investments.[42]

Imperial Oil, a subsidiary of Exxon, is the senior partner in this venture. Like other Canadian oil companies in its early years, it sold out controlling shares to a U.S. firm because it could not gain adequate access to markets dominated by big U.S. corporations; nor did it have Canadian government protection on the domestic market. Though Exxon now owns 70 per cent of its shares, the actual capital provided by Exxon over the years has been considerably less than the capital provided by Imperial to its parent firm. According to Douglas House, who conducted a probing study of Imperial in the early 1970s:

> Exxon has contributed only a small part of the subsidiary's capitalization. Even in the major expansionary period following Leduc, Imperial financed its development mainly by selling two of its own subsidiaries (The Royalite Oil Company and the International Petroleum Company – the latter to Exxon), and by borrowing in financial markets.[43]

House goes on to describe capital inflows, and argues on the basis of company reported statistics that from 1947 to 1951, a period of rapid expansion for Imperial, Exxon supplied only one-fifth of the required capital. He says further: "No manager interviewed could remember Exxon's having supplied any capital to Imperial since that time."[44] Expansion is now financed entirely through retained earnings, with minimal utilization of financial markets for such extraordinary ventures as Syncrude. At the same time, Imperial has paid in dividends alone, between 1935 and 1974, some $1,094 million, and the amounts rise each year. In House's assessment: "The subsidiary now finances itself, while paying annual tribute to and building up the equity of the parent, which in turn uses the money to help finance its international expansion and to enrich its shareholders."[45]

Throughout the early stages of development, Alberta government advisers urged that Canadian capital, technology, and companies not only be involved but have control of the project.[46]

Their position was countered by the "international" company. Between them the four U.S. parent companies held combined assets in 1973 of over $40 billion; they controlled most of the world's oil supplies, refineries, storage and pipe-line facilities, and had a world-wide marketing network; subsidiaries of the subsidiaries, moreover, had various contracts for specialized services on the Syncrude project. There was no room here for Canadian companies or Canadian technology. Larry Pratt quotes a Bechtel construction company official as stating; "Canadians know fuck all," in response to arguments that more Canadians should be in charge of the project.[47]

If one were to take that sentence at face value, one would have a hard time explaining the predominance of Canadian employees on the project. Canadians apparently know enough when their wages are dependent on American companies: it is as independents attempting to operate in a market dominated by American companies that they founder. In short, it has considerably less to do with knowledge than with monopoly control of export networks.

House, in the study cited above, has demonstrated that Imperial in 1974 was staffed almost entirely by Western Canadians: some 70 per cent of its professional and managerial positions were held by these, only 8 per cent by Americans. He also discovered in his interviews with company employees, that most Canadians had been actively trained and provided with technical skills by the company, sometimes by Exxon in its U.S. facilities. During the course of his investigation, he found that the U.S. parent shared its technical information with its subsidiary, and that this central pool of information was important for subsidiary dominance in host countries. However, he also found that technological development and research facilities were carried on only in the parent country: Canada did not generate its own knowledge, and was therefore dependent on U.S. sources for information.[48]

In addition, Canadian firms are engaged on a contracting basis. As noted earlier, there are risks connected to a particular division of labour and heavy capital investments in plant and equipment. A less expensive means of having exploration and some specialized work done, while retaining control of a project the size of the Tar Sands, is to "farm out" specialized jobs to small companies. House has noted this:

> They farm out much of their exploration to smaller companies, particularly for marginal prospects; they contract out most of their geophysical exploration and drilling to specialist firms; they rely upon a host of small companies to provide numerous services and supplies ranging from helicopter services to catering; and they turn to "consulting firms" to supply

extra geologists and engineers during peak activity periods. This makes for great variety and flexibility in the overall organization of the industry. For the small specialist companies, it provides a socio-economic niche and a chance to make it in an exciting industry. For the majors, it is a basic technique for minimizing risk.[49]

The same process is evident in the forestry industry in British Columbia. There small businesses engage in trucking, marginal logging, and special custom-cut milling for the majors and provide some portion of the major's wood-chips for pulp mills in the process. Large forestry companies contract out areas of their tree-farm-licensed property to "stump-to-dump" operations, and these first-line contractors subcontract yet further to the owner-operators of logging trucks, skidders, and other equipment. These small operators have no claim on the company in times of recession. The company relieves itself of its labour commitments and retains its control over the resource itself. A similar pattern is evident in the manufacturing industries discussed elsewhere in this book. During the early growth and experimental phases, agents and parts-suppliers are components of the corporate complex; once the market is contained and relatively stable, the corporation begins to buy out its suppliers and sales-outlets and to provide its own internal service arrangements. Though contracting out is ultimately in the interests of corporate growth, the procedure does lead to high employment and an entrepreneurial climate during early phases of a project such as the Tar Sands. Through this procedure, corporate and non-corporate employees increase not only their wealth but as well their technical skills. A wide range of companies and individuals becomes knowledgeable about the technical and marketing aspects of the project.

American companies had argued in the early 1960s that Middle Eastern producing countries could not possibly run their own oil companies. With the full development of OPEC, this claim has proven false. A large number of employees for the corporations together with independent contractors and their employees were technically able to produce oil. The hurdle state-run corporations have to jump is the marketing stranglehold of the oil companies. It is not know-how or management expertise that gives the companies their edge: it is market control. It was in recognition of this market control that OPEC negotiators chose to organize a bargaining cartel which permitted the oil companies to retain control but at a higher price, rather than to nationalize their separate resource companies. Alberta's negotiators, whether because they believed they could not break the marketing network on their own, or because they were unwilling even to consider alternatives, did not pose as one possibility during bargaining Canadian ownership and control of the tar sands project.

The demands of the oil companies in early negotiations with the Alberta government were these: (1) that Syncrude be permitted to deduct operating costs, depreciation losses carried forward, and 8 per cent interest annually on 75 per cent of its overall investment, plus other interest allowances, from net profits – before determining the royalties shares for government; (2) that labour stability be guaranteed – no strikes during construction; (3) that federal tax laws which assess taxes on total profits be waived, so that the consortium would pay taxes only on the "net profits" after all deductions and Alberta government royalties; and (4) that the federal government not regulate the prices of synthetic crude oil "below the levels attainable in a free international market."[50] Throughout 1973-74, the demands of the oil companies reached the Canadian public indirectly, through a public squabble between the Federal and Provincial governments over condition (3), the royalties taxation. In the course of this fight, the oil companies threatened to withdraw altogether, arguing that oil by its nature is a "risky" business, and that anyway they could move into other oil-producing areas which provided fewer "disincentives."

The outcome was predictable. Given the general presumption by both governments that continentalism was in Canadian interests, given the nature of the financial investment class in Canada and its long-term involvement with American multinationals, and given the unwillingness of either government to consider seriously government-controlled exploitation of the Tar Sands, the oil companies gained most of their demands.

The partners in the ownership complex have changed as a consequence of these squabbles. Imperial upped its share to 31.25 per cent, Gulf increased its share to 16.75 per cent, Cities

Service reduced its share to 22 per cent, and three levels of government became financial partners: Ottawa, for 15 per cent; Alberta for 10 per cent; Ontario for 5 per cent. Imperial Oil has enough equity to outvote the three governments combined; the three companies have 70 per cent of ownership equity. What the governments end up doing is providing capital without gaining control. Not only do they provide capital at this level: Alberta "lent" Gulf and Cities Service $100 million each, and agreed to pick up the entire cost of Syncrude's utility plant and pipe-line (without ownership). In addition, the province must build the entire infrastructure of roads, schools, and services. Syncrude can write off its investments from taxable income, and is exempt – as demanded – from federal royalties-tax legislation. In the view of author Larry Pratt:

> The organized influence of international oil in Canadian society, as seen through the Syncrude episodes, extends to the highest levels of our political life. The American corporation has indeed become a central cog in the national politics of Canada. Thus, if private oil is corrupting democratic principles in the United States, in Canada it is also corrupting the possibility of national sovereignty and independence. For the source of the power which lies behind the successful political manoeuvres and pressure tactics of Canada's oil lobby is not to be found within Canada itself; this power is foreign. In the last analysis the politics of Syncrude are the politics of imperialism.[51]

## V

The transportation of wheat and other resources from the West to St. Lawrence ports and central Canadian industrial populations required the construction of both a national government and a national railway. A century later, it is oil and gas which need transportation. Again the need is for construction of a government and a transmission line, but this time the required government is not one based primarily on national interests or even the specific interests of a national financial class, and the transmission lines are intended to run from north to south rather than west to east.

Proposals to build pipelines are proposals to ensure steady

supplies of energy to existing industries in United States and their subsidiaries in a constricted belt of South-Central Canada. Without steady and secure supplies of oil, gas, and electricity, U.S. manufacturing industries would founder. Thus it is not only the oil companies which have an interest in ensuring American control and American priorities: it is the entire complex of multinational corporations centred in the Northern United States. Such pipelines, owned by Americans together with guaranteed rights to oil and gas reserves, would ensure that industrial development elsewhere on the continent would be impeded. Though this eventual result seems obvious enough, the federal government of the 1970s has consistently operated on the assumption that such pipelines should be built and that American "participation" to a level of effective control should be encouraged. In 1972 the Minister of Indian Affairs and Northern Development invited U.S. applicants to submit proposals for pipeline construction, stating that "everything that is reasonable to facilitate this particular development" would be done by the government. In 1974 the same minister reiterated his belief that joint U.S. and Canadian involvement would be required.

> The discovery of large oil and gas reserves at Prudhoe Bay, followed by indications of large reserves in the Mackenzie Delta has convinced us that pipelines will be built during the '70s from the shores of the Arctic Ocean to Southern Markets. It is no longer a question of whether pipelines will be built. The question has become when. There is no doubt, however, that a gas pipeline will be built through Canada.[52]

As pipeline applications proliferated, each from a consortium of oil companies and their subsidiaries, public protest erupted. A similar protest had emerged around the James Bay project, with native Indians, environmentalists, academics, journalists, and others expressing and publishing hostile arguments against the construction of infrastructure which would facilitate further foreign domination and destroy a local environment. The James Bay controversy had been expensive, not so much in terms of the final settlement that was eventually extracted for compensation of lost hunting territories for native inhabitants, but in terms of public confidence in governments acting in the interests of national or provincial citizens. Revelations regarding

American interests came to light which were not erased by a cash settlement. They came to light, moreover, at the same time as the economy was entering a recessionary period, unemployment was beginning its steady ascent, and inflation was beginning to affect all classes. At such a time governments are already in weak positions. They are unable to perform successfully their two major mandates: to provide channels for the accumulation of capital, and to provide legitimation for the system and its modes of operation. The "oil crisis" provided a temporary release from public skepticism, but as this, too, came under public attack and knowledge of its lack of substance became widespread, governments suffered a marked loss of public faith as they pursued American capital for the apparently not so necessary pipelines.

In 1973 a team of independent economists published a detailed study of the Arctic gas proposal in which they concluded: "Without assuming abnormally high rates of discovery, or of extraction from proven reserves, we calculate that production from non-frontier sources will be sufficient until 1988, and will continue into the next century."[53] This was the academic end of a debate that would not have occurred at all in the Canada of the affluent 1950s and 1960s. It was over the basic assumptions of economic growth and government policy: not about means, but about ends. In response, a government bent on complying with American industry demands would have either to apply force or to seek some means other than bravado for inducing the population to accept the imperatives of American growth. The appointment of a series of investigatory committees or royal commissions has a long history of use for purposes of "cooling" attitudes: it was the method chosen again on this occasion. What clearly was not anticipated was that the commission, headed by Justice T.R. Berger, appointed to enquire into the social, environmental, and economic impact of a proposed Mackenzie Valley gas pipeline, would elicit such strong opposition to pipeline construction in the North and such articulate support of Northern rights in Southern Canada that it could not be shelved or ignored. Berger recommended no immediate development of a Mackenzie line, and urged that native land claims and needs be given priority over American demands for oil; priority even over Canadian demands.

We look upon the North as our last frontier. It is natural for us to think of developing it, of subduing the land and extracting its resources to fuel Canada's industry and heat our homes. Our whole inclination is to think of expanding our industrial machine to the limit of our country's frontiers. In this view, the construction of a gas pipeline is seen as the next advance in a series of frontier advances that have been intimately bound up with Canadian history. But the native people say the North is their homeland. They have lived there for thousands of years. They claim it is their land, and they believe they have a right to say what its future ought to be. . . . What happens in the North, moreover, will be of great importance to the future of our country; it will tell us what kind of country Canada is; it will tell us what kind of people we are.[54]

To have ignored not only this appeal but the reservoir of doubts about growth-at-any cost would have been suicidal for a government. One of the government agencies (the National Energy Board) subsequently agreed with the Berger recommendation, and the Mackenzie Valley route was – at least temporarily – dropped from the agenda.[55]

In February 1978, Commissioner Andrew Thompson reiterated reasons for preventing construction of a pipeline, this time via Kitimat and across north-central British Columbia. The Thompson commission was able to provide only a preliminary report because the pipeline companies, recognizing that even more hostile opposition was mounting along the B.C. coast where oil-spills would destroy fishing habitats and dependent villages, withdrew their applications whenever Thompson's group came too close. The preliminary report argued that "a compelling and unavoidable need (for a West Coast oil port) has not been established."[56] The Kitimat port debate is not concluded: the oil companies appear to be waiting out the opposition before resubmitting yet another in a series of proposals. Meanwhile an interior route parallel with the Alaska Highway to bring Beaufort Sea supplies through 2,000 miles of Canada for the Midwestern states is going ahead. As Jean Chrétien promised, it was when and not whether pipelines would be constructed in Canada which formed the basic question.

While the pipeline debate continues, the same oil companies are renewing their claims on government aid in the Tar Sands; this time in a context which includes a world oversupply of oil (the crisis being remarkably short). Shell Oil announced in 1978 that it was "interested" in building a third oil-sands plant, but the senior vice-president of Shell Canada made his bargaining stance quite clear: " . . . expressions of interest are subject to acceptable commercial terms being established with governments."[57] At the time of writing this, the federal government is still preparing its oil-sands and heavy-oil policy statements for further development; having pledged itself to a policy dedicated to "self sufficiency by 1985" it appears unlikely that the policy will disappoint the oil companies.

Overall, the level of foreign ownership in Canada is steadily increasing. According to the Foreign Investment Review Agency, established originally to screen potential foreign take-overs and reduce the degree of Canadian dependence on foreign firms, proposals by foreign investors to establish new businesses in Canada were up 74 per cent in 1977 over the previous year; applications to take over existing businesses rose by 56 per cent. The agency's approval rate rose to 90 per cent in that year, suggesting that it lacks either the will or the capacity to restrain foreign take-overs.[58] The incapacity or lack of will is supported by the leading financial elites within Canada, who continue to depend on U.S. multinationals for their own profits. Though an increasing number of economists argue that Canada could be self-sustaining and would grow in a more healthy direction if foreign investment were curtailed,[59] bankers and spokesmen for international business interests express contempt for the Foreign Investment Review Agency and demand its dismissal. Earle McLaughlin, chairman of the Royal Bank, is one who argues that "at this stage of our development" Canada should be a major international borrower. He asks, "Can we not insure our Canadianism in corporate affairs by other, less meddlesome-means?"[60] The Royal Commission on Corporate Concentration shared McLaughlin's views in this respect, though not with respect to banking legislation. For banks, that Commission recommended measures to bring about greater competition, but for non-financial industries it recommended measures congruent with ever greater concentration. The stated reason for this is a lack of savings sufficient for investment by Canadians: the same reason financiers provided for investing in American business in the 1880s, 1920s, and 1950s. The investment class in Canada considers national sovereignty as much of an outdated concept now as it did then.

This, then, is the context within which large corporations operate in Canada. With control over technology, capital, and world markets, with the active support and participation of a Canadian financial elite and the continuing compliance of both federal and provincial levels of government, but with a decreasing rate of expansion in the industrial countries, they have a great deal of power to determine what kind of a country this is, if not, in Justice Berger's noble terms, what kind of a people we are.

## VI

The charge that this history constitutes American imperialism does not carry with it an explanation for the compliance of both federal and provincial governments in Canada. One of the means of explaining this is to describe the extent to which such governments are actually composed at the cabinet and policy-making levels of members of the financial class or their direct representatives. Though the congruence of personnel as well as of interests is less startling than at the period of railway construction, it has been persistent and strong throughout the post-war period.[61] However, there has been a change in government policy in the current period which appears to be incongruous with that explanation.

This is the direct participation of a federal government in exploitation of resources and construction of transportation lines with a provincial government and American capital. The national elite whose interests that government has represented for a century appears to have been deprived of its traditional position as intermediary.

What appears to be happening in the 1970s is that the national financial class as a distinctive class has receded in importance. Its interests have merged so completely with American capital that it no longer has a separate "internal colonial" role to play. That part of it which has remained outside the magic circle of international capitalism has lost power. The federal government, always combining with established power, as a member of the "disestablished" elite has phrased it,[62] is obliged to work directly with American capital if it is to retain political control of the country. It no longer has an independent base within Canada, so successfully has that base sought profit outside the country. In moving toward this conjunction, it must combine forces with new internal powers at the regional level, represented by their provincial governments and financiers. This is all the "crisis of federalism" is about, but not all the "crisis of government" is about because such governments still have to persuade their constituents to accept the existing power structure: Syncrude, pipelines, foreign ownership, unemployment, inflation, and all else that is contained in it. The task of persuasion was much lighter while capitalism expanded and provided jobs and mobility.

# PART TWO

# SOCIOLOGY OF INDUSTRIAL ORGANIZATIONS AND THE CLASS STRUCTURE

# CHAPTER 4

# SYSTEMS FOR MANAGEMENT

*What I shall attempt to bring about is that nothing shall be dependent upon the life or existence of any particular person; that nothing of any importance shall happen or be caused to happen without the foreknowledge and approval of the management; that the past and determinate future of the establishment can be learned in the files of the management without asking a question of any mortal.*

– Alfred Krupp[1]

Contemporary multinational corporations are characterized by highly efficient management systems. The systems did not develop automatically or easily. Although some companies were models of efficiency with respect to their division of labour before World War I, they were few in number. The phenomenon of the multinational corporation, and particularly of the corporation which is both decentralized with respect to its daily operations and centralized with respect to its financial and policy decision-making, is largely a phenomenon of the post-second-war period.[2] There was a considerable time-lag for most companies between early dominance in the market and creation of an internal system of management for control of the established empire.

These companies emerged first as manufacturing or resource companies with a somewhat unco-ordinated system of sales outlets. Often the sales agencies were on a commission or contract basis, and not integrated into the central concern. Merchant houses and agencies abroad representing domestic business were important to growth because they generated considerable wealth to be reinvested in manufacturing at home (Britain, Europe, and subsequently the United States and Japan). They were also important in establishing early connections between domestic firms and foreign nationals. These links frequently became the essential means by which domestic companies, having grown sufficiently wealthy to expand their production units abroad, obtained foreign currency and the support of foreign bankers, and gained knowledge of foreign cultures and economies. In addition, portfolio investment (which carries with it no rights of ownership), especially in raw materials, sometimes cemented the base for direct purchase of these materials at a later date.

But these merchant houses and agencies did not form, in themselves, the basis for integrated manufacturing-resource complexes. Companies gained control of markets, gained capital for expansion, took over the technical capacities of smaller firms or otherwise gained control of a technical process, yet frequently held themselves together only through the momentum of entrepreneurial activity. When markets dipped, they were unable to organize their resources. Not a few large businesses developed terminal diseases with such events as the 1930s depression. World War II saved many American and Canadian "empires" by providing defence-production contracts. The companies emerged from the second war with expanded capacities for production on a more integrated basis than they had hitherto enjoyed, and with this some discovered the merits of "efficiency."

The advantages of systematic organization were recognized long before these companies became dominant economic units of capitalism. Writing in the first decade of the twentieth century, German sociologist Max Weber observed:

It is primarily the capitalist market economy which demands that the official business of the administration be discharged precisely, unambiguously, continuously, and with as much speed as possible. Normally, the very large, modern capitalist enterprises are themselves unequalled models of strict bureaucratic organizations.[3]

Over a century before Weber wrote this, Adam Smith had argued that the division of labour would increase in direct relationship to the market demand for products.[4] This general relationship is accurate at a crude level: obviously the need for such specialization increases where the market expands, but there are inhibitions to its implementation. One of these is the stability of such markets. A market may be large, but it may also be exhaustible, temporary, or potentially subject to controls by governments and legislation or other "unfavourable" political climates. It may be large only if producers are able to vary the product to meet local demands across different territories. It may be large, but the product itself requires such extensive detailed work that mass production and standardization are not possible.[5] These characteristics of markets vary for products, and a company which invests a great deal in an extensive division of labour without an assured long-term market may so tie up its capital in specialization that it loses its flexibility.

Thus, the creation of a highly specialized system either at the production level, which involves a considerable investment of capital in machinery and training of workers, or at the managerial level, which also involves an investment in people and training, depends not only on the extent of a market but on certainty about the long-range stability and growth of such markets. This may be otherwise phrased as the reduction or elimination or risks.

Entrepreneurial activity involves individual risk.[6] It requires actors who are willing to make quick decisions where high stakes are involved, and who will do this on their own authority with limited information. It not infrequently obliges such actors to engage in salesmanship or something akin to it, not simply obtaining customers but usually obtaining capital backing as well. Entrepreneurial activity has as its goal the creation of capital by any means whatsoever, and it is by its very nature a short-term individual undertaking.

The transition to a company with long-term interests that transcend individuals is a transition from entrepreneurial activity to corporate organization. The organizations, unlike individuals, may live (if not forever) a long time: they can afford to lose immediate profits if they gain the power to increase their wealth in the long run. They can do this only if they find a means of identifying risks, and if they can obtain sufficient information about markets, competitors, and technical developments so that their decision-making is relatively "safe." This process is generally slow to develop, partly because it takes time to assemble such an organization, but partly as well because most organizations begin with entrepreneurial leaders whose talents and objectives are not conducive to long-term planning. The organization must outgrow its origins in order to become the corporation described by legal fictions. Few industrial organizations had reached this stage before 1945.

The DuPont Corporation was an exception, and it subsequently became the model for other corporate re-organizations.

## I

The DuPont Corporation of 1900 was a family-owned and family-controlled enterprise with stock in other firms and with considerable influence over the explosives industry. The company in effect operated as the leading voice in a combination of companies. Yet Alfred Chandler in a detailed and probing study of DuPont's early development observed that the family at this time did not actually control the combination.[7] They did not control it because they had no systematic information about what the other firms produced, about the price structure for various products, about the production capacities of the total combination. Nor had they developed a systematic marketing network. The various firms in the combination sold through agents in a mercantile arrangement.

The combination was re-organized when a new generation of DuPonts decided to expand their operations. According to Chandler's account, this involved the following steps:

1. Properties were inventoried, and all were transferred to a new consolidated shareholding company initially under the control of three cousins. This company became the sole owner, the sole manager, and the sole decision-maker for the companies which were previously loosely organized in combination.

2. Three committees were established with distinct tasks and functions. These were the Finance, Executive, and Administration Committees. The Finance Committee consisted of the largest stockholders and concentrated on consolidating properties, creating a rationalized system of financing and providing financial information to the Executive Committee. The Executive Committee concentrated on policy rather than operating decisions, and planned long-term growth, rationalization, personnel policies, and allocation of funds. The co-ordination tasks on the field and in the plants were undertaken by the Administration Committee, composed of departmental directors.

3. The entire company, now consolidated as one, was re-organized on a "line and staff" basis. The lines, beginning with the three family partners, included several vice-presidents responsible for particular functional areas, through department directors and assistants to plant managers and supervisors. The sales organization included branch managers and field officers. The manufacturing divisions included plant managers and their deputies. The staff functions were professional, and the duties of these technicians were explicitly defined for each of the functional areas.

4. Communications systems were deliberately designed in order to ensure a maximum of information flowing up the line of authority while orders flowed downwards. Regular meetings of superintendents and managers and circulation of information pertaining both to administration and technical developments were means of maintaining the communications effectiveness.

The three cousins who engineered this transition from family to managerial corporation became dominant board directors rather than single owners, but it should be noted that they also became board members of several other companies, including General Motors.

After World War I, with a much-expanded company due to war production facilities and profits, the DuPont Company underwent yet further centralization. New and younger executives were given top management positions, and the company was re-organized into four "functional" divisions each headed by a vice-president. Subordinates reported to the vice-presidents rather than the executive committee. The guiding concerns in the redesign were the need for co-ordination at levels not hitherto problematic, and the need to ensure that one person would take full responsibility for the actions of different production sectors of the company. The report submitted by the redesign team, following an investigation of practices in several other large firms, stated: "The principle of individual responsibility and undivided authority has been recognized by the Company and consistently followed in the cases of its established divisions." This principle meant that each department head was held responsible for results, and he was given authority and autonomy "subject only to the alternative of having someone replace him if his official judgment is not good." In turn, branch office managers and plant superintendents were responsible for their spheres of operation, subject to the principles and methods of their superiors.[8]

The centralization was accompanied by an extension of the division of labour: as authority was concentrated, so too was it dispersed and turned into a delimited, specific aspect of jobs held by persons always subject to removal if unfit for office. However, this reorganization did not work as well as anticipated. While the firm was rationalizing a structure suitable to a single product line, the company was simultaneously diversifying its products.

One wonders what impetus a successful company has for diversification. In this case, as in so many others, it was the sheer size and existing resources of the company. Technicians, technical knowledge, personnel, finances, production facilities, and a massive administrative structure were an assembled society looking for new territory to conquer. Even before the war, the search for territories had begun. Canada was a major foreign territory for DuPont. In the post-war era, DuPont bought out controlling shares in Canadian Industries Ltd. and thereafter maintained heavy investments in Canada.[9]

Chandler quotes an executive order to an appointed subcommittee in 1908 charged with investigating what steps might be taken to develop further uses for gunpowder or related production in view of "the likelihood of our having a considerable idle capacity at our smokeless powder plants."[10] Among the alternatives investigated were increases in services to government, and industries with a nitrocellulose base – artificial leather, artificial silk, photographic film, dyestuffs, vegetable oils, paints and varnishes, water-soluble chemicals, and cellulose purification. With the end of the war, these investigations were intensified and resulted in the process of diversification, enlargement, vertical integration of plants, take-overs of small firms in allied fields, and still further enlargement. What began as an effort toward utilization of excess capacity became a means of exceeding existing capacity many times over.

It became clear in the process that the unified command structure could not handle the enormous increase in different kinds of industries. The problem lay in the lack of "logical marketing connections" between product lines. A sales department under a single vice-president was adequate for a single-product line, inadequate for several industries even where these were feeding into one another. In particular, it became impossible to market goods intended for different populations and requiring vastly different approaches. For example, paints intended for private consumers could not be sold in a fashion similar to defence products intended for government. The committee of 1920, established to determine where the problems lay, concluded that no natural disadvantages lay in the company's technical capacities or resources, but rather that the organization itself was the critical factor. The solution proposed and, after a lengthy delay, adopted, involved a shift from "functional" units to "product" units. Each division included its own purchasing, accounting, manufacturing, and sales departments; an Executive Committee oversaw managers of the divisions, and each division had its own line of authority. This new structure came to be the dominant form of American industry after the 1920s. The organization chart for the corporation indicates the nature of the product-line form (Figure 5).

This organization as depicted in the chart appears to have four different presiding bodies. The Board of Directors does not include all of the executives in the organization, and includes a large number of people whose formal employment ties or financial conditions indicate that they are not regularly involved in the operation at all. The next two bodies are committees rather than single persons, and they are equivalent in formal powers. The president is not the head of the corporation, and he is officially responsible to only one of the committees which head the

138

Figure 5: Proposed Organization for the DuPont Company,
August 31, 1921

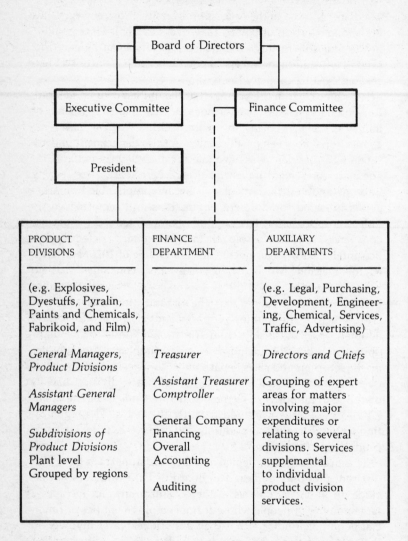

SOURCE: Based on Chart 5 in Alfred Chandler, *Strategy and Structure*,
Boston, Mass.: MIT Press, 1962, pp. 108-9.

organization. The precise relationship between product divisions and auxiliary departments is not clear, nor is the relationship between the finance committee and the treasurer's office and all other departments. There appears to be, instead of the precise vertical hierarchy suggested by Weber, a series of horizontally placed departments each with its own vertical hierarchy, and the relationships between all of these is left open to further interpretation.

Officially the interpretation is something like this. The Board of Directors provides broad guidelines, financial contacts and support, and tie-ins with other corporations. The operating power lies with the Executive and Financial Committees which have complementary powers. Actual administration, as distinct from policy formulation, is carried on by divisional managers and their deputies. Product and functional departments negotiate with one another according to need.

One might reinterpret this by observing that the Board of Directors appears to have taken on the position of "class monitors," in a rather literal way. Its task is to ensure that the activities of this or that corporation among its various directorships is toeing the line. It acts as a standard-bearer for class interests, maintaining class morality through presence, contacts, persuasion, and ultimate financial control, but it does not exert a daily control on operations. The executive and financial committees are actively involved in policy formulation and retain (but in what precise balance is left open to negotiation) overall control of corporate activities. It might be noted that in terms of the society at large, it is these executives who have the power to channel resources, establish priorities, restrict financing, employ or disemploy populations, and choose the moral codes by which corporate growth will proceed. They are constrained (but to what degree is apparently also left to negotiation) by the real financial control still wielded by bankers and other corporate directors, and by the class ideology which permeates that group and its decisions.

Past this point, we find a somewhat ambiguous mixture of centralization and decentralization. Financial and policy control are centralized; actual operations are decentralized. In order to maintain this relatively flexible organization and still retain control, the central offices have their own hierarchial staffs and auxiliary services. They have, for example, an independent information-gathering service which Chandler discusses though it does not appear on the chart. Its function is to provide "independent" information, which is used to "correct" or "balance" that given by the decentralized departments. The establishment of such auxiliary services is predicated on an implicit recognition that there will be a struggle over scarce resources. The need for a "balancing mechanism" is occasioned by these conflicting demands on resources. The concept "in the interests of the total organization" is one which arises in this circumstance precisely because it cannot be taken for granted that separate divisions will treat the total organization as a single entity with interests that diverge from those of their internal operations.

## II

DuPont was a leader in systems management. Most American and Canadian companies which are now multinational actually went through more growing pains. Most were established by the turn of the century or within the next decade, but grew unevenly before the 1940s. They emerged from World War II, often as a result of extensive defence-production contracts, possessed of vastly enlarged capacities and the opportunity to move into Europe for new markets, but hampered by internal deficiencies in organization. During the 1920s these companies had reorganized their production systems at the level of the factory or shop-floor, but it was not until the post-war period and into the 1950s that they developed systems to co-ordinate internal operations on a multiregional basis.

Ford Motor Company is an example. Ford (established 1903) was neither the first nor the most prominent of automotive manufacturers in the United States during the early years of its operation.[11] Nor was the United States the original home of the automobile. A forerunner had been created in 1875 in Europe, but not manufactured "because its inventor saw no future for it."[12] The first commercial automobiles were produced in France. British manufacturers were prevented from entering the field prior to the 1890s by prohibitive legislation against highway use and speed pushed through by railroad and carriage companies.[13] American companies, however, became successful in the production of cheaper mass-produced cars, in large part because they early developed the machinery for production and thereby saved on labour costs. As noted in an earlier chapter, labour-saving devices were perceived as necessary in the United States because of a labour shortage and high labour costs, whereas plentiful labour and relatively cheaper wages in Europe inhibited such technical advances. In common with the Colt gun, one of the advantages of mass-produced cars was the inter-changeability of their parts.

Ford's first venture into manufacturing abroad was in Canada. By an agreement signed in 1904, Ford provided patents and technical information to a Canadian subsidiary, and the sub-sidiary gained exclusive rights to manufacture and sell Ford cars in Canada. Over 60 per cent of the financial support came from Canadian investors. The Canadian company, having access to British Empire markets, also gained control of sales throughout that market. Indeed, this was one of the reasons Ford and General Motors, along with other American companies, were eager to locate plants in Canada.

The parent company retained control of the enterprise. The president of the American company was also president of the Canadian company; Henry Ford was vice-president, and the American treasurer remained treasurer for the subsidiary. The Canadian entrepreneur who had negotiated this arrangement held the highest Canadian position as general manager.

In the early years of the Canadian operation, the parent com-pany appears to have allowed this offspring considerable in-dependence. It expanded its production facilities rapidly, and its sales – aided by the buyer's market in a growing coun-try – steadily increased. Both Canadian and American opera-tions, however, centralized their control over sales outlets abroad, and maintained strict control over distribution. The American company established and wholly owned a manufac-turing plant in England in 1911, and maintained close supervi-sion over its development.

All of these plants were engaged in mass-assembling of parts which were produced in various locations. Some parts were pro-duced by machine-shops and other contract producers. Shortly before the war, Ford developed a genuine mass-production pro-cess utilizing a continuous conveyer belt and similar other mechanical devices for assembly lines. This was not essentially a technical development. It was rather an achievement in management. Ford had taken the mechanical potentiality that already existed and had been developed several decades earlier for other purposes and applied it to the production of automobiles in such a way as to produce entire products in a single factory at startling speed. With this development, Ford outstripped competitors in the United States and was able to produce automobiles much more cheaply. Ford turned this capacity into cheaper costs for buyers and shorter hours at higher wages to employees. The result was a prodigious enlargement of the potential market for automobiles together with an upsetting of traditional wage-structures for workers.

Through the war and into the 1920s, Ford ensured that all foreign subsidiaries with the exception of the Canadian one would be wholly owned and tightly controlled by his family. The Canadian company had public ownership of its stock, though it remained firmly within the American empire. After the war, the empire included branches in Argentina and Brazil, as well as throughout Europe. The nature of control is evident in this quotation, from an executive in the Detroit parent to a subsidiary manager in Spain: "the Spanish Company is owned by the Ford interests and subject to instructions from the home office the same as any branch house."[14] Financial transactions, accounting procedures, investments, marketing, employee management practices, wages (explicitly designed to offset the appeals of unions), and all details of manufacturing were under direct supervision of the Detroit firm. All subsidiaries were treated as "branches" regardless of their constitutional status as incorporated companies.

The tight control was one of the defects of the Ford system of management. In common with the early development of IBM, under Thomas Watson, the company expanded territorially but retained an individual decision-maker at the top: the procedure for operating was unwieldy. Ford failed to develop an adequate bookkeeping system. The company had no division of labour between its top executives with respect to personnel, accounting, marketing, or production. By the end of the war, Ford owned steel mills, soybean-processing factories, rubber plantations, glass manufacturing plants, ships, and an automobile and truck empire, but had no better idea of what each produced and how

**Figure 6: Ford Motor Company, International Holdings**

---

Consolidated Holdings
Under U.S. Parent[1]                          Canadian Holdings[2]

---

Ensite (Canada)                           ┌─ (88.1%)
Ford Motor Credit of Canada               │  Ford Motor of Australia
Ford Motor of Canada ─────────────────────┤  Ford Motor of South Africa
                                          │  Ford Motor of New Zealand
Ford Aerospace and                        │  Ford Motor Private Ltd.
  Communications                          │    (Singapore)
Ford International Capital                 │
Ford Motor Credit Co.                     │  In Canada: 75 subsidiaries
Ford International Finance Corp.           │  listed in sales, property
Ford Motor Co. (England)                  │  holdings, leasing, rentals.
Ford Motor S.A. (Mexico)                  │  Sales companies market
Ford Motor (Belgium)                      │  cars, trucks, tractors,
Ford-Werke A.G. (Germany)                 └─ and other equipment.
Ford Motor Argentine S.A.
Ford France S.A.
Ford Nederland N.V.
Ford Brasil S.A.
Richier S.A. (France)
Ford Espana S.A. (Spain)
Ford Motor Co. (Denmark)
Ford Motor Co. (Sweden)
Ford Motor Co. (Finland)

Ford Philippines
Ford Pacific (Australia)
Ford Motor Co. (Thailand)
Ford Lio Ho Motor Co. (Taiwan)
Ford of Japan
Ford Mid-East and Africa

(Non-consolidated holdings not
listed; smaller subsidiaries
also omitted.)

---

[1] As listed in *Moody's Industrial Manual*, 1977.
[2] The four international subsidiaries are listed in *Moody's*.
Holdings within Canada are given in *Inter-Corporate Ownership
Directory*, 1972, and may be updated by *Financial Post* listings.

much profit each made than had the elder DuPont at the turn of the century.[15] The change came in 1946 when Ford's son, together with a new president, began the process undertaken by the DuPont cousins between 1910 and 1925. Defence contracts during the Korean War years increased the profitability of the automotive industry, and simultaneously increased the pressure to rationalize not only production but marketing and accounting as well.

Essentially the same story may be told of IBM, with allowances for the personality differences of the two "fathers." International Business Machines was an outgrowth of the Computing Tabulating Recording Company, established in 1911. The original company included on its staff Herman Hollerith who actually invented the tabulating machines and held the original patent. He had awarded licences outside North America for their manufacture and distribution before Thomas Watson became involved in the firm. Watson, a former salesman with National Cash Registers, and one who at the time of initial employment was facing a jail sentence (later suspended) for his share in violations of American anti-trust legislation, became chairman and later president of the company. On the death of its technical genius and owner, Watson changed the name of the company and extended the market for business machines outside North America. The fall of the German mark in 1922 provided the company with reason to take over the German company which had received licences from Hollerith, and Watson then began manufacturing or assembling products abroad in order to ease cash shortages caused by transportation and European import restrictions. During the 1920s, IBM encountered competition from a technically equal business which later became part of Remington-Rand, and Swiss Bull Company which IBM later took over.[16]

Watson recognized the need for a division of labour and often talked about it. The main action he took in this direction was to organize the company into two divisions, a domestic unit to be headed by himself and later his oldest son, and a "World Trade" division to be headed by his second son. Up to his death in 1956, he held all effective power himself, and the result was that this extensive business was running into the same problems as beset Ford. As in the Ford case, the son decentralized the organization, and created a management system that effectively divided areas of responsibility and authority. In this system final control still rests with head offices, and ultimately with the board of directors and executives, but certain operating decisions and day-to-day functions are carried on by lower-level management.

The Massey-Harris-Ferguson story illustrates a similar case, but in this instance the problem did not lie with a particular father figure, so much as with an executive group that, before the merger with Ferguson in the mid-1950s, simply failed to divide their labour effectively. Vincent Massey, president of the company in the early 1920s, wrote that: "there was little, if any, departmentalization in the Company. There was no well-defined sales department, or department of production. Officers of the Company moved easily from one division to the other. . . . "[17]

The 1930s depression brought the company close to financial ruin. The company had never developed its own technology, and had depended on the expanding market for agricultural machinery in Canada together with purchases of smaller companies with proven technical advantages for its growth. In 1941 it finally gave birth to a new product: the self-propelled combine. This, together with defence production contracts (especially with the American government) during the war permitted it to become a diversified company with assembling operations throughout North America. With the decline in mass markets for agricultural implements and machinery early in the 1950s, its lack of specialized organization and its dependence for manufacturing operations on contracts undermined its capacity to expand much further, indeed threatened its very survival. As late as 1950, re-organization schemes failed to implement the innovative management techniques developed by DuPont three to four decades earlier. Company biographer E.P. Neufeld observes that control consisted of demands for periodic submissions of balance sheets and income statement data and "on periodic personal visits by the President, for which masses of materials usually were specifically prepared. . . . There was no market research of a continuing nature."[18]

The merger with Ferguson in 1953 was the crucial turning-point for Massey-Harris.Though both organizations were in financial trouble, their combined assets made them the second highest sales volume corporation in the field (International

Harvester retained top position). Their merger provided Massey-Harris with the Ferguson integrated tractor, and Ferguson with a sales organization. Though on paper the new company was enormous and potentially most profitable, the lack of internal organization suffered previously by both parties to the merger prevented it from capitalizing on its position for several years. Says Neufeld of the 1953-56 period, "Policy emerged piece by piece as emergencies were encountered one by one."[19]

Ferguson left the organization (or was ousted, depending on whether one maintains the official interpretation that this was a merger, or understands, as did Massey-Harris negotiators, that it was a take-over)[20] the following year. The company re-organized its management once in 1954, and again in 1956, at last moving closer to the systematic forms adopted in more successful corporations around the world. This meant both increasing specialization of responsibility, and increasing centralized control. The management group which had directed the company through its many acquisitions, its war growth, its difficult years in export and domestic markets, its negotiations with Ferguson were gradually pushed out by what Neufeld calls "a new breed of men." The "new breed" included Argus holding corporation's executives which up to that point and since World War II had dominated the board of directors: hardly new to the corporation, but now moving into active command of operations. The resulting organization of Massey-Ferguson, 1956, clearly indicates the functional, product, and regional divisions of the company. This was further systematized through the following decade, and by 1966 the organization had a division of labour much more typical of successful companies than it had in the pre-1954 period.

The 1956 plan was accompanied by a detailed and demanding memorandum from the new chairman and chief executive officer. This made clear two principles: that there would be extensive delegation of responsibility and authority, and that, simultaneously, there would be "continuous supervision and control": "The fact that RESPONSIBILITY has been delegated does not in any way lessen the accountability of the Executive who delegates."[21] Line and staff functions were spelled out. The 1966 plan extended these functions into several more specialized

147

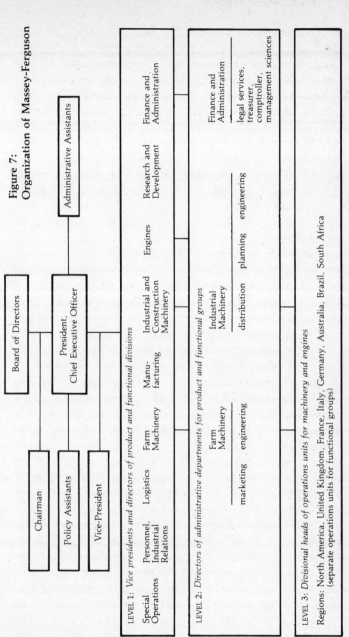

Figure 7:
Organization of Massey-Ferguson

LEVEL 1: *Vice presidents and directors of product and functional divisions*

| Special Operations | Personnel, Industrial Relations | Logistics | Farm Machinery | Manu-facturing | Industrial and Construction Machinery | Engines | Research and Development | Finance and Administration |

Chairman

Policy Assistants

Vice-President

Board of Directors

President, Chief Executive Officer

Administrative Assistants

LEVEL 2: *Directors of administrative departments for product and functional groups*

Farm Machinery

marketing    engineering

Industrial Machinery

distribution    planning    engineering

Finance and Administration

legal services, treasurer, comptroller, management sciences

LEVEL 3: *Divisional heads of operations units for machinery and engines*

Regions: North America, United Kingdom, France, Italy, Germany, Australia, Brazil, South Africa (separate operations units for functional groups)

SOURCE: based on E. P. Neufeld, *A Global Corporation*, Toronto: University of Toronto Press, 1969, pp. 234-35, chart 5.

areas, including advertising, specialized operations (a unit designed specifically to investigate potential extensions of operations into countries not already served by branches), and new product developments in industrial and construction machinery.

As the organization chart indicates, the primary divisions here, as in other large companies, were not regional. Regional units were and are subservient to product and functional division heads. Policy and finance were centralized functions, the responsibility of vice-presidents and the executive committee subject to the Board of Directors. On the other hand, manufacturing and marketing were so organized as to permit decentralization of decisions.

### III

Initial success is not in itself a guarantee that a company will maintain its dominance. But it is a pretty hefty advantage, because the capital accumulated in the process is sufficient to buy further technology, expand marketing operations, and withstand temporary set-backs such as general recessions, saturated markets and overproduction crises, and trade barriers established by foreign governments. The company which has successfully developed such capital reserves typically hedges its bets and secures its permanence not only by buying out its supply sources and sales-dealers, but as well by moving into related and even unrelated industrial and servicing fields. The result is not so much an organization as a massive co-ordination of many separate yet each complex units.

Canadian Pacific is one such massive complex. It obtained its start through government grants on such a scale that even in the 1970s the amount appears staggering.[22] This was an example not of a particular family having wealth but of a particular group of financiers creating a government in order to tap the public purse. Still "owned" in Canada, Canadian Pacific has holdings outside the country though these are not extensive. Its domestic holdings, which are extensive, are shown above in Figure 1. It may be seen that the company includes a major subsidiary, Canadian Pacific Investments. This in turn owns many other companies in a range of product and industrial sectors. In addition, Canadian Pacific Investments has holdings sufficient to provide positions on the boards of directors for many other large corporations.

By comparison with Canadian Pacific, most large multinational corporations have much more extensive holdings in the manufacturing industries. Indeed, their central concerns are with manufacturing, and other areas – such as transportation, finance, real estate, and even the extraction of resources – become means by which the manufacturing capacity is ensured and enhanced. Canadian companies, like Canadian Pacific and Noranda (Figure 2), are concentrated in the transportation, finance, and the forestry and some mining resources sectors. Two of the most powerful Canadian companies are mainly financial holding complexes: Argus (with interests in Massey-Ferguson, B.C. Forest Products, Dominion Stores, and Hollinger Mines) and Power Corporation (Figure 4). The majority of manufacturing companies in Canada are foreign-owned, and of these the majority are American.[23]

Multinational manufacturing firms may be organized in various ways because there are several organizational means of integrating a production empire. The most formidable is probably that in which separate research, manufacturing, and marketing units of the same company are assigned highly specialized tasks such that none of them completes a product and all are dependent on a central authority for co-ordination and direction (e.g. IBM). A second type is that in which subsidiaries trade parts amongst themselves, forming an integrated production system on a regional basis similar to other production systems for the same items in other regions, the entire network being co-ordinated by a central authority. A third type involves a series of production units turning out essentially the same and interchangeable components which may be assembled into final products in a central location. Few companies have developed their production systems to such a high degree of integration and interdependence of parts as IBM. But many are mixtures of this process together with the second and third types on different continents. Some are in transition from "identical" factories to "interdependent" ones. Some which are now interdependent are creating parallel copies in regions where they fear too great a dependence on component units. On an international scale, these variations are similar to those of assembly-line factories, and companies experiment with alternative ways of maximizing economies of scale across national borders.

International Business Machines, now the sixth largest corporation in the world with assets worth more than the Gross National Product of several European nations, controls about two-thirds of the computer market in the "free world." It employs some 260,000 people around the globe, about 25,000 of whom are engaged in research and product development.[24]

IBM maintains seventeen manufacturing plants in thirteen nations, and twenty-six separate laboratories in eight nations. Its 360/40 computer was developed in Britain, and eventually put together in France and New York from component parts manufactured in Scotland, Paris, the Netherlands, Sweden, and Italy. Two of the three fundamental research laboratories are in the United States, the third in Switzerland. These engage in basic research in the physical sciences, computer technology, and mathematics. The remaining laboratories are engaged in research on practical applications and manufacturing designs: seventeen in the United States, six in Europe. Each of these is assigned specific tasks, and none may compete with the others or engage in tasks which do not have approval – and funds – from U.S. headquarters. Each country specializes in a particular range of components.

Marketing is also centralized. The head office co-ordinates a number of regional offices, and national and branch offices feed their orders and requirements through regional headquarters. The European market, for example, is serviced entirely by the British regional office. Orders are sent to the British office by private line and computer tape from other centres. There are 331 sales offices and 228 service bureaus and data centres in 104 countries, all co-ordinated in this way and kept in close contact through the communications network.

Automobile manufacturers also create integrated production and marketing systems. The nature of the integration varies with the size of potential markets, the levels of technical skills in a region, the infrastructure of roads and auxiliary services available in a country, and consumer tastes and incomes. Unlike computers, cars are not yet exactly the same the world over, so that complete integration is not feasible. On a regular basis, however, such manufacturers as General Motors, Ford, and Chrysler work in much the same way as IBM. The British subsidiary of General Motors makes all trucks outside America; the German subsidiary exports all passenger cars. Component parts for these are manufactured on an integrated regional basis and shipped to their final assembly plants from the "in-company" suppliers. Most models for North America are manufactured at plants in the United States. Prior to the *Autopact* agreements, American subsidiaries in Canada manufactured a slightly smaller range of the same cars for the Canadian market in order to avoid import duties on American manufacturers. With this barrier removed, Canadian subsidiaries manufacture fewer models on an exclusive basis. Both these models, which are not produced in the U.S., and U.S. models which are not produced in Canada, are sold regionally throughout North America. Thus the production system is geared to an integrated marketing strategy. As one executive put it:

If the South African assembly operation and its recently added manufacturing facilities are to function smoothly and efficiently, they must today receive a carefully controlled and coordinated flow of vehicle parts and components from West Germany, England, Canada, the United States, and even Australia. These must reach General Motors South Africa in the right volume and at the right time to allow for an orderly scheduling of assembly without accumulation of excessive inventories. This is a challenging assignment which must be made to work if the investment is to be a profitable one.[25]

Massey-Ferguson, now maintains a similarly integrated empire, although less specialized in its units. Economies of scale may also be achieved through multiple manufacture of identical components, so that all parts can be interchanged, and plants can be utilized according to local demand, financial environment, and political advantage. A managing director described it this way:

(We have) interchangeability of product and common design everywhere as far as possible, so that components can be produced from a high volume centre to be exported to an overseas factory making the same finished machines. . . . We can now, for example, take a transmission and an engine from England, a rear axle from France, sheet metal parts and other components from Detroit, and assemble tractors for the domestic market. Or we can vary the sourcing of components as costs of currency dictate.[26]

Another example is the world's leading manufacturer of ball and roller bearings. SKF (Akteibolaget Svenska Kullager-fabriken) manufactures bearings in fifteen countries, has sales offices in 120, and like IBM, is tightly controlled by head offices in Sweden. It has worked on the principle of identical manufacturing processes in all plants, achieving economies of scale through interchangeability of parts and maximum exploitation of local markets. SKF boasts of its policy of "sharing out" the available work. It switches export orders from one plant to another, depending on local employment situations, financial climates, and political considerations. A senior executive is quoted with reference to a re-allocation of orders from Germany to France at a critical point in French history, when French production dependent on the French market might otherwise have created problems for that subsidiary: "These orders together with others from several different sources within the SKF group helped the French SKF factories considerably after the events of May, 1968."[27]

Most large corporate enterprises dominant in the 1970s have grown through their use of mechanization, new chemical bases for production, automation, and other technical developments: one cannot pin-point one single technical change as the critical one in their growth. Take for example the aluminum industry.[28] Aluminum in its raw state can be found almost everywhere beneath the earth's surface, but until the mid-nineteenth century no one knew how to extract it in sufficient concentrations to make it a profitable mining venture. A French chemist identified the chemical "bauxite" in 1821, a substance in which a very high aluminum oxide content exists. When other chemicals – aluminum fluoride, synthetic cryolite, and carbon – are applied to bauxite the aluminum content can be extracted. In order to separate the aluminum in large quantities, very high electrical currents are driven through alumina (the initial extract from bauxite), causing molten aluminum to sink to the bottom of containers and thus become usable for industrial purposes. This electrical process was discovered in the late nineteenth century. It is now undertaken via electricity from dammed rivers in northern Quebec and British Columbia, in large smelters near hydro-electric power stations. Mechanization is evident in the smelters in a series of shuttle-carts and various cranes and conveyors which situate the various chemicals, mix them, and through which the electrical current is fired. In the last decade, some of the processes have been automated, and in one section of the Alcan smelter at Kitimat, B.C., much of the electrical firing and chemical mixing is now done by automatic controls. Workers are employed at the controls and in servicing the machines rather than in manning the conveyors and carts.

Alcan's operation involves the extraction of bauxite in nine countries, including Australia and the Caribbean countries. Bauxite mines are owned and entirely controlled by Alcan; their production schedules, rates of extraction, employment volume, and costs are determined in the Montreal offices. The initial processing of bauxite usually occurs in the extraction regions. This involves refining bauxite into alumina. The alumina is then exported to smelters in industrialized countries (Canada and Norway, both of which have available electrical power and a skilled labour force) in quantities and on terms determined in Montreal. Following the smelting process, the ingot is turned into manufactured products – kitchen foil, heavy-duty cables, industrial materials – in Europe, Canada, the United States, South Africa, and other regions.

These manufacturing firms are organized into regional (not national) units, each with a general manager who reports to the Montreal office. Within the regions, subsidiaries of Alcan import and export amongst themselves and may form an integrated chain in a manufacturing process. Sales offices and resident agents are located around the world. In this empire the head office maintains control over the production, distribution, and price of the materials, and financial appropriations for all major projects. Jounalist Christopher Tugendhat summarizes the Alcan system this way:

Within the parameters established by head office Alcan's managers have considerable freedom of action to run their own affairs. The company's senior executives emphasize that they do not want yes-men. . . . But just as a military unit cannot operate without supplies of food and ammunition, so the subsidiary of a multinational company cannot survive without money. In the words of Nathaniel V. Davis (President): "We sure have it on financial control."[29]

This statement is not made in jest. It is precisely the careful division of labour, so that operations decisions at the plant level on a day-to-day basis are made by local management, but policy and financing decisions are retained at head offices, which characterizes the successful multinational corporation. In IBM phraseology: "As in the United States, IBM operates abroad under a philosophy of decentralized operations. However, due to the nature of the business a great deal of coordination and standardization is required between countries and functions."[30] The author of this statement goes on to say that the objective of the planning system at IBM is to increase integration and continuity, optimize the allocation of resources, and "communicate these aims down through the line and staff organizations." This is to be done through a "decentralized framework" which will provide flexibility and responsiveness to a rapidly changing technology and changing environmental conditions.

What IBM means by decentralization is the allocation of certain kinds of decisions to subsidiary managers and their staffs, subject to policy, planning, and financial decisions made at head offices, or made at head offices after consultation with field managers. Two analysts who conducted extensive field research on multinationals noted that most such companies claim to have decentralized operations. After surveying their data, however, they concluded that "a decentralising ideology masks a centralising reality."[31] The reasons for this are not hard to locate. The pace of technological change in companies that by their nature are very heavily engaged in research and product development creates enormous pressures for central decision-making, central information-gathering, and central financing, even if there were no additional pressures such as the financial interests of the head office or parent company. Planning for technological change and adaptation of markets is a long-term process, involving extensive consultation and data collection on a continuing basis: for an integrated chain such as IBM, a central authority must inevitably exert ultimate controls.

These pressures are enhanced by the ease of facilitating them. The introduction of electronic data-processing makes central file-keeping not only possible but highly profitable, since it alleviates top executives of the need to depend on field-offices for information, and provides a rapid back-check on field operations. Instant communications systems such as that developed by IBM allow for a very high concentration of decision-making power in head offices without loss of time for subsidiaries; and also allow subsidiaries to maintain contact with, and controls on, one another.

Certain industries tend toward centralized control because their products depend on consistency: drugs and photographic equipment, for example. Other products, such as oil processing, have always been centralized because they depend on co-ordination in their phases of exploration, production, shipping, and storage. Resource corporations, of which oil companies in their extraction phases are examples, are typically centralized because there are no profits to the company likely to be realized from dispersion of control. Manufacturing corporations have been more likely to decentralize some functions where their product allows for regional differences, and they must take into account cultural preferences, or where they employ professional personnel in regional centres. However, the increasing tendency toward integration of product manufacture on an inter-regional basis, together with centralized data control. exerts strong pressures toward concentration of decision-making power in headquarters.[32]

U.S. firms have one other reason to centralize decision-making, planning, and research and that is the overwhelming size and consumer-demand of their domestic market. Whatever other factors dictate centralization for IBM, the fact that by far the larger share of its computers is sold on domestic markets is a significant one. By contrast, Alcan, Massey-Ferguson, and Mac-Millan Bloedel – to name three of Canada's multinationals (all much smaller on world ratings) – are obliged to aim at the U.S. and European markets. Their domestic sales cannot support them. Similarly, SKF (Sweden) depends on external markets for survival. In recognition of this dependence, SKF is reported to operate in English rather than Swedish, even though its head offices remain on home territory.

There are certain functions most likely to be guarded by central offices of all corporations. These include decisions regarding the location, nature, and inputs of production and sales; location and scale of research and development; movement, recruitment, and training of higher level personnel and subsidiary managers; determination of salaries for higher executives; and negotiations with international labour unions. In addition to these, the one function which is universally retained is control over financial transactions. Subsidiaries generate their own profits and have access to both international and local sources of outside funding for current operations and extensions, but their discretion is strictly limited over the uses of these funds. Their allocation, remittances to head offices, accounting to local governments, investments, purchases of supplies of component parts, and "adjusted" profitability are all matters over which parent companies exercise considerable control.

Subsidiaries are not gauged on their profitability as autonomous producers. Their profitability is determined by their utility to the parent firm, and this may mean that "in company" transfers take precedence over purchase of supplies on an open market. Open market purchases might be much cheaper for the subsidiary but lose money for the parent. Likewise the shifting of resources for the benefit of one subsidiary at the cost of another may cause the first company to appear "unprofitable" though it increases the parent company's total profitability. As one financial adviser observes: "Any time the Canadian subsidiary utilizes a resource from which a large profit could be extracted by an associate firm elsewhere, it does so at the expense of the corporate family."[33] That is, an action may be in Canadian interests, but disadvantageous for the American parent firm. A more revealing statement is that of a contributor to an International Management Association publication:

The chief accounting officer is fully responsible for local financial matters subject to the financial policy of the company, but problems affecting corporate finances must be referred to the financial officer [at head office] for approval. For instance, very few overseas employees understand or appreciate the influence U.S. taxation has on local problems. It is perfectly reasonable to expect the overseas manager to propose the revaluation of fixed assets or the creation of special reserves to diminish local taxes. But what is the overall goal? Are dividends to come forward with regularity to the domestic company? If so, each dividend becomes subject to U.S. income tax. The effective rate of reduced taxation on earnings out of which the dividend is paid, when taken as a tax credit by the parent company, may result in the parent company's paying more tax in the United States than would have resulted otherwise; therefore, the efforts of the overseas manager are fruitless. This is a good illustration of the type of responsibility and authority which cannot be delegated to people in the field under a decentralised organization for financial activities.[34]

In order to keep track of finances, head offices tend to demand continuous flows of information of a uniform nature from all subsidiaries on activities, expenses, and marketing. These reports are frequently a source of extreme irritation for subsidiary managers, as much of the information is not essential to their own operations, takes a good deal of their time and energy, and serves as a constant reminder of their subservient status. Yet head offices, by centralizing financing activities, allocate resources and determine funding on the basis of these reports – buttressed, of course, by the information provided in their own offices and stored in central computers.

The financial reporting requirements of head offices frequently involve minutely detailed instructions to foreign-office managers. Brooke and Remmers quote a number of such instructions included in accounting manuals which establish procedures, schedules, definitions, format specifications, and various corporate rules and regulations.[35] The existence of such manuals and the detail included in them suggest rather strongly that Weberian-style bureaucracy is the model: hierarchical control over essential functions is retained with the regional division of labour.

## IV

In spite of all this planning, this minutely detailed division of responsibilities and authority; in spite of their ability to shift liquid capital and eliminate problems of resource supplies or transportation; in spite of market planning and advertising: in spite of all these, large organizations incur new risks in the very act of eliminating old ones. The deliberate process of rendering obsolete those goods which can be superseded by new products creates the risk for the producer that it will fall prey to its own logic.

The same technological processes which provide corporate strength while their products dominate a market are themselves subject to obsolescence. Alternative sources of raw materials, new kinds of raw materials, changes in energy base, and new ways of organizing techniques for production are all on the agenda of research units in large organizations. Those which are most successful at any given time are not necessarily those which can innovate most rapidly. Indeed, the most successful organizations for one technical phase must have an enormous amount of capital and organizational expertise tied into a particular mode of production: they cannot simply sweep away existing facilities and their existing division of labour in order to move into completely different kinds of product output. It is for this reason that corporations undertake "contracting out" relationships with small businesses. But this in itself would not prevent a massive collapse in the event of a genuinely radical change in industrial fuel or processes of production. Huge pulp mills, oil extraction plants, gas pipe lines, manufacturing assembly factories are major investments made on the assumption that the future – that is, their life-span – would more or less resemble the present.

The most obvious potential risk for multinational corporations is investing in plants that can only be run on oil, gas, or electrical energy. This is a risk if sources of such fuels and power cannot be absolutely guaranteed. Since the sources cannot be so guaranteed, though every conceivable means of guaranteeing them has been taken, there is incentive to "invent" new energy sources. The oil companies themselves are perhaps less likely to risk their capital in this situation than manufacturing companies, since it is the oil companies which are engaging in the research and buying out of alternative sources of fuel. Their bets appear to be well hedged. They, in any event, are likely to be the best-informed agencies about the nature of the transition, its timing, and its predictable impact. Meanwhile they have discovered the considerable merits of having national governments pay for oil exploration, research, capital equipment, transportation, and environmental protection services.[36] This is especially the case where the national governments can be counted on to protect the interests of major constituents which are also the oil companies' best customers, that is, other multinational corporations.

But manufacturing corporations, unless they are party to research on alternative fuel sources, are less likely to have predictable outcomes to their present actions. They cannot know, any more than governments and private citizens know, what alternative sources of energy will cost, how installations can be accommodated to such flows, and whether new sources will render their present plants obsolescent. New sources of energy could also render their products obsolescent if the products are geared to present fuel supplies.

The implications of such changes create an unstable and risk-prone situation to even the most sophisticated and highly integrated corporations. The time required for technical adjustments, the costs of maintenance as well as initial capital investment, the consequences for labour and the division of labour: these are all unpredictable. Because these are unpredictable, large corporations are taking considerable risks if they invest further in technology dependent on current fuel sources and supplies, but are also taking risks if they hold back and competitors proceed. Competitors, in this context, means those other large corporations which share and not infrequently divide up markets and which do not normally engage in genuine competition, but which have the potential capacity to oust one another if any one of them obtains a significant technical advantage.

To put this in other terms, multinational corporations by the very nature of their size and capital investment, have a considerable stake in the status quo. It is not in their interests to encourage social change. As suggested at the beginning of this chapter, the division of labour is tied not only to the extent of a market but as well to the certainty that such a market will still be there for another generation.

# CHAPTER 5

# THE MANAGEMENT OF LABOUR

*Every day he repeats the same movements with monotonous regularity, but without being interested in them, and without understanding them. . . . He is no longer anything but an inert piece of machinery, only an external force set going which always moves in the same direction and in the same way. Surely, no matter how one may represent the moral ideal, one cannot remain indifferent to such debasement of human nature. . . .*

– Emile Durkheim[1]

*By being able to identify in advance the work groups that will support or attack management or union programs, the administrator gains a major tactical advantage.*

– Leonard R. Sayles[2]

The industrial revolution was undoubtedly a barbaric era of management. The degradation of the poor, the unholy working conditions of the men, women, and children who staffed factories, the overt force applied when they resisted: all are documented features of the eighteenth and early nineteenth centuries. There have been changes, and some of these changes were introduced by members of the same class as benefited from the exploitation of workers, through the developing democratic institutions of national parliaments. But the emphasis on the political platforms which initiated change can be overdone, as it often is in textbooks on the development of industrial society. There were some very good economic reasons for change. In particular, the various mechanical inventions which reduced the need for unskilled labour while increasing the need for educated office workers and technicians made it disadvantageous to employ women and children in factories. Women were persuaded to spend more of their time raising school children, and children were induced, through compulsory legislation, to spend more of their time learning the skills of a disciplined, literate, work force. The state paid for this training, but expanding industries paid part of this cost indirectly by increasing the wages of male workers beyond subsistence rates. Such workers then became consumers of the products being created by such corporate enterprises, and in addition became defenders of the system by which they benefited in high wages and a high standard of living.

Workers are by definition managed people. The right to manage workers belongs to those who invest capital in a production technology and their appointees, or, in a state-capitalist system, to those who control the capital of the state. The owners or controllers of production corporations and the executive officers or their deputies are permitted by the society at large to hire, fire, deploy, reward, and punish the vast majority of the adult population, and to do this with reference primarily to their own needs and interests. They do not do this through overt force. The primary mechanisms for management are material incentives combined with an absence of alternative means by which a large number of people can survive.

Those who own or control productive facilities purchase labour as a commodity, much as they purchase raw materials, machinery, financial loans, and other "factors of production." The production system could not operate without labour, but labour does not invest its time and energy and skills in the operation as a collective undertaking: if this were the case, labour would be equally involved in voting, decision-making, and responsibility for production. On the contrary, labour is sold for an income. The income varies according to how useful the labour is to those who own or control the productive mechanisms which require labour for their operations. Thus we have a labour force with members receiving differential benefits from the sale of their labour.

This situation is widely regarded as a natural state of affairs. It is normally regarded as apt, sensible, and proper that an employer hires whom he wants at prices determined primarily by his needs on a "labour market." The price is modified by the availability of labour, which is referred to as the "law of supply and demand." Supplies can be affected by collective action on the part of the labour, as in the withholding of labour until an agreement for wages is reached. This form of collective bargaining is practised by about a third of the industrial labour force in Canada: others accept the wage employers offer, given the current availability of persons with their skills. The naturalness of this situation is so widely assumed that workers become angry at the unemployed (those who are not currently selling their labour); and the reply "Because they own the place!" is seen as adequate in response to the question "Why do employers have the right to make decisions about technological change?"

The phrase "a free labour force" is not perceived as an irony. The labour force is obliged to work for a paycheck, must contract itself out to employers: that is the meaning of the phrase. Instead of questioning the legitimacy of a contractual society in which employers (as the investors or controllers of capital) establish the terms and workers (as the investors of labour) are obliged to accept those terms, workers concentrate almost exclusively on the appropriateness of the differential pay benefits for their class. Should plumbers receive more than postal clerks; should kindergarten teachers receive more than domestic servants; should university professors receive more than industrial researchers; should fallers in the forestry industry receive more than pulp-mill workers? These are the guts of most debates, and the vast majority of strikes in industry are concerned with stratification by income, not with the rights of owners.

This widespread acceptance of the situation comes about because workers do not have alternative means of economic survival. The technical capacities of the industrial society permit it to provide food for large urban populations with a relatively small agricultural labour input. At the same time, few farm families can provide enough of their own needs through their farming activities that they can avoid the "market economy." In order to survive and obtain a cash income, they must become involved in market operations, but the market operations are largely controlled and managed by large corporate enterprises. In the higher value-producing sectors of agriculture, large corporate enterprises have moved increasingly toward the actual production of the food as well as the marketing of it. The overall consequence has been a steady reduction in the number of people who can survive as independent farmers, as well as a reduction in the number of wage-workers dependent on agriculture for their cash incomes.[3]

Mining, logging, and sawmilling have all undergone similar historical developments. Each in turn has become an element in a market economy first controlled at the market level by large corporate interests, and then controlled at the production level by the same interests. Most independent sawyers, for example, cannot control the conditions of markets or obtain sufficient supplies to maintain a steady cash income, and so sell out to large corporate sawmills or else go into bankruptcy with one slump year. Likewise, independent fishermen cannot easily market their fish and so turn to the large canneries which eventually gain control of the fishing boats and equipment so that the fishermen become wage-workers rather than independent owners.

The wage-worker in the corporate situation may easily earn a good deal more money than the independent entrepreneur. In fact, once the process is well underway the disparity in incomes between corporate employees and independent, small businessmen and their employees increases very much in favour of corporate workers. Materially, a population is quite likely to be better situated within a corporate economy than within a "competitive" or small-business one. The increasing wealth of workers, indeed, is one of the incentives by which the system operates. What is lost is independence, or alternative means by which people can survive. One has to have control over the means of production in order to live independently, and there are ever fewer means of production which an individual can control.

If one must sell his or her labour, then one tends to view a steady income for the sale as a legitimate outcome, and to then defend that income in the face of any objections. Those who are unemployed have been permitted to survive by the introduction of social insurance and welfare benefits since the 1930s, but they are permitted to survive only at a level that will persuade them to get into the labour force again at their earliest opportunity. One of the most frequent arguments against providing sufficient income to welfare recipients to raise them from poverty is that such an income would discourage their participation in the labour market. Private corporations pay incomes to those employed by them; society at large pays welfare benefits to those who are unemployed. When there are not sufficient jobs available for all members of the society, then some members must be unemployed and it is merely then a matter of which members; yet this does not prevent both employers and employees from chastising the unemployed for what is perceived to be laziness. The facts that technical innovations will cause some workers to lose present employment and that such innovations will allow the corporations to produce more at lower labour costs do not cause the society at large to demand that corporations pay the subsistence costs of the unemployed. On the contrary, the unemployed are blamed for their unemployment, given enough to keep them alive but not enough to permit them to overcome their poverty, while politicians talk abstractly about whether a 4.5 per cent unemployment rate is "an optimum level." Optimum is defined by the needs of large enterprises for an elastic labour force, that is, a reserve labour pool which can be drawn on in times of expansion, but disemployed in times of contraction.

Nonetheless, the unapologetic era of management-by-force is past. Workers are still managed people, but the terms of the management have changed. Let us consider how they have changed, and why.

## I

If a production system is mechanized or automated in such a way as to eliminate human labour from a range of tasks while still increasing productivity, then we might expect that technical progress in this sense means loss of employment. The argument against this apparently obvious correlation is that while unemployment was the lot of workers so displaced between the 1900s and the 1970s, the application of new techniques also created new jobs and thus permitted the re-absorption of some of the technologically unemployed. It created new jobs in terms of skilled positions for attendance of the machines which had never before existed, in terms of semiskilled or unskilled jobs which came into being because of the rapidly expanded production possibilities, and in terms of office jobs to service the consumer markets for mass-produced goods. Its capacity to do this depended on the growth of markets for new products.

An example is the introduction of a continuous conveyer belt for automobile and similar manufacturing industries from the 1920s onward. It eliminated a wide range of hauling and handling jobs, but also created the possibility of mass production of automobiles and this in turn created a demand for new labour to man the conveyer belt system. Workers in such a system are situated at junctures along the belt, assigned particular and repetitive tasks on materials brought to them at regular intervals by the belt, and sent by them at equally regular intervals to the next workers. With goods moving continuously along a conveyer-belt system such as that introduced into the Ford automobile factories, it became possible to employ three shifts of workers to process the goods continuously. The need for designers, engineers, technicians, and other experts increased steadily as mass production of automobiles created a consumer market. Sales organizations came into being, and entire supplementary and service industries were created, including service stations, used-car markets, parts manufacturers, and publicly financed construction operations for roads and facilities that mass transportation required. In addition, during the initial expansion phases, the system of mass production and consumption created a demand for additional workers in raw-materials extraction and preliminary processing industries. Thus a new technology, while it undoubtedly eliminated a range of skilled and unskilled jobs associated with the earlier automobile manufacturing industry, created a large number of new jobs. Automobiles, of course, were relatively new inventions even at that stage; in other industries, skills of much longer duration were displaced even if the overall consequence was greater employment.

In the printing industry, for example, technological unemployment is only in the 1970s becoming an effect of computer technology. In this case it is highly skilled workers who are displaced. Printers have for over a century retained a genuine crafts base in their trade. They controlled recruitment and training through an apprenticeship programme, and in every industrial country they formed one of the first trade unions and remained one of the more cohesive and militant organizations. They retained a high degree of autonomy and bargaining power even where they became employees in large publishing companies. However, the capacity of computers to print automatically large volumes of information accurately with only manual input from keypunchers renders much of the craftsmanship of printers obsolete. Books, newspapers, periodicals, and other publishable material can be produced at lower labour cost and in high volume without recourse to printers. The trade-off here in terms of employment is for relatively unskilled workers at the level of keypunchers and clerks, and skilled computer technicians and programmers. Not incidentally the first group consists almost exclusively of women, and their pay rates are equivalent to those of clerical workers; that is, much lower than the pay scales for skilled craftsmen.

Not all processes created a need for more labour. Some both reduced the labour requirements at a plant, and indirectly caused unemployment in related industries. The shift from human to coal energy and then to electricity and gas or oil reduced the number of people engaged in hauling and handling tasks, as well as the number engaged in construction of facilities for production, the extraction of raw materials such as coal, the hauling and handling of fuel, the service trades dependent on large numbers of workers coming and going from plants. Various surveys from the 1920s to 1940s produced alarming statistics on unemployment, but actually measuring the rates was problematic precisely because new techniques not always directly involved employees who lost jobs and the links between industries were not easily assessed. One very careful study in the steel works and rolling mills, where electrification of drives and controls eliminated labour, introduced the possibility for continuous production, and facilitated the development of standardization in shapes and chemical specifications, noted that: "for the sheet steel industry as a whole, the complete adoption of strip-sheet rolling will mean the displacement of ten thousand men and the concentration of sheet and tin plate production in the hands of a few dominant concerns."[4] This was in the 1930s. According to that survey, there were five electric main roll drives in 1905 and 1,806 in 1931, each with an enormous horsepower capacity and all producing far more than had been possible with more manpower, and producing this within relatively few large plants.

In resource extraction industries, the initial increase in labour was followed by the development of machinery to displace labour. Over the past decade many of the most skilled logging jobs have been eliminated as machines for felling, bunching, and landing timber have been introduced. Hydraulically powered drums for pulling in nets in large commercial fishing boats have eliminated labouring jobs in that industry. Parallel developments have reduced the labour force in mining. These are the most important industries in Canada, and such technical developments have had their impact on Canadian workers in the form of unemployment or mill-employment at reduced skill levels. Unemployment affects particularly the young, for whom new jobs are not available in these fields. Older workers may retain employment after the introduction of machines that effectively displace them and their skills, but they are not replaced when they drop out of the labour force.

It is difficult to measure direct unemployment effects due to mechanization or automation because neither process is a "once only" occurrence. Parts of production processes are mechanized, others remain unchanged over the same period of time; the same plant may displace workers in a section which has been mechanized, but employ many new workers in its offices when the increased sales of articles produced by the mechanized plant demand greater numbers of clerks.[5] This, indeed, would seem to be what occurred over the period from 1920 to 1970, and the shift is evident in the dramatic change in composition of the labour force. By the mid-1950s, the proportion of all workers engaged in clerical, sales, and administrative work exceeded the proportion engaged in skilled or unskilled manual work. Of course these two sets of workers were not necessarily (or even probably) the same: many workers were unemployed and permanently disabled by technological change. It was their children, schooled by the system for a changed industrial society, who moved into clerical jobs. And this shift is part of the reason for a widespread belief that there was great mobility within the system, and an absence of classes. Clerical and administrative or sales work retained from an earlier period their higher status: they, unlike factory work, were regarded as "middle-class" occupations. We will consider some aspects of these middle-class occupations later on.

In addition to unemployment, a negative feature of some kinds of technological change is the introduction of mindless, asocial, monotonous, and uncomfortable work. This feature, too, is subject to debate, because again there are different phases and kinds of technological change and by no means all change involves such a transition, and never for all workers.[6] The technology which appears to have created the highest degree of repetitive and unpleasant work is that in which some phases of the work are mechanized and workers fill in other phases in jobs that are mainly unskilled and demanding of no personal control over the process. These occur particularly within assembly-line processes where discrete items such as cars, telephones, or other "hard" commodities are produced. They are also found in smelters, large sawmills, and preliminary-processing plants where a high division of labour, a strict stratification of workers by seniority and experience, and a high degree of repetitiveness in tasks are designed to increase plant productivity.

Published studies of the relationship between technological situation and conditions of work are not numerous, and of those that report empirical findings almost all are concerned with the manufacturing industries. For these it would appear that workers in small crafts shops which produce a range of custom products or small batches of similar products, tend to be interdependent, highly specialized, and in close contact with one another throughout the production process. Supervisors tend to be co-workers, so that management itself is not very specialized and there are not several levels of supervision between workers and owners. Research on continuous-flow plants in which automation has become a feature of at least some of the production processes indicates that here, as in the unit-production shops, workers are interdependent, specialized, and in close contact. Lower-level supervisors are co-workers, but more levels of management are involved in the total production system including a rather large number of personnel specialists together with engineering, chemicals, and other technical and accounting experts. In both systems, there is a high ratio of skilled to unskilled workers, and skilled workers are the dominant group in the actual production tasks (as contrasted with servicing and maintenance tasks). Both systems apparently require, not merely permit, a great deal of communication between workers.[7]

Between these two kinds of production system, mass production systems of various kinds appear as the anomalies: they involve the least amount of necessary interaction, the highest degree of repetitive tasks, the least amount of interdependence in tasks, and the greatest amount of direct supervision by persons who are not themselves involved in actual production tasks. Unskilled workers predominate in production itself, skilled workers being more in evidence in machinery maintenance and managerial tasks.

The differences in various technical systems for workers have been reviewed in detail by Meissner in a study of the literature up to the 1960s. In his summary he states: "altogether, work at the technically undeveloped, almost pre-industrial level and the most advanced and perhaps post-industrial level (automation) appeared to permit the widest range of choices when it came to the integration of voluntary and necessary cooperative and communicative acts."[8]

Meissner warns that these conditions of themselves do not indicate any necessary increase in job satisfaction or commitment. All systems have their inherent problems, but the problems encountered in the in-between technologies of hand-work combined with machine-line work are rather different from those of the more exclusively hand-work or automated systems. Meissner suggests that the mechanized forms in which men and machines are mixed are in a sense "incomplete states of technical advance. . . . "The result of this incompleteness was that workers performed partial operations as stopgaps, as it were, to an imperfect technical design. The characteristics of social behavior were correspondingly lacking in one aspect or another."[9]

Researchers in Britain, in assessing the differences between plants with a wide variance of dependence on machines and mixture of production systems noted that labour relations in the unit or crafts-style systems and in the more automated and continuous-flow production systems were relatively amicable. The most hostile relationships were to be found in the mechanized mass-production systems.[10]

Studies of steel workers in a non-continuous plant and in a plant undergoing transition to a continuous process support this argument. The transition plant was operated by relatively "satisfied" workers who developed a capacity, in the researchers' words, to "think and act as a unit." They had greater necessary communication links in their work, were obliged to act co-operatively, and were generally concerned with maintaining their own high productivity. They were also more highly skilled and fewer in number than their counterparts in the non-continuous production line.[11]

Many sociologists, studying one factory or a group of factories in which technology itself has not been taken as a variable, have failed to explicate the relationship between types of work and experience of work by the worker. A significant exception is Blauner's study of four groups of workers in very different industries: automobile assembly lines, chemical continuous-process operations, print shops, and textile mills.[12] Blauner identified very different kinds of skill required for employees in these industries: in printing and other craft technologies, workers required manual skills; in the chemicals industries with continuous-flow technologies, they required capacities for taking on responsibility for monitoring automatic controls and inspecting machinery; in mass-production technologies such as the automobile systems, they required neither particular manual skills nor responsibility. This accords with the studies cited above, and again the mass production technology appears as an "in-between" form of production even where it is a terminal stage for many industries. Blauner investigated the relationship between these different technical conditions and the presence of "alienation" amongst workers. Alienation is a many-sided experience, including feelings of powerlessness, meaninglessness, isolation, and self-estrangement. He argues that these various dimensions of alienation vary to some degree independently, and will always be in part related to specific organizational and cultural contexts of work, but that of the four industries he studied in depth the machine and assembly-line technologies gave rise to higher degrees of alienation overall than did the craft or continuous-process industries.

These studies do not exhaust the possibilities: all were conducted or written prior to the full development of automation potentialities in a wide range of industries, and none of these studies includes information on the still-developing computerization of offices. They are mainly concerned with the plant-level of manufacturing industries, whereas much of current technical development is occuring either in offices or in resource extraction industries. They do, however, help us to understand that the relationship between a technological system and its workers is a complex one, and that generalizations about workers are not deducible from studies of single plants embedded within a single form of technology. Nonetheless, much of what has been written about the management of workers at the plant level is based on just such studies. Indeed, much of what was written during the 1940s to 1960s, which we review in the next section, signally failed to mention the technical constraints of work. Still less did it come to grips with the power arrangements for the conduct of work in expanding corporate organizations. Not incidentally, these studies were conducted mainly in the United States, Britain, and Western European countries. Canada has produced very little by way of management studies of workers in manufacturing industries for rather obvious reasons: there are relatively fewer manufacturing workers and their places of work are more often extensions of parent firms where personnel management is centred. Most studies done in Canada have been replications of American studies, or extensions of them based on the same theoretical frameworks. The assumption is that Canadian workers are in no essential respect different from their American and British counterparts.

## II

In the earlier phases of mechanization it was actual wage costs that were the concern of management when they sought technological innovations. A large work force meant a high wage bill, and if the capital costs of mechanization could be amortized by higher levels of production over a short period, then long-range wage bills could be reduced. As productivity gains from earlier forms of mechanized production created high profits, the direct wage costs of labour became less problematic. However, the difficulties of "managing" a labour force became more problematic, because high capital investments in equipment could be profitable only if the equipment was in constant use. Shutdowns incurred by an organized labour force on strike for higher wages or changes in working conditions could be considerably more expensive than the actual increased cost for wages. Turnover rates in extraction, processing, and manufacturing industries became major problems not only because they incurred costs of training and replacement but because a high number of inexperienced employees increased the rates of accidents and down-times, and generally led to lower rates of production. As long as labour remained an essential ingredient in the production process, employers were obliged to concern themselves with the management of a labour force, and with the costs of mismanagement.

The management of workers is made more difficult by the mixture of technical conditions in any one large production plant, let alone by the vast mixture across the industrial spectrum. No single principle for "good management" is equally applicable in all situations, though researchers on behalf of management have searched assiduously for such principles. Schools of business administration and commerce were established in the mid-twentieth century, a large part of their task being to conduct research into "good management" techniques. Such techniques were frequently translated as "increasing the productivity of labour" or, as indicated in the quotation at the beginning of this chapter, "predicting and controlling" workers' behaviour. Scientific management was the natural corollary to scientific technology. A brief review of some of these research results and theories will indicate the concerns of twentieth-century management.

Scientific management of workers is a term normally associated with the name, Frederick W. Taylor.[13] In the 1900-1920 period, it was his theories which were most widely approved by management and disliked by workers. The basic argument was that every task in the organization could be refined so as to provide maximum output at lowest cost. The objective was to reduce each job to a fragment of the total process, a fragment which could be easily learned and efficiently reproduced by any worker; and then to create a chain of these fragmentary, repetitive jobs so that the total production was the outcome of many specialized yet simple imputs. Workers could be replaced easily in such a system because they were essentially interchangeable; productivity was increased; and cost for skills over and above physical labour was reduced.

This thinking has essentially the same objectives as those described by Henry Ford in his principles for mass production technologies: "(1) the planned orderly progression of the commodity through the shop; (2) the delivery of work instead of leaving it to the workmen's initiative to find it; (3) an analysis of operations into their constituent parts."[14]

Such principles create jobs in which the pace of work is mechanically determined, any one worker is required to undertake only one set of actions but to undertake these actions repetitively at predetermined intervals, and the actions involve very little discretion on the part of the worker. Minimum skill is required for such jobs, and in general, no group co-operation or interdependence. Workers are located side-by-side, each performing a simple and single set of tasks for which no social interaction is necessary. The entire production process is planned in advance and, if possible, mechanically maintained. Workers become part of the production process and as individuals are interchangeable. The epitome of this is found in the automobile factory, but in processes which are not as mechanized as the assembly line the same principles can be applied provided workers are co-operative.

Workers are by no means always co-operative. Long before Taylor, Andrew Ure was arguing that the major problem in "automating" industry was not in the creation of machines but in the disciplining of a labour force:

The main difficulty did not, to my apprehension, lie so much in the invention of a proper self-acting mechanism for drawing out and twisting cotton into a continuous thread, as in the distribution of the different members of the apparatus into one cooperative body, in impelling each organ with its appropriate delicacy and speed, and above all, in training human beings to renounce their desultory habits of work, and to identify themselves with the unvarying regularity of the complex automation.[15]

Taylor, it is clear, was not introducing radically new ideas. Nonetheless, it was to Taylor's philosophy that such criticisms as this were directed:

> To aim at pressing all workers into the same mould is not only to destroy individuality and to encourage needless monotony, but also to run counter to known psychological principles. It is the outcome of so-called "scientific" management, mechanically formulated by the engineers in which the mental factors of personality, sentiment, and sympathy are sacrificed to purely physical considerations.[16]

This particular criticism is quoted because it repeats so much of the ideology that was "taken for granted" as scientific management procedures actually became a regular feature of much of production. Even the criticism was embedded in its technique. The argument against it was not that it was essentially coercive, nor that it obliterated the skill distinctions between workers, nor even that it destroyed working groups with interdependent members – all of which might have been reasonable criticisms. It was rather that the process destroyed individuality, and that was further elaborated as personality and sentiment.

Where skilled craftsmanship and highly individual talent become unimportant contributions to a production process, what else is there about the individuals working there which might distinguish them from one another? The answer is a vague one, though it is often said as if it were perfectly clear. It is personality. If people cannot differ in any other respects, they can differ in how they laugh, whether they lose their tempers, their expression of emotions and sentiments, and what they believe. The quotation cited above, then, implies as much an acceptance of the situation as a rejection of it: it demands not the maintenance of work groups and the importance of distinctive skill capacities, but the maintenance of respect for the personalities and sentiments of workers. This statement was typical of the response to scientific management, and it did not go

unheard by management. Overt coercion was not an un-
mitigated success in creating a disciplined work force. Were
there alternatives?

Two schools of thought emerged and not infrequently merged
though philosophically they were from different roots, in
response to management's need for productive workers. The
first of these was oriented toward "human relations" and based
on a recognition of the social "needs" of workers. The other was
oriented toward personality, and based on a recognition of certain psychological "needs" of the same workers.

The human relations school had its modern beginnings in a
study of plant workers in the Western Electric Company known
as the Hawthorne works.[17] Certain apparently paradoxical findings were uncovered in research on productivity rates under differing environmental conditions, and subsequent interviews and
further studies with the workers caused the researchers to conclude that productivity rates were affected by informal group
pressures. This led to a series of enquiries into the nature of informal groups and the reasons for their development. The
leading philosopher of the movement – for such it
became – was Elton Mayo,[18] whose many sermons to management argued that workers in industrial society needed the security and moral integration of small cohesive groups which
developed in the industrial plant. Management, he argued,
could best fulfil its destiny by encouraging the existence of these
groups and by recognizing, in other respects, the sentimental ties
and emotional needs of workers.

One of the chief criticisms of the human relations school was
that it gave precedence to the group over the individual. Classi-
fying it along with the Catholic Church and aristocracy in
France prior to the revolution, Edmund Burke in his antirevolu-
tionary phase, German Nazis, and Communists, one critic said
of the movement: "This is the most modern episode in the attack
on reason in the name of harmony, cohesion, and a traditional
culture."[19]

There is truth in the argument that the human relations school
advanced an ideology that in some respects was contrary to
prevailing trends, specifically with respect to its concern with
group interaction. However, the social context being proposed
was an occupational society wholly contained within the work-

place, and not a total community in which work might be integrated into a wider social context. While Mayo and his followers were concerned with the happiness of workers within this restricted setting, the appeal of the theories lay in the connection of happiness with productivity. The case was stated by one of the leading theorists of the 1950s in these terms:

> Although there is some contradictory evidence, the preponderance of evidence indicates that production is actually increased when social conversation is allowed. . . . Restrictions that have the effect of diminishing the pleasantness of the work situation rob the workers of a significant source of satisfaction and can be expected, therefore, to reduce their efforts.[20]

The original studies at the Hawthorne plant are often treated as "serendipitous" findings, that is, findings that come along unexpectedly and which were followed up even though they fell outside the intended research design. They were fortunate for employers, whether or not intended: they occurred in the late 1920s and proceeded through the 1930s and 1940s during a phase of continuing organizational efforts by unions.

The research that grew out of the human relations orientation was manifestly directed toward aiding management in its efforts to obtain a disciplined work force. Teams of researchers invaded industrial plants of all kinds, interviewed workers, and observed them both on the job and in their leisure periods in order to determine how informal groups developed and what effects they had on productivity rates. They isolated such variables as ethnicity, status, status congruence, leadership formation, degrees of interaction on the job, and individual characteristics outside of work in order to see whether these "caused" differences in group pressures and "worker satisfaction."

One team discovered that some informal groups in a plant had higher status than others, and that membership in the "preferred groups" was attached to an ethnic status which at that time was high among these particular workers, together with stable if not high status in other respects.[21] Another team discovered that where workers could interact with one another frequently, they were more likely to create strong informal groups.[22] Yet another research venture indicated that certain factors did not affect group cohesion, specifically age, educational level, or occupational prestige.[23]

One study, directed "primarily for administrators whose understanding of the social structure and function of work groups determines in large measure the effectiveness of communication with workers regarding the common goals of the organization,"[24] involved two hypotheses. One was that work groups would establish themselves so as to achieve a minimum level of production required by management and a level required to maintain their social needs. The other was that such groups tended to become "frozen" at these production levels unless they experienced some kind of leadership challenge to do otherwise. The author advised administrations to create favourable conditions for group development, and to employ first-line supervisors who are sensitive to group needs and "who are capable of helping those individuals unable to function comfortably as members of a group."[25]

But sensitive supervisors could not cure productivity problems. Another researcher noted that some work groups persisted in being "atypical in their behavior" even after there were changes in their supervision and membership, union leaders, and management policy.[26] This suggested that the reason might lie in the technical constraints of the jobs for such workers. Unfortunately his research failed to provide clear indications for measurements of different technologies, though he arrived at a conclusion nonetheless to the effect that workers who were able to talk with one another and between whom there was little job differentiation were inclined to develop cohesive bonds. If they shared grievances, these bonds might lead to hostile groups; otherwise to productive ones.

All of these studies indicate that groups form in industrial settings if potential members have opportunities to interact but they do not indicate what the role of the group is or even whether it is systematically related to workers' satisfaction. In addition, they fail to demonstrate that productivity is linked to informal groups in a systematic fashion. High status informal groups were found to be as likely to exert pressure on their members to reduce productivity rates as to increase them. In fact, isolates and deviants from the informal groups system were found to be among the highest producers.[27] Managers interested in "predicting and controlling" behaviour were not given very succinct or persuasive guidelines for how this might be done through manipulation of groups or conditions favourable to group formation.[28] However, the studies indicated something about informal groups that did not support the general persuasion of the researchers in human relations. This was that informal groups might not only reduce high productivity, they could as well be the means by which resistance to management directives is created and hostile unions formed. Human relations in its focus on the group ended up providing fuel to those who argued in favour of more coercive action and prohibitions on communication and interaction on the plant floor.

The original human relations approach was perhaps too simple-minded in its assumptions about the direct relationships between pleasant working relationships and either satisfaction or productivity. A more sophisticated approach paid attention to such variables as size of group, personal attributes of members, and actual tasks. Small groups laboratories were established in Canada as well as the United States where social psychologists used experimental techniques for manipulating people in laboratory conditions, and measuring various kinds of co-operative, conflictual, co-optative, coercive, and submissive behaviours. Groups consisting of dyads, triads, mixed pairs, and many persons were subjected to various tests for determining group behaviour. Personal and selected social variables were introduced: status, status congruence, income levels, sex, age, ethnicity, sentiments, beliefs, and group homogeneity in these respects. These experiments were informative about interpersonal relationships in groups to the extent that such relationships were independent of culture, historical development of groups, and technological conditions. These variables could not be imported into laboratories.[29] The university researchers who conducted these experiments in the 1950s and 1960s were interested in forming theories about social interaction rather than producing new methods for the manipulation of workers, but their findings were utilized in more applied research and embedded in much of the subsequent human relations work.

Another direction for research involved study of biographical variables which might affect workers. Research on particular groups of workers revealed such tidbits as that waitresses who could best cope with the pressures of a very demanding restaurant situation were people who had grown up with high degrees of personal responsibility, whereas "the girls [sic] who grew up as followers tended to find that they had great difficulty handling the tensions of work situations."[30] Nightwatchmen were people with a history of isolation and paranoia.[31] Supervisors who did well in hierarchical organizations came from urban and "sociable" backgrounds.[32] While these studies isolated specific work groups, their findings could be applied to other workers with similar job requirements.

In a study of clerical organization within the French government, Michel Crozier discovered that "class background" had more to do with employees' attitudes toward their jobs than such other factors as age and seniority.[33] Working-class women who handled routine clerical tasks were generally satisfied; middle-class women were satisfied only where they were group leaders. The explanation offered by Crozier was that class background creates expectations, and that the clerical status of the jobs was less congruent with status expectations of middle-class people than of working-class people. American theorists were generally disinclined to consider class as a variable influencing workers' behaviour. In an ideological environment which insisted that America was a classless society, they tended rather to seek explanations in terms of random childhood experiences, personal "needs" translated into social behaviour, or universal psychological needs which could be satisfied with varying success through manipulation of the work environment.

This concern with psychology was manifested in two streams of research which used opposite methods for investigation. One involved formal testing of populations and the development of "average" scores for intelligence, various personality traits, skills, and aptitudes. A test of abilities for prospective workers was developed in the 1940s[34] and subsequently improved to inform managers about a wide range of aptitudes and personality conditions for job applicants. Personnel testing had become a commonplace aspect of job interviews by the 1950s, and by the 1970s there were many consulting firms whose main business it was to test applicants and advise management about the suitability of prospective workers for jobs. The process of measurement has become considerably more sophisticated over time, now including tests of intelligence, logical capabilities, skill in conceptualization at abstract levels, sociability, ability to work under stress, and motivation. These measures, however, are most useful in the selection of supervisory and management personnel; they are limited in their utility for hiring and keeping production workers.

The second stream of research focused on psychological characteristics of workers was more generally useful, in spite of a lack of evidence for the validity of its assumptions.[35] This involved numerous theories about the normal and natural needs of all human beings and the obstacles or facilitating circumstances for satisfying these provided by different organizational environments. Individuals are perceived as having various kinds of needs which they satisfy in various ways through interaction with others, in return for which satisfaction they reciprocate with rewards to others. Groups of workers can join together to seek group rewards or inflict group punishments on management or other workers, and within the group they will give and receive in ways that either allow the group to become cohesive or cause it to disintegrate.[36]

In one test of this general thesis, Argyris interviewed employees in both highly skilled and unskilled or semiskilled jobs within a single factory, other factors of the organization such as supervision, formal policies, and the like being identical.[37] He expected that the skilled group of employees, having more outlets for their mature capacities would be happier, healthier, and more satisfied with their work. The second group would regress to infantile behaviour of various kinds. By a process of translation from what is "mature" to what in fact the employees said, he concluded that this was generally the case. However, he was puzzled by the fact that the unskilled workers were no more likely to be absent, leave their jobs, or join unions than the skilled workers. He came to a creative explanation for this similarity: both groups had adjusted well to their work situations and so both groups were equally satisfied with the work environment, even though one group suffered high subordination and responded in infantile ways. His conclusion was that the research shows "that the employees modify the organization by creating an informal employee culture which coerces and sanctions behavior that helps to guarantee employee actualization."[38]

These studies, still being carried out, are not far removed from the original informal groups investigations. As one writer summed up the progress:

> human relations, in resolving the Hawthorne paradox, has created its own. The happy unproductive worker and the unhappy, productive worker have been discovered; permissive and employee-centered supervisors have not always bossed the most productive groups; and consultation with workers has often created more problems than it has solved.[39]

Meanwhile managements of mass production firms apparently operated on quite another principle to obtain workers. Quite simply the principle was to pay workers much more than they could obtain either as independent producers or as workers in small businesses. While human relations experts pondered about the effects of group actions, another admitted bluntly "We may have created too many dumb jobs for the number of dumb people to fill them."[40] Woodward noted that in Britain of the mid-1960s, within the firms she studied, the earnings of semiskilled production workers were approaching those of skilled workers:[41] this was apparently the trade-off for dull and repetitive work. A decade earlier in United States, Harvard researchers had discovered that high wages were the critical factor in maintaining a labour force in assembly-line systems. In a survey of automobile factory workers, Walker and Guest found that over three-quarters of the workers surveyed said they took the jobs and stayed at them because the wage rates were considerably higher than elsewhere. The jobs were secure and steady, and were supported by collective bargaining agreements. Although the authors did not say so, and indeed wrote prolifically on differences in job satisfaction, the data themselves suggest that loyalty in mass production firms is achieved through material incentives. These incentives have their limits: absentee quit rates reported in this study were twice as high among workers in mass assembly production jobs as among workers in maintenance and other jobs, a finding supported by larger surveys of workers in industry.[42]

## III

The solution to "labour problems" is much the same in resource industries, though here it may require other material incentives besides high wages. Although early settlements in Canada and other countries were situated close to natural resources, depletion of these made it necessary to move farther away from settled areas to obtain raw materials for industry. One of the chief problems for management as a consequence has been to induce a labour force either to work far from home for long periods of time, or to settle in isolated towns close to the resource.

The town created by Ambrose Crowley, described in an earlier chapter of this book, was not remarkably different from new towns being created in Canada today. Kitimat, Mackenzie, and Fort McMurray are examples of instant towns created by companies in resource and preliminary processing sectors, all with substantial grants of land and other forms of aid from provincial governments. Communities such as Inuvik and Churchill have emerged as uneasy fusions of precapitalist societies and resource towns. Employers have persistent difficulties in obtaining and keeping labour. Skilled tradesmen are in scarce supply, unskilled workers will not stay. Turnover rates at the Alcan plant at Kitimat run in the neighbourhood of 65 per cent every year.[43] In logging, pulp-mills, and sawmills, estimates – and no doubt the reality – vary according to the larger employment context from well over 100 per cent through the 1960s to half that in the mid-1970s.[44] In mining, estimates of turnover run from 120 to over 300 per cent.[45] Turnover is expensive to employers, because it involves lost costs in training, additional costs for seeking replacements and training them, and the costs associated with too high a proportion of the labour force lacking experience. Employers in this sector therefore seek advice on how to reduce turnover, and this frequently means paying attention to the living conditions in resource towns.

While all employers have experimented with variations on human relations styles of management in order to retain workers for these industries, internal studies of turnover and managers' occasionally frank comments make it clear that the reasons for high turnover are seldom related to specific supervisory practices or management-employee relations. They are related to the monotony of the work, the noise in the plants, the isolation, the impossibility of social contacts because of the nature of the work or environment, and the physical discomfort associated with the work. Workers here, as in manufacturing industries, have no stake in the outcomes of their work.

In response to the problem as it is perceived by management, Canadian researchers have spent a good deal of time and both industry and government money investigating the relative benefits (as measured in reduced turnover rates) of various housing and town development styles. In addition, they have done extensive research on the "problems of women," by which is meant boredom, a sense of being cooped-up, and general frustration with their lack of employment opportunities in resource-based towns. Northern towns have high frequencies of violent crimes, mental health problems, alcoholism, and suicide: the solutions proposed by researchers are attractive houses on crescent-shaped streets, recreation facilities, and community activities.[46] The solutions so far devised by management include preferential hiring of married men (who are more likely to tolerate discomfort for the sake of a steady pay-cheque),[47] and material incentives (housing at low downpayment rates, subsidized transportation to the town, and hourly wages slightly higher than wages in urban centres.)

Employers in resource towns have a means of controlling workers which is not available to employers in urban centres. It is control over recruitment of town residents which accompanies selection of workers. Known union militants can be prevented from moving in where employers own houses and effectively control municipal councils (as is often the case in these towns). In addition, preferential hiring of immigrant groups known to be passive or unwilling to strike is a recognized procedure (and is one of the reasons for racial conflict).[48] Control of housing, control of community membership through recruitment, and control over employment are effective means of ensuring a co-operative labour force. Lucas argues that these, combined with the high turnover rates, effectively emasculated unions in the Canadian resource towns he studied.[49]

Another means of controlling workers in both resource and manufacturing areas is to shift some of the disciplinary tasks onto established unions. International unions are not in general militant organizations; they have opted for "business unionism," whereby their members receive high wages in return for guaranteed supplies of labour over the duration of negotiated contracts. As long as industry expands and resources or manufactured products have strong markets, this arrangement suits employers or is at least preferable to wildcat strikes, accumulation of hostilities, and individual bargaining by workers.

Resource towns, unlike manufacturing regions, are frequently tied to seasonal cycles of work. This presents management with the problem of maintaining a stable labour force while retaining the right to lay off workers during low-production seasons. Here government (public) financing and management of an unemployment insurance programme provide a means. At relatively low cost to employers, and partly at cost to themselves through compulsory contributions, workers are paid enough during layoffs to encourage them to remain in the region until production begins again. This is especially effective during periods of high unemployment elsewhere, when there are few alternatives to waiting out the down-time.

## IV

As the term indicates, management of human relations means manipulation of workers. The objective is not satisfied workers, it is higher productivity. There is another means by which higher productivity might occur, but there is not a great deal of research on this for the reason that it is not a means likely to maintain the power of management or the profits of investors. This is full and equal participation in management of all workers; otherwise phrased, it is the taking over of management tasks by production workers.

Early experiments in consultation are documented in the literature of the "free world." A ball-bearing firm in London, for example, attempted to avoid industrial relations problems during the war and following it by establishing a workers committee composed of elected representatives of various work groups.[50] This experiment involved the publication of a manual instructing managers to be sensitive and accessible, but it concluded with the statement "nothing in the foregoing . . . shall interfere with the right of the executive to make final decisions concerning all matters within the orbit of his responsibility, subject to the over-riding authority of his own boss."[51] In subsequent studies by outside researchers, the firm was found to be "a good place to work," but at the same time workers suspected management of underhanded activity, and management suspected workers of laziness. In a dragged-out debate over piece-rates in the service shop, workers confronted management with a dilemma. They argued that if consultation was to be a policy of the firm, then it had to occur prior to any major undertakings. Consultation does not mean being informed after the fact. However democratic the internal procedures may appear to be or however democratic some managers might wish them to be, when management continues to be a prerogative of managers, and managers continue to be responsible to a board of directors and to shareholders rather than to workers, consultation becomes merely another form of manipulation.

Another model of worker participation is evident in the "industrial democracy" developments in Sweden and Germany. In both countries, trade unions have become participants in the decision-making process. In Sweden both employers and unions have formed highly centralized bargaining units with virtually all businesses and workers covered by agreements. In Germany a process known as co-determination likewise involves centralized bargaining between highly organized trade unions and employers' associations. In neither case are workers at the plant level engaged in policy decision-making, and the prerogatives of management are not contested. In fact this is explicitly stated by the trades union federation of West Germany:

> . . . it is by no means the intention of co-determination to destroy the authority of the management. Nor is it intended that the workers, acting through their delegates, should take over management. It is rather the intention that management should be placed institutionally under an obligation to exercise its authority in the sense of a trusteeship, not to abuse its authority, and to act at all times responsibly. . . . Co-determination, therefore, means primarily that the fate of an undertaking cannot be determined by the owners alone.[52]

The German policy has been advanced as one worthy of emulation in Canada. Like the Swedish arrangement, it successfully avoids strikes. Individual firms and groups of workers within individual firms are unable to stage strikes, and complex forms for working out disagreements and grievances substitute for withdrawal of labour by dissatisfied workers. Neither productivity nor profits are threatened, though the cost to employers is high wage bills.

Critics of the co-determination model argue that this is still a long way from genuine industrial democracy, and that ultimately it is primarily owners of industry who profit from industrial peace.[53] While the process has brought trade union leaders into a consultative relationship with management, it has not provided the rank and file with any non-material benefits. Instead, it has strengthened the existing power structure, rigidified the class structure and a system of stratification by income for workers, and has produced a bureaucracy capable of exercising extremely repressive and authoritarian rule. These criticisms demand further attention in Canada where initial advances toward a similar system have been made in the form of invitations to labour and business by government to engage in a "tripartite" system of industrial government, and the introduction of wage and price controls.

One further example of participation in decision-making is worthy of note, and this occurs in Canada. It is not the result of grand schemes by government, business, and trade unions; on the contrary, it is the result of decisions by corporations to spread their risks by contracting out phases of their work to small companies and owner-operators of equipment. In resource industries, particularly, these small companies are recognized to be generally more productive and efficient than direct employees of large companies doing the same work. In the forestry industry, a recent Royal Commission report argued that they were also inclined to be more innovative in technique.[54] The probable reasons for this are that they compete with each other for contracts, and more workers in each unit are actively engaged in decision-making and profit-sharing. Large companies, combined with large unions, create an industrial situation in which the employed worker has no private interest in the outcomes of common work: the products are not his or hers, they are anonymous whether done well or badly. In a small operation, an employee and an owner are likely to work side by side: they share their problems and objectives. If a machine breaks down, they are obliged to repair it or do without work: consequently they take pride in their inventive capacities and skill. Moreover, since there are fewer specialists, all workers are obliged to take turns at various jobs. In the absence of both a union, which delimits jobs and creates an adversary situation, and a hierarchy of management, which defines jobs and creates a power situation, the work gets done with a minimum of conflict.[55] A system of much smaller enterprises would appear to have its advantages, but neither management nor unions are inclined to propose such a system as a solution to the "management of workers."

Industrial democracy as it is proposed is not to be confused with community control. Workers are also members of a regionally-based community, and their families are not necessarily paid workers. Proposals for reform of the collective bargaining process have not so far included means by which all members of communities affected by industrial production can express their wishes or even gain access to all relevant information where new industries or other changes are planned. More typically, communities find themselves the hosts to new industries because either a company buys a local resource and in the process destroys alternative modes of existence, or alternatives have already been destroyed and governments pay the costs of establishment and maintenance. Mathias has documented five cases of government-sponsored industrialization in Canada, all of them disasters because the companies set the conditions and operated on their own terms.[56] Leyton has documented the case of the fluorspar miners in Newfoundland when they accepted industrialization and discovered that it led to lung cancer.[57] Other Newfoundland writers have studied the effects of external control of the fishing industry and government-sponsored or government-aided attempts at industrialization in Newfoundland, the apparent net effect of which has been the dissolution of viable communities and the creation of a chronically unemployed industrial labour force.[58] In all of these cases, the local communities provided labour but they did not control any of the conditions for their own transformation into an industrial labour force.

Not all communities are passive when confronted with these prospects. There are agricultural communities in industrial societies, for example the Hutterites in Canada, which have established successfully their own living conditions and which have resisted outside control as well as industrialization. The Dene of the Northwest Territories have postponed industrialization, gaining time to establish at least some of their own conditions for subsequent industrial development. The Nishga of northern British Columbia have also resisted outside control and mass migration of their young people by organizing their members and demanding some control over their own educational system.[59] Some older towns which have come under the control of large corporations have developed strong community groups which are opposed to "growth at any cost." Even some new towns, Kitimat for example, have spawned opposition to corporate control. While none of these cases represents a major redirection of power to local communities, they do indicate that communities are not passive pools of manipulable workers. A genuine form of industrial democracy would have to include means by which full communities could exercise decision-making rights. That is a long distance from the present order or present proposals for tripartite government.

## V

As mass production of goods became a means of expanding corporate organizations, the mass production of services within the organization was, inevitably, introduced. In the early stages this shift meant simply the employment of ever more workers in clerical, sales, and office service jobs. This had its impact outside the office on the creation of training schools by the state for clerical and other office workers, the establishment of various service businesses for offices, the creation of an impetus for new technical developments to speed up office work, and the gradual restructuring of the entire labour force. It also affected the overall distribution of income.

With respect to technical changes, a certain amount of mechanization of the office coincided with similar phases in the plant. Bookkeeping and file-keeping services were speeded up with the introduction of office machines which allowed for faster reproduction and more systematic location of materials. Like conveyer belts, these required a combination of machines and people for their operation. Typewriters were constantly improved so that typing could be done more rapidly and with fewer errors. Typewriters, indeed, became the most important mechanical device in the office. A feature of mass-production organizations in which office work has also become bulky is the "typist pool." The co-ordination of activities for an increasing number of divisions and the support services required for the utilization of expertise at all levels led to a demand for the mass production of typed materials: a room full of typists whose sole task was the production of documents at high speed was the "solution." A similar production line was created in telephone companies, where batteries of operators served multitudes of customers simultaneously. In both situations, workers shared many features of assembly-line production systems: their discretionary time was limited, the workload was determined entirely by supervisors, the pace was steady, and the spatial and other freedom available was limited.

It might be noted here that it is not the level of technical skills possessed by workers which determines the change from a simple organization to a more complex one, although technical skills may create a limiting condition for change. Automobile repair shops in the 1970s are – theoretically, at least – geared to a very high level of technical complexity. Workers supposedly have mechanical skills of a high order, and their skills are directly dependent on the development of the automobile industry. However, the shops themselves are not producing the automobile: they are merely producing a service to automobiles. The service itself does not involve complex production processes, and is, in fact, closer to the crafts-shop production situation than to a mechanized process. Their office arrangements are typically minimal, and involve a very low degree of complexity and a small number of workers. This situation alters only if the service shop turns itself into a mass-servicing production system, with workers specializing in particular aspects of the service operation, and a large number of "items" being produced on a routine basis.

With respect to employment and income, this development of large bureaucratic offices and sales staffs had a far-reaching impact. Since the early 1950s, more workers in all the industrial countries have been engaged in the "white-collar" occupations than in any other kind of work. White-collar work had been accorded a higher status in popular thinking during the early stages of industrialization simply because jobs in this sector were performed largely by the owners and their families, and then by the more literate (and therefore higher class) members of the population. As mass schooling was introduced and as mass production of office services became the norm, this status was retained through the belief that white-collar workers used their brains, were better educated, and didn't have to rely on manual labour, as did factory or "blue-collar" workers. The truth underlying this belief gradually eroded: more and more clerical jobs became as routine, as machine-oriented, as lacking in demand for mental skills, and not infrequently, as "manual" as factory jobs.

The change in real conditions for office jobs was manifested in a steadily deteriorating income position relative to manual workers, even while the "prestige" of office work continued to be marginally higher. The average income of all workers in all clerical occupations in Canada ranked third in 1931, fourth in 1961. The relative dollar incomes for managerial, professional, and clerical employees dropped steadily. For example, the average incomes of managers dropped from five times that of labourers in 1931 to less than three times that of labourers in 1961. While clerical workers of 1961 earned one and a half times as much as labourers, in 1931 they earned two and a half times as much.[60] In the manufacturing industries, office workers earned over 30 per cent more than other wage earners at the onset of the war; 6 per cent more by the end of the war; and almost the same amount by 1951. By 1967, their incomes were slightly lower than those of other workers.[61]

As income declined and office work became more factory-like, women were brought back into the labour force. The low cost of woman-power and the large supply of female labour which could act as interchangeable office employees served to reduce overall per-capita labour costs for offices. By the end of the 1960s, over three-quarters of all clerical workers were women, and of all women in the labour market, 62 per cent were engaged in office jobs of one kind or another.[62]

As this dramatic change in labour force composition occurred, and as the income distribution ceased to favour office employees, the distance between upper level managerial and professional workers and the bulk of office employees increased.

In a survey conducted in 1969 of "white-collar" workers in British Columbia, the author of this text found that such employees recognized their changed status: one-third of a sample of over 300 identified themselves as "like industrial workers"; another third as somewhere between industrial workers and management but not quite like either. Only one-third identified with management in the sense of seeing themselves as "like" management.[63]

One of the basic differences between the upper level executives and the production crews in offices was sex: at the upper levels, there were seldom any women. In fact, by the 1960s it was apparent that the sexes formed two almost exclusive labour forces. Though an increasing proportion of women were becoming employed for income, they were entering a segregated labour market in which the range of jobs available and their income positions were virtually determined by sex rather than skills or education. In fact, a higher proportion of men with elementary school education than of women with university degrees held managerial positions.[64]

Middle-class women, in common with those economists who think in terms of a consumer-choice theory for economic actions, tend to explain their re-entry in terms of personal preferences, that is, a desire to be useful in the adult world of work, boredom with household chores, a need for adult company and sociability with co-workers, and a desire for additional family income. If one studies the data on working women, however, one concludes that there is a very strong co-relation between entering the labour market and a declining income for male marriage partners. The lower the male income in a family, the greater the probability that a woman will become employed for wages.[65] This is not best described as a desire for additional family income: it is a need, and apparently it is a need widely experienced. The proportion of two-income families in the middle to lower deciles of income-earners in Canada has steadily increased. Johnson argues that the majority of these families could not maintain a level of subsistence which would permit them to participate in the society (e.g., to educate children so that they, in turn, can obtain employment to provide adequate shelter and food for the raising of a family) without at least two wage-incomes.[66]

## TABLE 4

### Average Weekly Earnings for Male and Female Clerical Workers in Manufacturing Industries, Selected Years, 1959-69*

| Year | Number Employees | | | Dollar Earnings | | | Women's Income as Percentage of Men's |
|------|------|------|------|------|------|------|------|
| | Total | Men | Women | Total | Men | Women | |
| 1959 | 147,033 | 76,830 | 70,203 | 69.91 | 84.04 | 54.44 | 64.7 |
| 1963 | 158,267 | 82,170 | 76,097 | 79.14 | 94.49 | 62.56 | 66.2 |
| 1965 | 170,233 | 86,996 | 83,237 | 87.19 | 105.72 | 67.83 | 64.2 |
| 1966 | 190,796 | 95,122 | 95,674 | 92.40 | 111.52 | 73.39 | 65.8 |
| 1967 | 195,413 | 97,778 | 97,635 | 99.08 | 120.01 | 78.11 | 65.0 |
| 1968 | 216,587 | 103,408 | 113,179 | 103.03 | 126.05 | 81.99 | 65.0 |
| 1969 | 194,270 | 97,283 | 96,987 | 116.48 | 142.50 | 90.39 | 63.4 |

* Data not available before or after this decade. The series has been discontinued because employers point out that the separate tabulations required of them imply discrimination by sex. The nadir of clerical employment appears to have been reached in 1968 in the clerical occupations, with a marked drop for both sexes in 1969. However, one cannot assess a trend without continuing data into the 1970s. Total dollar earnings are computed by multiplying the number in each sex group by the average earnings for each, adding, and dividing by total number of employees.

SOURCE: Dominion Bureau of Statistics. *Earnings and Hours of Work in Manufacturing Industries*, 1959, Table 7; 1963, Table 7; 1965, Table 7; 1967, Table 7; 1968, Table 3; 1969, Table 7. Ottawa: Queen's Printer, annual (cat. no. 72-204).

The data on two-income families fly in the face of much contemporary thinking. If corporate employment provides higher incomes than non-corporate employment, and if employed workers are relied on as a significant consumer population for the massive array of goods being produced by the corporations, then how is it possible that an increasing number of families find it essential to put both parents into the labour force?

One of the possible explanations is that the absolute cost of living has steadily increased, so that wage increases for men have not maintained parity with them. Inflation pushes women into the labour force. Another possible explanation which does not exclude the first is that while corporate employees in production and managerial or professional jobs earn relatively high incomes, an increasing proportion of potential workers is either excluded from participation altogether or restricted to the marginal work world of small businesses operating on the fringe of the corporate economy, seasonal work, and temporary work performed by the "elastic" portion of the labour force. In addition, while unemployment has been increasing amongst workers who are either unskilled or skilled in ways no longer useful to employers, up to the 1970s it was not increasing amongst clerical or most service workers. Provided productivity increased, the bureaucratic apparatus continued to expand. For some families this meant that women who had been taught clerical skills could obtain employment while men who had relied on resource sector employment were laid off. If inflation pushes women into the labour force, so will unemployment or underemployment of male marriage partners.

A third explanation is that the expectations and material demands of families have increased. Consumerism has become a primary means of self-expression; families measure their quality of life in terms of house ownership, nutritional foods, and children's educations as well as expensive gadgets. To increase their family's material status, not only because they desire more goods but because they perceive these as essential to family welfare, women move into the labour force.

These are explanations for women's motivation, and all may be true of some women, but they do not explain the increase in availability of jobs for women over the twentieth century. To explain that, one needs to consider the basic principle of employment policy: to employ productive labour at least possible cost. Employers hire workers at wages dependent on their needs, not those of the workers; if there is a high supply of equivalent workers, no matter how high the level of skill, they will obtain their workers at lower (competitive) costs. Women provide an oversupply of potential labour in clerical, sales, and service sectors, coincident with the high demand for workers in these occupations. As women competed for jobs, the overall wages in these occupational categories declined. One might expect that if the initial cost of hiring women is lower in any other occupational category, and in the absence of union, professional association, or legal restrictions, an increase in proportion of women hired would likewise occur. The only other obstacle would be either the reality or a perception of probable lower productivity by women, and this would affect mainly work which requires great physical strength.

The re-introduction of women into the labour force creates a number of basic changes in the organization of society. It is ironic that the earning of two incomes, intended, presumably, to improve the quality of life, frequently means the foregoing of community activities, family interaction, leisure time, entertainment of a kind that requires planning or active participation, and daily involvement in the raising of children. Thus, wage-work increasingly becomes the almost exclusive activity of adults: even the raising of children, via day-care, kindergarten, and schools, becomes wage-labour. The whole of existence is determined by the organization of industrial production, and the family unit is the first to feel the effects of shifts in labour demands and reductions in wages. Studies on the effects of women's employment outside the home on the division of domestic labour suggest that there are very few effects on men's time, however.[67] Employed women continue to do the household chores when they return home from their places of employment, in this fashion conforming to the ideological beliefs of a period that has passed.

There is a "double-bind" for women confronting these changed conditions, which is evident in the ideological developments of the "women's liberation movement." The movement, like most movements, views itself as self-propelled: it developed because women themselves were tired of being exploited as service station attendants in the home by husbands and by their husbands' corporate employers.[68] They joined together in order to fight the system and to gain recognition, status, and equal incomes as full-time workers in the system. To do this, they had to seek full-time employment outside the home and to argue that such employment was their "right." Yet when we consider the larger context of corporate development which involves an increasing demand for bureaucratic workers combined with a variable demand for production workers, and when we consider the advantages to employers of hiring women whose initial wages would be much lower than those of men for similar jobs, then we might begin to suspect that the "women's liberation movement" is a very inexpensive way of changing the labour force to the advantage of corporate employers. Equality comes cheaply when its initial thrust is to lower the overall income levels of those with whom the new employees compete.

# VI

The high employment period for women in clerical jobs, however, may be in its final phases. An automated office need not employ so many people in the subsidiary and hinterland operations.

The first and perhaps most obvious change for offices with electronic data processing is the recentralization of file-keeping and decision-making, together with the re-integration of product divisions. The sheer bulk of paper work associated with assembly-line production systems, when combined with diversified product areas and regional dispersion of manufacturing plants and offices, makes some decentralization essential. But when data can be stored on tapes and maintained in a small physical space yet be instantly available, centralization becomes equally inevitable. Information can be more efficiently organized, and head office managements can gain immediate access to financial and operational data.

The regional dispersion ceases to be a genuine distance in space where data processing is possible. A central office is no longer so many miles or a continent away: it is immediately available via computer in a much more powerful sense than by the telephone and telecommunications which preceded computerization. Thus centralization affects regional as well as product divisions, and while regional offices continue to be physically located away from home, they are centrally directed on a day-to-day basis.

As one manager stated it:

> We were moving in the direction of decentralization, but are now definitely recentralizing. This is because no matter how widely spread out the branches and districts are, if you have one company you need one record-keeping department. The modern tools of bookkeeping make recentralization possible."[69]

In line with this centralization and integration of product and regional divisions, the structure of management and communications networks must be altered. Multiple hierarchical pyramids are no longer necessary. Some divisions are eliminated altogether, as computers and head office personnel take over their functions. Others lose their need for middle management personnel, people who once interpreted head office to their divisions and their divisions to head office.[70] Much of their work becomes subject to programming, the Weberian model finally coming into its own via "simulated brains" rather than depersonalized workers. Communications networks for management personnel who remain – that is, specialized workers familiar with computer techniques and still essential to the operation – are likely to become horizontal and diagonal rather than vertical since authority at the production and marketing levels becomes more dependent on knowledge than position. The computer itself becomes a central part of the "radial" flow of information.

Computers, combined with such earlier telecommunications developments as telephones and telex, increase the possibilities for the concentration of power in a single location and a single executive group. At the other end of the authority scale – the hierarchy is not obliterated by virtue of changes in its operation at middle-management and expert staff ranks – there is an elimination of jobs which formerly dealt with filing and accounting, but an increase in some complex tasks involving groups rather than autonomous individuals. Apart from the jobs of keypunchers, which remain in the mass-production era and are already disappearing as alternative methods of entering data are developed, the tasks of the computer unit require interdependent activity. In addition, more jobs rather than fewer may be created in personnel divisions. Computerization so increases the productivity of the company that costs attributable to bureaucratic labour need no longer be a high component cost of production. If the utility of labour depends on the permanence of trained personnel, then costs for maintenance of such personnel are worthwhile.

All of these increases in management and supplementary personnel affect labour-force composition, just as did the earlier accelerated demands for labour in mass-production systems. The apparent trend is toward an increase in the proportion of all workers engaged in supervisory and lower managerial tasks where the main production operations are actually carried out by machines. This tendency implies a reduction in jobs for unskilled workers again. In addition, if these plants are part of integrated production systems covering multinational territories, and if production scheduling and accounting and filing systems have become automated, then the mobility for administrators is limited to the plant level: there is reason to suppose that mobility upward from the plant level would be restricted because of the concentration of control at head offices. In fact, some writers have expressed a fear that as these processes continue, the omission of genuine middle-rank management positions will give rise to a subsequent crisis of control because there will be few trained executives able to move into top positions at a later stage.

None of these events occurs suddenly at a given moment in time. Automation in the plant is a gradual process, affecting the labour force this way and that in apparently contradictory ways as it first creates a demand for skills, then a renewed demand for manual labour, then another wave of demands for skills. Likewise, the expansion of offices creates a demand for skilled clerical workers and managers and professionals, and this demand may steadily increase while the plant undergoes many fluctuations over time in requirements for workers with different combinations of skill. Researchers entering plants which are at any intermediate stage of automation (and not all industrial organizations will ever become fully automated since some processes by their nature preclude this) inevitably study a partial process. Thus the British researchers supervised by Woodward, whose studies were described earlier, provided a series of conclusions for the difference between mass-production and continuous-production organizations which should be understood as observations subject to revision as the technical conditions continue to change. Likewise, Blauner provided a detailed account of the conditions of work for printers just a dozen years before the entire printing trade was completely undermined by computerization.

The author of this book conducted a study of office workers during the late 1960s, and was struck by the low level of job control possessed by the vast majority of women in office and sales occupations.[71] The income of these workers was also very low, and these two conditions, low control and low income, were equally characteristic of women who were unionized and of those who were not. In fact, unions at that time served mainly to systematize the existing inequalities between the sexes: they evaluated jobs in terms traditionally used by employers, and their interpretation of jobs reserved for women, if not officially then unofficially, was that these were relatively unskilled. Table 5 describes the kinds of work done by men and women.

Since that time some of the offices visited for that research have undergone preliminary transitions to automation. The job structure has changed. Men and women have not yet changed their relative positions, and unions have only begun to take an active role in supporting employed women in the private sector of the economy (though they have become, in the meantime, much more active in the public sector). Like those who have studied production systems in the plant, this researcher would no doubt have to revise many of the job descriptions in line with these technical changes in offices. In particular, it would be helpful for our understanding to determine how many of these low-control jobs of the 1960s are being phased out, and what the consequences of that phasing-out are for the employment of women in offices.[72]

One further point in this connection might be considered. That is, that though the availability of recognizably "unskilled" jobs is decreasing, it may be incorrect to assume that the remaining jobs are particularly skilled, or that the employed labour force consists of highly skilled workers. Lower-level supervisory jobs, administrative positions, many clerical positions, many

## TABLE 5

### Job Descriptions for Sample of White-Collar Workers by Sex, British Columbia, 1969

#### Job Descriptions (Percentage at each level*)

| | Male | Female | | Male | Female |
|---|---|---|---|---|---|
| *Machine Work* | | | *Decisions Involving Materials* | | |
| machine-controlled | 7 | 20 | none | 15 | 44 |
| op. some control | 6 | 17 | little | 31 | 44 |
| op. controls | 22 | 30 | fair amount | 36 | 9 |
| no machine work | 65 | 33 | great deal | 18 | 3 |
| *Verbal Skills Required* | | | *Idea Generation, Discussions on Ideas* | | |
| not at all | 20 | 42 | not at all | 45 | 80 |
| not very much | 41 | 46 | not very much | 37 | 11 |
| fair amount | 27 | 8 | fair amount | 8 | 6 |
| much | 12 | 5 | great deal | 10 | 3 |
| *Task Complexity* | | | *Extent to which Worker Completes Own Product Process* | | |
| simple procedures | 21 | 48 | not at all | 41 | 66 |
| some complex tasks | 32 | 35 | little | 7 | 17 |
| fairly complex | 39 | 14 | fair amount | 21 | 8 |
| very complex | 8 | 3 | great deal | 31 | 10 |
| *Extent to which Knowledge of Particular Company Important* | | | *Extent to which Job Integrated in Main Production Process of Firm* | | |
| not at all | 27 | 36 | not at all | 21 | 54 |
| little | 25 | 29 | little | 23 | 12 |
| some, fair amount | 32 | 9 | some | 32 | 22 |
| great deal | 16 | 7 | great deal | 24 | 14 |

* In some instances, percentages do not add to 100 because of rounding errors.

SOURCE: Patricia Marchak, "Women Workers and White-Collar Unions," in *Canadian Review of Sociology and Anthropology*, vol. 10: 2 (May 1973), 134-47, Table 1.

technical positions, personnel functions, and an increasing array of computer-attendance jobs are not really very skill-demanding. They do not require the level of expertise, precision, experience, training, for example, once required of master carpenters or tailors or typographers. Their incumbents have lengthy, rather than skill-creating, educations. They may have learned to be punctual, polite, co-operative, conscientious, and literate (although these cannot be guaranteed by schools and universities, where even a philosophical essay can be purchased on the open market and a grade obtained by proxy). They need not have learned how to do very much of anything. If there is one attribute of an industrial urban labour force which is most noticeable, if fact, it is its relative inability to survive without the vast underpinning of technological development that provides its wages.[73]

# CHAPTER 6

# THE MANAGEMENT OF MANAGEMENT

*. . . I question, explain, prove, disprove, comfort, threaten, grant, deny, demand, approve, legalize, rescind. In the name of legal principles and provisions I defend law and order for want of anything better to do. The order I defend is brutal though fragile, it is unpleasant and austere; its ideas are impoverished and its style is lacking in grace. I can't pretend to like it. Yet I serve it, it's law, it works; it's rather like me, its tool. . . . My highest aspiration is that a medium-rank utterly insignificant civil servant should, as far as possible, live with his eyes open.*
— George Konrad.[1]

The effects of a division of labour are not limited to productivity increases. Confining our attention to the internal effects, we are struck by the capacity of large and complex corporate bodies to engender loyalty in their higher-ranking members. One argument is that loyalty is increased where workers are brought into consultative relationships with one another in the absence of external authority. But loyalty is displayed equally intensely within obviously hierarchical organizations, and in any event, corporate bodies by their nature always involve a hierarchy of power.

The argument advanced instead is that within the context of organizations which are hierarchically arranged and rationally ordered toward the pursuit of profits and social power, there exists a stratum of workers whose specialized functions require them to work interdependently even where they must also compete over scarce resources. Through their separation of function, their respective spheres are secured; through their necessary interaction, their solidarity is created.[2] Essentially the same process occurs at the level of organizational units. Though they may and even must compete over scarce resources, the entire political process is one which creates a moral community within the organization – a community with rules for competition inside a framework of common organizational objectives.

Thus the line of reasoning from Durkheim to Simon and March and Burns provides an explanation for loyalty, but it is a partial explanation. The other half is in the ideology contained in this same explanation. By ignoring the power structure within and the power of corporate organizations, theorists and the managerial-professional workers for whom they produce their theories intensify their commitment to a heavily veiled reality.

The other half of the reality is labour engaged in the actual production of goods and services. The division of labour in the plant is predicated on the ever-increasing demand for greater productivity. This is not necessarily, nor usually, met through encouragement of genuine expertise. It is met, rather, through minimizing the total skill range of each worker, increasing the similarity between workers and machines, machines and workers, who can hardly respect one another's area of specialization when it is so obvious that untrained workers can master the skill in very little time. Though organizations theorists on behalf of management investigated the plantworker with great thoroughness in order to predict and control his behaviour, only one conclusion from their mass of studies could be substantiated. This was that the production worker's loyalty is a function of steady pay-cheques.

In this chapter we will consider the position of the "first" half of the reality: management personnel and the staff of experts who steadily infuse large organizations with their specialized skills and receive in return benefits that considerably exceed (even where it is adequate) their income.

## I

The bureaucracy described by Weber was necessarily hierarchical. Each position was connected to another above it, each person was accountable to a superior officer. Each person was to know which others he or she was accountable to and for which others he or she was responsible. No person was to be permitted to make decisions not falling within a programmed task. However, the precise context of any task need not be spelled out. Indeed managerial tasks of necessity involve the making of decisions within the programmed area of discretion.

Thus we find examples of dilemmas between conflicting demands in mechanistic or rule-bound hierarchical organizations just as we might in what we will subsequently call "organic" organizations as described by current theorists. Crozier studied the large bureaucratic operations of the French government in the 1950s, and noted that the rules themselves created a need for the exercise of discretion and power from managers in their dealings with subordinates. Managers, in his opinion, were obliged to treat rules as weapons. They would insist on observance of rules where subordinates exceeded their authority or challenged a manager's power, but too great an insistence on too many occasions would reduce the discretionary opportunities for the manager as well as others. Thus good management involves careful balancing of rules and exceptions to rules within a context of power relationships.[3]

The system of power relationships, in Weber's view, began with a corporate leader:

> A social relationship which is either closed or limits the admission of outsiders by rules, will be called a "corporate group" so far as its order is enforced by the action of specific individuals whose regular function this is, of a chief or "head" and usually also an administrative staff. . . .[4]

Flanking such leaders were specialists, paid on a regular salaried basis and subject to the administrative rules of the organization. Again we will quote Weber on this because contemporary theories tend to neglect these same power and rule-governed relationships:

> Bureaucratization offers above all the optimum possibility for carrying through the principle of specialized administrative functions according to purely objective considerations. . . . The "objective" discharge of business primarily means a discharge of business according to *calculable rules* and "without regard for persons."[5]

... And as far as complicated tasks are concerned, paid bureaucratic work is not only more precise but, in the last analysis, it is often cheaper than even formally unrenumerated honorific service."[6]

The "machine" described by Weber is a fairly simple and stable organization. It appears to have straightforward objectives which are shared by all persons and groups contained within it, and to have a large number of functionaries at lower levels whose strict obedience to authority is beneficial to the operation. Its interaction with an external environment is apparently predetermined and inflexible. It is not required to respond anew to a constant influx of novel demands. Its technical components are likewise fixed. There is no strain involved in adjusting to them, and they do not create any needs to re-structure the system. Perhaps most noticeable about the model is its lack of provision for struggle over scarce resources. Apparently there is enough for all or, if not that, the portions to each have already been allotted and are not open to debate.

This simple and stable organization chart does not appear to describe adequately an expanding industrial corporation. In such an organization there are jobs which not only permit but absolutely require the exercise of considerable discretion. Interaction with environments is not altogether predictable, and bureaucratic officials are required to engage in bargaining, manipulation, initiatives, and response actions which cannot be programmed. By the nature of expansion, the technical conditions for production are changing, and these changes do create strains both on roles and rules and on the people who perform roles or obey rules. In addition, the structure of a multi-divisional organization necessarily involves a struggle over scarce resources. Personnel, time, commitments, overall objectives, financing, and even ideological persuasion are all scarce resources in this situation. Different groups within the organization – quite independent of their personal objectives, which form yet another set of complications not under discussion here – are obliged to compete with each other in order to properly manage their own departments.

The greater flexibility and discretion available to managerial and professional personnel, together with their increasing numbers in expanding organizations, puts too great a strain on the Weberian model. As organization charts became increasingly difficult to use as genuine representations of authority or communications, both theorists and corporate administrators proposed alternatives. These alternatives focused on the dynamic properties of interaction and organizational decision-making, and on individual behavioural responses to situations involving risk and uncertainty. Such concerns have given rise to a vast literature on influence processes, decision-making, interaction, the utilization of expertise, and the relationship between private goals or career objectives and organizational goals.

The properties of bureaucracy as cited by Weber have not actually been superseded in this literature. What these theorists do, rather, is redefine the terms, although often they appear to be arguing that their models and theories are novel departures from classical theory. The redefinitions take into account the variable nature of productive enterprise when the underlying techniques of production are undergoing extensive change and when the external environment is unstable. Rational decision-making, for example, may be most easily undertaken by rules when the objectives are clear, the alternatives are known, the consequences of various alternatives are identified, and the personal qualities of both decision-makers and those subjected to the results of the decisions are predictable and manageable. The organization is no less concerned with rational decision-making, however, when it encourages extensive consultation between its various experts and administrators, deliberate "search processes" regarding alternatives and consequences, committee deliberations, and experimental conditions. Given an uncertain environment (e.g., market acceptance of new products), an uncertain technical component (e.g., an office undergoing transfer of filing systems to electronic data storage), and a staff of specialists who can realistically consider alternative employment, rational decision-making becomes a process of negotiation, trial-and-error, and calculated risk.

Efficiency, likewise, undergoes a change in definition. The organization is no less concerned with the most accurate and rapid performance of tasks relative to its overall goals. However, it becomes more efficient to recognize the sub-unit goals of divisions and individuals than to ignore them; and it becomes more efficient to entertain extensive committee consultations over specific objectives and employee morale than to insist on single lines of authority and rules for behaviour.

A typical bureaucratic condition in a large and expanding industrial corporation involves several different departments or divisions in a company each with its own perspective on the total organization, and its own set of needs and demands. The accounting department is designed so that its members will seek ways of reducing costs throughout the entire operation. Yet the research department is designed so that its members will seek innovative techniques without considering total costs. The two are obliged to negotiate their differences, and there are no organizational programmes which can prevent such negotiation, no organizations which could survive unless the respective personnel were prepared to undertake such negotiations.

In negotiating, personnel find themselves with somewhat contradictory objectives. They must consider the short-run efficiencies versus the long-run costs of any undertaking; the relative weights to be placed on financial and human factors; company goals versus environmental considerations; and the various sub-goals of different departments involved versus the total organization.

In addition, various functionaries of organizations tend to develop different approaches to problem-solving, meeting objectives, dealing with outsiders, and organizational rules, not because they have different personalities but because their jobs necessitate certain perspectives. Some jobs by their nature depend on fairly rigid adherence to rules, concern for stability, safety, strict file-keeping. Others by their nature depend on a high degree of flexibility, innovative action, risk-taking, a cavalier attention to formalities. A mechanistic organization would not allow these various personnel to co-operate, nor could it anticipate their differences. Organizations in fact stay alive precisely because their members are willing to negotiate the terms of their roles and modify regulations in the light of circumstances.[7]

Much of this negotiation occurs between persons in organizations whose positions are roughly equivalent. This is currently called the "horizontal" level of bureaucracy. One American study of negotiation at this level involves the job of "purchasing agent" in large organizations, as reported by George Strauss.[8]

The official programme for agents is to receive requisition orders from various experts in other departments, primarily engineers, and to obtain their materials from suppliers on the best possible terms. However, this programme fails to take account of the structural conflicts between different departments, and with the perspective of these conflicting demands available to the purchasing agent. Strauss quotes one purchasing agent on the problem:

> Production scheduling wants quick delivery, engineering wants quality, manufacturing wants something easy-to-make, accounting wants to save money, quality control has their own interests. And then you've got to deal with the supplier – and present the supplier's position back to your own organization (sometimes you think you are wearing two hats, you represent both the supplier and the company). Everybody has his own point of view and only the agent sees the over-all picture.[9]

Undoubtedly the same situation would be described by the engineers or quality-control personnel from their own perspectives. But for the purchasing agent, the problem is to satisfy as many demands as possible while performing adequately what he sees as his task. What he sees as his task is not included in the official programme. It involves negotiation not only with suppliers for the best terms, but negotiation with organizational personnel regarding technical specifications. Those purchasing agents who wish to expand their influence or status in the organization define their task in ways that cause them to be vital sources of information about best buys prior to the issuing of requisitions, and to have some means of vetoing orders that do not meet with their approval. They seek to be considered the "experts" within their own sphere of operations.

If they did not seek to be experts, the organization would lose one of its sources of ultimate efficiency and economical operation. Their ability to translate the desire for status and influence is one of the sources of loyalty to the company. Yet these benefits to the organization are to be weighed against the conflicts that an expansionary agent can create in his negotiations with an engineer who defines the agent's job in much narrower terms and who jealously guards his own prerogative to state specifications. These various factors cannot be built into programmed roles and rules without an overall loss to organizational strength: they must be left open to negotiation, limited by a relatively vague set of regulations that establish perimeters rather than job contents.

It is instructive to consider some of the techniques used by purchasing agents in their dealing with engineers. Where engineers are reluctant to recognize this other source of expertise, excessive compliance with rules by agents can ensure that problems recognized by them in advance will not be avoided and the engineers will be obliged to accept blame. Pressure through allies in other departments, appeals to higher authorities, demands for explanations in writing, appeals to formal rules which are not normally enforced, and pressure to reorganize departments and revise standard operating procedures are all tactics observed by Strauss in this study.

Strauss discovered that large organizations with many divisions tended to engender greater expansionary designs amongst agents. This is not surprising. By their nature these organizations have different units struggling over scarce organizational resources (funds, personnel, promotions, influence). In addition, these different units engender different terms of reference for their members. It is inevitable, and from the perspective of the organization, highly desirable, that the personnel negotiate their relative positions on a regular basis. As far as administrative jobs are concerned, flexibility appears to increase with complexity of organization.

The appearance may, however, be short-lived. The entire structure undergoes another change with the introduction of electronic data-processing equipment. Such equipment, when fully installed and in steady operation, provides the means for filing documents in small spaces, thus avoiding the need for enormous office space and many locations for different divisions. Regional offices can be reduced in both size and number because much of the regional data-collection and file maintenance can be relocated at the central offices, and it will still be – indeed will even more be – quickly available. The number of people required to staff a data-bank library is considerably smaller than the number required for regionally dispersed and large filing systems of the more traditional variety. In addition, many of the local decisions made by submanagers and product-division heads may be as easily made at head offices, on the basis of instantly available information in the data files. Personnel supervision becomes less vital as data-machine and library attendance become more central to organizational efficiency. Accounting systems, sales inventories, customer billing, many aspects of planning, and personnel services as an office division may be reduced in size, employee numbers, and autonomy. The flexibility needed for sprawling enterprises ceases to be so useful in a much more centralized operation.

According to one executive:

Thus the computer has been a major force for change. Its advent has mechanized a host of routine tasks, and the process has substantially diminished the administrative functions of the managers who supervised them. By shifting the center of emphasis from the supervision of people to the attainment of objectives it has caused managers to shift their areas of concern from procedural to professional matters – to the inquiry into the what and why of things rather than the how.[10]

Offices undergoing this transformation are overloaded with experts. The concern with "utilization of expertise" is no less than it was for the German bureaucracy; what has changed is the nature and extent of expertise in the total organization. Expertise becomes its own authority, and the organization must either find efficient means of utilizing experts so that they have independent authority, or must find an accommodation between an administrative authority hierarchy and the authority inherent in knowledge. When the matters under consideration are matters of production techniques or market capacities, the organization utilizes experts most efficiently by granting them authority. Typically, however, overall policy and financial control are retained by executive bodies, some of whose members are also experts in their own fields. Their authority is exercised not in the form of rules and hierarchies but in the form of ultimate restrictive capacities, the ability to establish the limits for experts or to facilitate expansion in desired directions.

The executive quoted above argues that the organizational change involved in extensive computerization of information retrieval systems results in a diminishing of executive direct control of many operating decisions. The top executive becomes more concerned with the quality of data base, systems analysis, decisions systems, and "the caliber of the associates and the character of the expertise that collaborate in making his decision."[11] Operating decisions are more likely to be made by a middle-management stratum which consists in a large part of experts in technical fields, through direct consultation with all others in like positions via computer-processed information. He outlines his concept of this process in a chart reproduced opposite (Figure 8).

It will be noted here that the hierarchy is not eliminated. Information is more dispersed and certain operating decisions are therefore possible at levels below top management (perversely represented at the bottom of these charts). The author phrases this in this way: "While the trend towards professionalism encourages an equality in dignity among managers, differences in function permit a few broad classifications even in a dynamic network."[12] Status based on administrative authority is less obvious here than in the traditional organization, but status based on expertise is enhanced. Administrators and experts become less differentiated, differentiation increases between specialized sub-units. As experts become more embedded in the organization and administration is carried on ever more by experts who in turn are served by a complex and instant communications system, management becomes ever more rationalized. Experts must be highly trained and they obtain this training typically in universities with specialized programmes not only in engineering, sciences, and law, but as well in business management itself. Management becomes, according to its view of itself, professionalized. Members can no longer learn the business by filling various positions along the way and having a general understanding of management practices. The "new breed of men" that Neufeld describes as taking over Massey-Ferguson in

## Figure 8: Businessman's Interpretation of Pre- and Post-Computer Information Organization

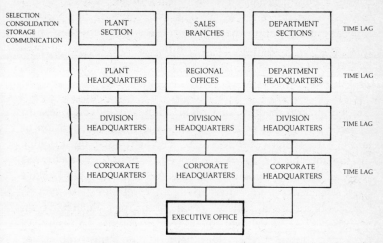

Standard Information Assembly System

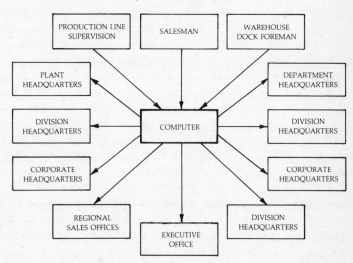

Computer Information System

SOURCE: Terrance Hanold, "The Corporate Manager: A Businessman's View," in Richard A. Jackson (ed.), *The Multinational Corporation and Social Policy*, New York: Praeger, 1974, p. 6.

the mid-1950s are directors with financial and engineering expertise, executives with professional degrees, managers trained by institutions established precisely for that purpose. In order to coordinate these specialized skills, means other than direct and heavy-handed hierarchical systems are required, and negotiation and information-sharing must be built into these new systems, rather than simply permitted at the fringes of programmes.

## II

Contemporary theories of organization are indebted less to Weber's analysis of power than to a theory of the division of labour in society proposed by French sociologist Emile Durkheim. This theory was developed at about the same time as Weber's theory of bureaucracy. Like Weber's work, Durkheim's was concerned with alternative interpretations of certain features of industrial society to Marxist theories which had been proposed and developed over the preceding half-century. However, unlike Weber, Durkheim avoided the problem of power in modern society and its organizations, focusing instead on the co-operative aspects of production relations.

Adam Smith, David Ricardo, and Karl Marx had proposed theories about the division of labour in which this development was viewed as the corollary of the development of a capitalist market. The function of a division of labour was increased productivity, and this pertained as well to machinery as to people. The optimum level of specialization was stated by Smith to be a function of market demand for products. This basic interpretation was accepted by Ricardo and Marx in their theories of class formation and class relations based on the division of labour in production organizations. Durkheim, however, chose to ignore this feature and to concentrate instead on the relationship between increasing population density and the division of labour despite his strong condemnation (as instanced in a quotation preceding Chapter 5) of the more degrading aspects of factory production systems. His argument was that the maintenance of societal cohesion and the reduction of both intra- and inter-societal conflict over scarce resources were the outcome and the function of an increasingly complex division of labour in circumstances of expanding populations.

Durkheim argued that the members of an overly dense population would, in the absence of a division of labour, engage in competition over scarce resources. In order to avoid such a potentially destructive event, and in order to preserve the social solidarity that characterizes society in its earlier and non-industrial phases, members of a society specialize in their production roles and engage in exchanges of goods and services, thereby increasing resources and interdependence. Thus, "Each of them can attain his end without preventing the others from attaining theirs."[13]

In this argument, Durkheim essentially ignores the function of a division of labour for productivity, and the deliberate rationalization of production organizations by those in control of the same for purposes of increasing either profit or power. This argument provides the basic assumptions for theories of organization which view these entities as essentially non-corporate bodies in the Weberian sense of that term, as, rather, coalitions of individuals who, through the division of labour and exchange of services, maintain a cohesive and mutually beneficial enterprise.

The coalition theory, proposed by American "behaviourists," treats individuals as the units and the total organization as a coalition of individuals. The basic premise is that individuals pursue private objectives in voluntarily joining large organizations, and their actions can be interpreted as exchanges in an essentially co-operative venture. Each person strives to achieve private objectives through various strategies which might include joining together with others where they enhance one's own positions. Individuals receive "side payments" in the form of authority, decision-making roles, or monetary incentives, such that they continue to view the total coalition as essential to their interests.[14]

The total coalition, or organization, consists of interdependent and interrelated units whose combined balance is achieved when contributions by members are perceived by them to be equal to payments from the coalition, and conversely, when the payments do not in fact exceed the actual contributions. Equilibrium can be affected by the environment, and part of the bargaining between coalition members involves adjustments of both payments and contributions relative to changing situational factors. The balance is summed up by one theorist: "Hence, an organization is solvent – and will continue in existence – only so long as the contributions are sufficient to provide inducements in large enough measure to draw forth these contributions."[15]

If the organization is a coalition of individuals, then the objectives or organizational activity become subject to negotiation along with the means of achieving them. This is what two authors propose:

> the goals of a business firm are a series of more or less independent constraints imposed on the organization through a process of bargaining among potential coalition members and elaborated over time in response to short-run pressures. Goals arise in such a form because the firm is, in fact, a coalition of participants with disparate demands, changing foci of attention, and limited ability to attend to all organizational problems simultaneously.[16]

Such negotiations can never result in total resolution of conflicts. Organizations may, actually, have contradictory goals, simultaneously hold mutually incompatible values, and make inconsistent decisions over time. This is inevitable in the nature of bargaining situations. Thus a theory of influence is required for explaining who gets what and why. How much influence is attributed to expertise, how much to financial control, how much to formal administrative authority, and how much to personal talent? Among the more important personal talents in bargaining situations would be the ability to negotiate terms in committees or to induce the personal loyalty of others through persuasion and example.[17]

Within such situations, information-processing or communication of information is critical not only to effective decision-making but also to the exercise of influence. Witholding of information or selective distribution of it can confer power on individuals or sub-units or the organization, but such power is negotiable only if some information is provided and certain goals are achieved. Thus organizations strive to maximize general pools of information, information services which are programmed and involve rules for distribution, and communications networks. They also create means which in effect take the place of direct authority transmission lines, such as weekly management meetings, regular conferences, encouragement of publication, the distribution of prestige, and esteem for those who communicate expert information to others.

Within the same general framework, British sociologist Tom Burns has proposed a theory which he calls the "organic" theory of organization.[18] He contrasts the mechanistic (Weberian model) bureaucracy with the organic system in terms of the latter's capacity to facilitate and even anticipate change.

> Organic systems are adapted to unstable conditions, when problems and requirements for action arise which cannot be broken down and distributed among specialist roles within a clearly defined hierarchy. Communication between people of different ranks tends to resemble lateral consultation rather than vertical command. Omniscience can no longer be imputed to the head of the concern.[19]

Burns' argument is that organic and mechanistic systems actually do exist as objective realities, and as polar extremes. They are, he suggests, not simply alternative ways to organize systems but respectively appropriate ways to organize particular systems. The particularity is given by the technological constraints and market or other external conditions. In addition, the specific functioning of either system will be affected by the congruence of conflict between its operation in any given organization and the career or personal goals of members.

Burns identifies a series of related properties of organic systems.[20] The first of these is that tasks are open to redefinition, are redefined in situational contexts, and are not so subdivided that individuals can work autonomously. The second is that neither the authority nor the responsibility lines are absolute, and they are also not primarily hierarchical. There is, instead, a "network structure of control, authority, and communication," and the head of the concern is not regarded as omniscient. All members may have special competences which they are expected to contribute to the entire organization, and in their own fields they are the authorities. Thus communication and responsibility may move in vertical, horizontal, and multidimensional ways according to the situation and the competences required. Although these organizations are not hierarchical in the mechanistic sense, they remain stratified. "Positions are differentiated according to seniority – i.e., greater expertise."[21]

The corollary of this open system of authority is that some other means of inducing loyalty and "obedience to the larger concern" is required which does not rest on formal power. Burns identifies this in the form of commitment. He asserts that "the extent to which the individual yields himself as a resource to be used by the working organization . . . is far more extensive in organic than in mechanistic systems. . . . the growth and accretion of institutionalized values, beliefs, and conduct, in the form of commitments, ideology, and manners, around an image of the concern in its industrial and commercial setting makes good the loss of formal structure."[22]

With loyalty and commitment as the basis of action, it follows that the unit of organization is a combination of individual and working group, and that co-operative enterprise is regarded and must be regarded as the appropriate form of behaviour where autonomous and regulated behaviours dominated the mechanistic system.

## III

The coalition, influence, and various communications and decision-making theories which provide this general perspective are both useful contributions to "objective" knowledge about organizations, and interesting contributions to current ideology on them. As ideological systems they are of particular use to corporations because they appear to explain organizational systems and thereby reduce curiosity. They cloak the nature of authority and explain away, rather than explain, the way in which expertise is utilized within organizations that remain hierarchical.

The essential rules devised by the DuPont cousins, the successors to Ford and Watson, and the post-war organizers of Massey-Ferguson were that managers and experts should be given complete authority in their sections, that nonetheless they would be subject to the next higher level of authority, and that they would be held accountable for their actions. In fact, they would be replaced if they failed to contribute to corporate growth and profit. These rules were critical to the continued growth of these organizations once they had established themselves in their markets. This division of labour allowed administrative and specialist staff considerable freedom, but it did not eliminate the hierarchical structure of the organization: on the contrary, it supported that structure.

These theories are concerned with the apparent freedom of this group of workers; they contribute to blindness about the context within which the freedom is played out. In particular, they ignore the hierarchy which exists not only inside one unit of a complex structure, but which ties subsidiaries to parents and the experts and managers in subsidiaries to the policies and authority of head office decision-makers.

For example, Burns mentions that several of the firms from which he drew evidence in support of his theory were branches of larger corporations.[23] Some of these had no local control over such functions as overall planning, policy direction, financial direction, or even purchasing. These subsidiaries were concerned solely with one or several phases of the actual production process. Occasionally this involved separate research and development departments. Some of the firms were engaged primarily in producing goods and services for internal use, that is, components that would be transformed or applied to yet further production methods in other subsidiaries. These different situations did not strike the theorist as problematic. Though some firms were and others clearly were not autonomous, and some firms contained the whole of management while others contained only plant-level administrators, he lumped all together in his description and analysis.

We have considered some of the structural differences between parents and subsidiaries in Chapter 4. From the quotations cited there, we are aware that however much the experts and management at the local level may interact and exchange information in an apparently collegial rather than hierarchical fashion, the constraints on their action are not of their own choosing. They do not make the final decisions about production rates, types of production, financing, location, or employment.

In some ways these firms might resemble the departments of a university. Each department operates to some extent autonomously, and its major task, the teaching of a particular subject matter, is its special burden. It is generally regarded as improper for administrative personnel to concern themselves with the actual production system. What they do concern themselves with is the cost of the production relative to costs elsewhere in the operation and the means of generating funds. They have similar controls on the hiring of personnel, research granting, and use of university facilities. Yet it is quite possible to study a department as if it were autonomous if one is interested in the actual production system, the teaching of a particular body of information. Seen in this way, some departments are extremely congenial companies. Members interact frequently, consult with one another, recognize one another's areas of expertise, enjoy a high rate of diagonal, vertical, horizontal, and multidimensional communication. The head of the department may act mainly as a chairperson, and have fairly circumscribed "housekeeping" duties. At most he or she may be regarded as a spiritual and intellectual leader (not particularly frequent in the mass production system that modern universities tend to be). If one does not concern oneself with the financial and other controls from administrations and boards of governors, one would completely miss the hierarchical nature of the authority system. It does not *appear* to operate at the level of the production system.

The same features may be noted for other enterprises. A study of the production of newscasts at a regional centre of the Canadian Broadcasting Corporation by Brian Campbell illustrated a similar situation.[24] Budget restrictions imposed on the newscast team by both central headquarters and divisional management precluded the possibility of a news-gathering service with any teeth. Campbell discovered that the CBC local news staff of necessity relied on local radio stations for their news sources. He noted other constraints as well, which have their counterparts in subsidiary operations of industrial corporations, such as the time allotted by the national decision-makers for local newscasting. Perhaps the most influential constraint is the least obvious: the fact that the only way "up" is toward the parent or national/international headquarters. The more ambitious local administrators and specialists are obliged to peg their promotion opportunities on their compliance with policies emanating from above.

Consider as an example the International Telephone and

Telegraph Company operations in Canada. ITT, which provides no consolidated sales or profit figures for Canada, would, if federally incorporated, rank about thirtieth in size for this country.[25] It ranks seventeenth in assets value in United States.[26] It has attracted considerable attention for its subversive activity in Chile prior to the overthrow of the Allende government, and has been the subject of a detailed biography with much unsavory revelation by Anthony Sampson.[27] In Canada, ITT is represented in two groups of companies; the first is a federally incorporated holding company with a number of electronics manufacturing firms under its general control; the second, numerous manufacturing, insurance, and service companies which are directly controlled by the U.S. parent. These two groups are joined at corporate staff national headquarters (Figure 9). A staff-writer with *Canadian Business* interviewed the Canadian president about his job. Sonja Sinclair's first observation in her article was that "the president of ITT Canada Limited does not enjoy the jurisdiction normally associated with the presidency of a major company."[28] She quotes an ITT official: "ours is a system of complementary relationships, not prerogatives." Rephrased by the president, Tom Savage, this comes out as: "First, we assist units in problem solving, monitor their performance against budget, interpret and apply corporate policy." It would be difficult to read this as the capacity to generate autonomous policy. Indeed, the organization chart makes it clear that each of the subsidiary companies reports to both ITT Canadian headquarters and U.S. management. Savage is quoted as emphasizing "Canadian content" in describing Canadian headquarters' task:

> To look at the performance and the operation of the units in the Canadian environment; to ensure, for example, that policies and procedures set up by the corporation are properly interpreted or properly postured to meet Canadian legislation; to give as much of a Canadian national flavour to the business decisions as is possible within the boundaries of making those particular decisions.

In short, the task of the national headquarters is to modify U.S. policies to fit or to appear to fit Canadian situations. In further delineating the various lines of authority, Savage makes it

Figure 9: Canadian Organization of ITT Corporation, USA

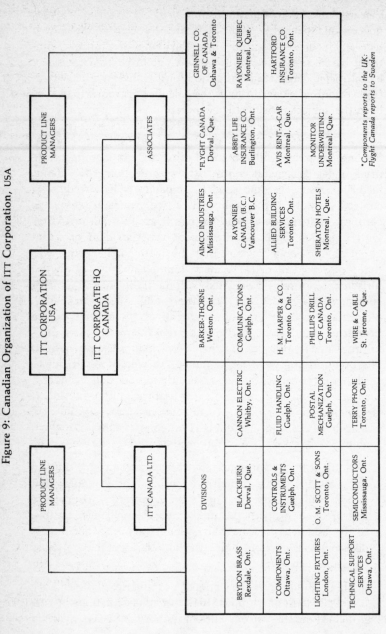

SOURCE: Sonja Sinclair, "ITT Canada: An Inconspicuous Giant," *Canadian Business*, March 1974, pp. 6-13.

clear that his own position is limited. Important subsidiaries, such as Rayonier, "consult" with the Canadian president; they report to their U.S. management. In explaining this Savage provides an outline of the "organic" organization: no single "boss," no single line of authority, utilization of expertise, joint responsibilities, and various lines of consultation between "horizontal" positions.

The directives for subsidiary managers are spelled out by an executive at Nestlé Corporation in a fashion that defies paraphrasing. No critic could be more devastating:

> Though running sometimes a very considerable business, the subsidiary manager must accept that he has not the final responsibility to the ultimately beneficial owners of the business and many of the obligations of the normal executive are being taken care of by Head Office, such as research, finance, etc. In a way he is a partly castrated top executive and it is as well he recognized this, lest he remains permanently dissatisfied. Secondly, in addition to the loyalty to his country, he must develop a loyalty to the international company; the two may sometimes come in conflict, for instance in matters relating to transfer of profits at a time of stress on the balance of payments or in questions, such as whether a company should have local shareholders, or in export matters, considering the obvious tendency of the international company to draw its export requirements from the cheapest available source. It is granted that such conflicts can also occur within a national company, but allegiance to a foreign company certainly has a particular touch of its own.[29]

These theories and the underlying order they represent are deficient as well in other respects. Among these is a consideration of the relationship between the corporate unit with its co-operative members and the external community. At best the outside community becomes a potential source of influence, a pressure point. But this ignores the fact that the participants in the internal system are members of the outside community. The question is whether they are inclined or encouraged to think of themselves primarily in terms of the internal system: is the problem a deficiency of theory or of reality?

## IV

The business executive quoted earlier, while extolling the virtues of professionalism and the participatory nature of computer-fed management, argued: "it is not the function of the businessman to create a separate ethos, differing from that of his society. . . . It is his function to maintain in his enterprise the ethical standards that our society observes and to assist in the general effort to advance those standards as new social aspirations indicate."[30] A United Automobile Workers Union executive responds to this: "This is an age of specialization in industry, and each specialist handles his own speciality. Unfortunately, no one ends up being a specialist in the ethical aspects of business activity."[31]

The theories, like the organizations they describe, are not addressed to nor specifically concerned with particular environments other than with respect to changing technology and markets as these impinge on internal decisions. The overall effects of organization decisions on nation-states, governments, natural environments, and people are not considered in the theories. It may be argued that such matters are beyond the scope of the theories, their objective is simply to describe how the internal organization is structured. This is a fair defence: it is also an ideological defence. The organizations themselves provide such a focus, and it is in their interests that organizations theorists concern themselves exclusively with individual behaviours, motivation, influence, decision-making, and communications within the firm. The firm can surely utilize such expertise, and does not pay the cost of enquiries into its full range of activities or their consequences. In a study of the Canadian arms manufacturing industry, Regehr quotes the President of an export firm: "We wouldn't be around here very long if we held very strong views about what we produce and what it's used for."[32] Canada ranks sixth among the world's exporters of arms.

The effects of a highly specialized organization so compartmentalized that no one is concerned with consequences, and of the incentives that success in such specialization incurs, are evident in many examples. One of the better known, because of its all too obvious and tragic outcomes, is the production of Thalidomide in the late 1950s and early 1960s.

In May of 1961 a baby born to an Australian woman in a clinic which had prescribed the new drug "Distaval" to pregnant women had upper-limb abnormalities and a bowel artresia. Three weeks later a second child with the same malformations was born in the same hospital. By mid-June of that year, with the hospital's rate of malformation in infants running three times that of the national average, the attending doctor at both these births reviewed the cases with utmost care and concluded that the drug was responsible. He immediately contacted the distributors and manufacturers of the pill, wrote an article for the British medical journal, *Lancet*, warning of the dangers, and instituted new laboratory experiments. Simultaneously, other doctors in Germany were arriving at the same conclusions, and were demanding the removal of the drug from the market.[33] Yet Distaval (known as Thalidomide in Canada) continued to be prescribed and sold to pregnant women until November 1961, and even at that date the corporations responsible for its manufacture and distribution withdrew reluctantly and charged their critics with manipulating a press campaign against them.

The doctor who pressed the case in Germany "had the impression that the Grunenthal people [manufacturers of the drug] showed no interest in the facts or arguments that pointed towards thalidomide being the cause of deformities." He said he was threatened with legal action by the company. Grunenthal employed a press agent to advertise the corporation's position, and sent out a memorandum to corporate members regarding their approach to medical doctors which read as follows: "It was decided that all doctors – especially those in a position to influence public opinion – who make critical statements must be persuaded by the strongest possible means to change their minds or at least be neutralized." They pressed for the suppression of a report by a pharmacologist employed by their British distribution firm, Distillers, describing the induction of the same malformations in rabbits which had ingested the drug. They referred to their own laboratory experiments prior to manufacture, experiments which they claimed had shown the drug to be entirely safe as a sleeping pill. According to a team of writers for the *Sunday Times* which investigated the entire case (and had its report suppressed for four years):

One of the mysteries of the affair is that these men reported experimental results which no other experimenter has ever been able to reproduce. Only in their hands were high potency as a sleeping pill and complete absence of toxicity brought together in experimental data."

The Thalidomide tragedy is now well known: at least 8,000 children throughout the world were born deformed as a result of their mothers' ingestion of the drug between the fifth and eighth weeks of pregnancy.

Other chemical companies were involved in the manufacture of napalm for use in Viet Nam, the company best known for its activity being Dow Chemicals. Dow bid on and received the U.S. government contract in 1967 to produce an "enriched" napalm bomb for use in Viet Nam. Napalm, developed at Harvard in 1942 and already used in World War II and in Korea, was known to burn on impact and adhere to skin. Dropped from airplanes, it could land on any civilians or army personnel below, burning them severely or fatally. Again one has to imagine the battery of specialists, armed with prestigious doctoral degrees in chemistry and allied scientific fields and backed by another group of specialists in business management and public relations, pursuing the research and engaging in the manufacturing process that led to a napalm war. The specialists were not concerned with the results, nor was there a specialist whose job it was to investigate such results and report them in grisly detail to the scientists.

When students across the United States began demonstrating against corporate recruiting of scientists for war production jobs, one of their chief targets was Dow Chemicals. Their protests, some of which incurred heavy penalties for the students and faculty involved, prompted the Board of Directors of Dow to consider – apparently for the first time – whether or not its actions were "moral." One board member summed up the result in stirring patriotic words:

If we believe our government is a democratically chosen government – and we do – then we have to support that government when it asks for our help. The really terrible thing for us to do would be to deprive those boys, who have been democratically drafted to go to Vietnam, of the weapons they need. We're not going to do that."[34]

The remainder of Dow's defence was provided by a group of

specialists, the Public Relations Department. This consisted in part of a press kit containing information of Dow's many other (non-war) products, its aid to the nation in its one-shot measles vaccine, and statements from military leaders and doctors regarding the country's need for napalm in Viet Nam.[35]

It is unknown whether the demonstrations had any serious effect on Dow's ability to recruit scientists. Dow recruiters (a group of specialists in that area) were of mixed opinion about this. In any event, they lost the defence contract in 1969.

There is no public record about the reactions of scientists involved in the production of napalm to student demonstrations. Dow reports that none quit their jobs. In the Thalidomide case, likewise, it was not the scientists who presented the company case. In fact, those who are engaged in research and actual production are not required by society publicly to account for their actions. That is what public relations departments are for, and by the terms of their employment public relations officers defend and justify company action whatever that action might be. The same story is true in public corporate organizations, whether they be government departments, universities, hydro and power companies, or publicly owned commercial operations. It is not private ownership as such which creates this decentralized specialization, it is rather the inherent nature of complex organizations of experts. But the inherent nature of such organizations need not obscure the fact that ultimately there are beneficiaries as well as victims. Experts have authority, and from authority derive many of their benefits: what they appear to lack is responsibility for the outcomes of their authoritative acts.

## V

The description of the system as one relying on participation, consultation, and communication rather than overt authority omits yet another critical factor: the obligatoriness of work. In the society of corporate production systems this means, for most people, employment. Robert Merton has phrased it succinctly:

> . . . one must be employed by bureaucracies in order to have access to tools in order to work in order to live. It is in this sense that bureaucratization entails separation of individuals from the instruments of production, as in modern capitalist

enterprise or in state communistic enterprise (of the midcentury variety), just as in the post-feudal army, bureaucratization entailed complete separation from the instruments of destruction. Typically, the worker no longer owns his tools nor the soldier, his weapons.[36]

The fact that people are experts does not imply their independence of bureaucratic organizations. On the contrary, the scientist is dependent on corporate laboratories, whether in private business or universities and government agencies. Expertise in the particular technological environment of the twentieth century is defined by and cannot exist independently of modes of production which no private scientist could possibly "own."

That the conditions are coercive is apparently clear enough to production workers, as evidenced in this statement by a long-time production worker in Detroit:

A lot of times the company has asked me if I want to be a foreman, but I always turn them down. I know I'd have to quit if I did. They'll come down and say, "We want you to do this particular job right away." And I'll say to them, "I can't. These men are tired and they already have enough to do." Then they're going to tell me. "That's not your concern. You just get the job done now." Well, I couldn't take that.[37]

The reality may be less obvious to middle-level experts and administrators, though few of them put into print their personal understandings, and one is not free to quote their private comments - which guardedly suggests they do understand where power lies and what would happen to them if they ignored that fact.

The nature of employment in large corporations, in any case, may ensure that strong-minded individualists likely to buck the system are seldom employed. The Dow Company, in reviewing its losses and gains during recruitment harrassments of the mid-1960s, offered this recruiter's opinion:

. . . Of course we are not looking for, nor would we ever want to hire all of the people in the top five or ten percent of their class even if we could get them. The genius is such an individualistic guy that he just doesn't fit in here. . . . Of sixty Ph.D.'s we hire every year we couldn't stand all geniuses even if we could get them. . . . We don't want too many top guys. The genius stands out as being different and being kooky. . . . So if these are the only ones we are scaring away, the napalm probably doesn't mean very much.[38]

What this might mean for technological innovation is another matter, but what it means for corporate capacities to overcome the limitations of specialization seems to be clear: recruits will not rock the boat. They, no less than production workers, are obliged to earn a wage-income. Nonetheless, experts have some alternatives – not to working within bureaucracies, but to working in this rather than that corporation or university or government laboratory. Their skills provide them with some options, at least as long as there are fewer people with the skills than there are jobs to be filled, and as long as their particular skills remain with the "human" domain and are not computer-programmed out of existence.

The organization which consists of negotiation and coalition is an organization of experts and administrators. It is not the organization of keypunchers, typists, clerks, middle management, assistants to the experts, laboratory technicians, janitors, fieldworkers, or production workers. These workers do not exercise discretion regarding their job contents and pace, and cannot negotiate their terms of reference. They need employment, and their motivation – while it may include many other factors – begins with a need for income. They remain subject to authority, programmed roles, and rules governing behaviour and output.

The version of coalition organizations, then, is a version suitable for the consumption and use of professionals and higher management officials. It is about these people. It is an ideological representation of organization as it appears to, or as some members wish it to appear to, a certain stratum within the organization. It accounts for influence within that stratum. It does not account for the larger organization's continuing authority system, nor the nature of bureaucracy for non-expert production and support workers. For privileged workers the division of labour creates means of achieving private goals and sharing in the security and power of the total organization. Their respect for and dependence on one another's areas of expertise for the performance of their common tasks and for the maintenance of the organization creates for them a social community to which they attach meaning and in which they have identity. A theory of coalition or exchange for such workers may be a useful tool for conceptualizing and investigating these social communities, provided it is situated within and does not ignore the power context of the organization. If one now rereads Weber's comments on the need to embed expertise in the organization, one suspects that he was considerably ahead of those who belatedly discovered the mutual benefit society of corporation executives.

One is reminded of phrases that have been part of every corporate body, from the Roman corporate enterprise through such forms as monastic orders and the church itself to the Hudson's Bay Company. The Catholic Church frequently represented itself as "the corporate union of all believers in Christ," or "the unum corpus," and "corpus Christi." The same phrase is found in all Christian churches: the "sacramental union of all believers in the body of Christ." A current historical account of the church adroitly reminds believers that the "unum corpus" is still in need of an authority system: "As a body the corpus Christi is in need of direction and orientation: although the many constitute this unum corpus, not all have the same functions within it."[39]

The "unum corpus" has its equivalents in "the academic community," and "solidarity forever" or "the union makes us strong." The business corporation relies on references to "one big family," "our company," and "participative management."

For those in middle management and professional ranks, either the mechanistic or the organic form appears to engender loyalty and commitment. Burns suggests that the commitment levels are higher in the organic forms because they include loyalty to the overall system rather than simply to the department of which one is a part. Strauss' study indicates that this may be a rather optimistic generalization, if the expanding corporations in Strauss' study fall within Burns' definition of "organic" systems. Since the two authors do not use the same language and criteria, one cannot properly compare them, although the Strauss observations suggest a fair degree of decentralization, and negotiation between managers at similar levels of authority. Even if the

Strauss data is excluded (and other, similar studies not discussed here in detail), there is no proof that commitment is greater in one organization than in another.

The mechanistic system appears capable of sustaining a high level of commitment to the overall goals of the organization. The German bureaucracy under both Bismarck and his successors apparently sustained the loyalties of its managers regardless of external conditions. The German army, a highly authoritarian system, engendered intense commitment from its middle-ranking officers. The Second World War Japanese army is well known as another example. The British army, under attack and in danger of "losing" Britain in the same war, is yet another example. The notion of a "higher goal" and corporate objectives, combined with a division of labour which provides one with identity and function, appears to sustain faith and effort with or without an *obvious* hierarchy of control.

Nonetheless there are undoubtedly real satisfactions and challenges in an organization which is not immediately experienced as authoritarian. For professionals and managers, the scope for individual initiative is enhanced, not reduced, by a sense of community and the encouragement to share knowledge. This provides immediate prestige, immediate acknowledgment of expertise. This is not new to organizations, it is merely novel in comparison with the mechanistic means of creating loyalty. It has its precedents in the organization of manorial estates, for example, in the thirteenth century. These excerpts from a list of "duties" for various estate personnel – all of whom might be regarded as the equivalent to middle managers and professionals – are remarkably "modern" in their appreciation of expertise and the exercise of discretion:

> The bailiff ought to be loyal and capable of turning the land to good account. He ought to be knowledgeable so that there is no need to send to his lord or to the steward to get advice and instruction on matters concerning his office, unless it were an exceptional case or one involving great risk: that bailiff is worth little in his office who knows little and depends on other men's knowledge. . . .[40]

The organization which engenders such loyalty from its executives is clearly not the same for manual and service workers.

The division of labour in the plant is not designed to enhance the identity or value of specialists or increase interdependence. It is designed solely to increase productivity through minimizing the total skill range of each worker and increasing the machine-like capacities of the total work group. It was this division of labour which Marx condemned and which, throughout the history of industrialism, has been recognized as soul-destroying, alienating, and degrading. Production workers are not expected to be loyal: they are expected to stay at the job only because they are obliged to earn incomes and have no alternative means of doing so. Historically, the means by which large corporate organizations have maintained, if not loyalty, continued acceptance of authority by such workers have been those thrust upon them by the workers themselves. United as a collective bargaining group, unionized workers created an institutional framework within which they might become part of the rule-bound competitive process with somewhat greater access to scarce resources than they would individually possess. A coalition model, in which workers are viewed as autonomous units bargaining for appropriate exchanges, is manifestly inappropriate: the units of the organization from the perspective of workers are not individuals, they are "workers" and "management."

It is for those who are part of management, or who perceive themselves as part of management, that the coalition and organic theories have most appeal. As they are further removed from the direct control of superiors, as their work becomes more integrated into group undertakings, as their departmental activities become more co-operative, they are inclined to suppose that the entire system lacks a head and control mechanism. It is represented to them and they represent it to one another as a political bargaining system in which all groups (or even all individuals) are engaged in negotiation, and yet one in which all members are loyal to the greater good.

What these theories bring to light is how the division of labour for that stratum of workers whose specialized function provides them with some shares in authority and decision-making powers creates *for them* a cohesive and meaningful society within the organizations.

# CHAPTER 7

# OWNERSHIP AND CONTROL

*Every class . . . has a definite function, which it must fulfill according to its whole concept and orientation, and which it actually does discharge as a class and through the class conduct of its members. Moreover, the position of each class in the total national structure, depends, on the one hand, on the significance that is attributed to that function, and, on the other hand, on the degrees to which the class successfully performs the functions. Changes in relative class position are always explained by changes along these two lines, and in no other way. . . .*

– Joseph Schumpeter[1]

*. . . And every class that has once enjoyed an elevated position is greatly aided in seizing on new functions, because the sources and gains of its prior function survive for some time.*

– Joseph Schumpeter[2]

If the labour force is managed, and the managers are managed, then one is obliged to ask: who does the managing? The answer to this is, a class of owners and directors, or those acting on behalf of the interests of a propertied class.

The answer, while true, is incomplete. Some of those acting on behalf of the interests of an owning class are appointed executives, and there are reasonable questions to be asked about their precise relationship to owners. The definition of "ownership" itself is sometimes problematic. There are also different kinds of ownership, or at least different valuable resources to be owned and used in the expansion of corporations, including fixed assets such as plants and factories, and cash currency. It is not always the case that the same groups own both at the same time. In addition, national governments own some fixed assets and cash currency, and the answer does not inform us about the relationship between private investors and public governments.

As well, the answer not infrequently is taken to mean that only class interests are at stake in corporate actions: that the corporation is but an extension of a class of owners and directors. While this is a more realistic interpretation of corporate action than the popular myth that owning class domination is a thing of the past, it ignores the internal momentum of corporations which include, besides executives and boards of directors, many others with vested interests in the on-going system. It is conceptually difficult to recognize a third possibility, that while members of a directing class harness the momentum of corporations and a corporate economy to their own interests, they are constrained ultimately by the nature of the system itself. The nature of the system is to alter the class structure as it proceeds from one phase of capitalism to another, even though the conditions that bring about the subsequent phases are predicated on class actions.

In this chapter we will consider various arguments about the nature of the class structure with respect to corporate ownership, control, and direction in both the United States and Canada.

### I

The first issue is whether there is, in fact, a class of owners. The founding families of commercial firms assumed that the firm and the family were necessarily mutually bound. The firm existed for and was managed by the family: the family's function was to manage and maintain the firm. As the DuPont case illustrated, consolidation of assets and diversification of product lines created a need for more extensive division of authority beyond even an extended family. The solution of the 1920s was to create a broad level of operations management subject to policy direction from a board of directors. The board continued for some time to be either a family affair or the affair of a group of interlocked families sharing policy functions across a range of formerly family firms.

This class of owner-directors expanded with increasing reliance of firms on outside sources of financing for growth. One of the costs of going public, in the sense of distributing shares on the open money markets, was to accept voting members on the board who represented the interests of outside shareholders. Not all outside shareholders were members of the original owning elite. Increasingly, in fact, they were appointed officers of banks and investment houses. In addition, boards contemplating massive expansions which involved expensive technical developments benefited from the presence on their boards of selected professionals in engineering, accounting, law, and occasional scientific fields. While these accretions dilluted the purity of a class of owner-directors, they did not significantly alter the general policy direction of the boards. Bankers, corporate lawyers and accountants, and professional engineers were normally recruited from the same class as the owning elite; they shared its interests.

In the early 1930s, Adolf Berle and Gardiner Means produced a research report which argued that the ultimate stock-owners had by then become so dispersed and numerous that they lacked cohesive decision-making power.[3] As a consequence, effective control of corporations in the United States had become a managerial prerogative. Such managers, Berle and Means argued, did not typically own large blocks of shares themselves, and so were not owners. Thus they represented a "managerial revolution" which would culminate in the elimination of owners as a genuine class.

Berle and Means based their argument on a classification of the top 200 corporations in 1930 by which private ownership meant 80 per cent or more of the voting stock, majority ownership meant 50 to 80 per cent, and minority ownership meant from 20 to 50 per cent. Smaller proportions of stock ownership were considered as incapable of conferring any control. According to their interpretation of stock ownership dispersion for the top 200 corporations, about 34 per cent of all non-financial corporations in 1930 were still under total or majority control of family or other identifiable small-group interests. The degree of control varied by industry: it was greater for industrial concerns (46 per cent) than for railroads (18 per cent) or public utilities (24 per cent).

In the same decade, an agency of the U.S government undertook a similar study, but theirs was based on information available through government access routes rather than *New York Times* and financial publications reports.[4] They took 10 per cent voting stock as a reasonable base for controlling interests in corporations. They argued that nearly two-thirds of the top 200 non-financial corporations were still under family or small-group control. This study was not widely publicized, and the Berle and Means study continued to be the basis of many theoretical works regarding managerial power.[5]

More recent studies provide equally contradictory evidence. Robert Larner studied the top 200 non-financial concerns for the U.S. for 1963, taking as his measure of control associated with ownership of shares to be voting stock in excess of 10 per cent.[6] He concluded that 14 per cent overall, and 18 per cent of the manufacturing and mining companies were family firms. In an expanded study, he found a higher proportion of private ownership: 27 per cent of the top 290 manufacturing and mining firms, 39 per cent of the 33 largest merchandising concerns, 13 per cent of the 45 biggest transportation companies, and 2 per cent of the 120 largest public utilities.[7] Robert Sheehan of *Fortune* magazine found 17 per cent of the top 200 were family firms, using again a 10 per cent measure of control.[8]

What would account for the divergences here might be different interpretations of control, different classifications, and different sources of information. Yet another author, Philip Burch, sharply criticized these studies and produced yet another set of estimates based on his own study of the top 450 corporations and additional groups from the non-industrial classifications.[9] Burch argues that just over 42 per cent of the top 450 non-financial firms were, by the mid-1960s, still under significant family or small-group control. Roughly 41 per cent were under management control, and the remainder, in his estimate, were either "probably family-controlled" or not clearly one or the other. His data come from *Fortune*'s listing of companies, combined with information gathered systematically from all leading financial publications for that period.[10] His data, unlike those of Larner and Sheehan, take into account voting capacities on boards of directors. Family control is, in his estimation, partly a function of ownership and partly a function of directorships. He argues that:

> control of a corporation can be exercised through either inside (i.e. management) or outside representation on a board of

directors, or through owning a very sizable block of stock in the company (other than a mutual concern), and many would contend, even more authoritatively through a combination of these corporate devices.[11]

Among the families identified by Burch are the DuPonts, Rockefellers, Fords, and Watsons. The DuPonts owned 30 per cent of a Securities Corporation which in turn owned 29 per cent of the central DuPont Corporation. Standard Oil of New Jersey (now Exxon) was some 3.6 per cent owned by seven different Rockefeller-controlled foundations. The Ford family controlled 39 per cent of the voting stock in Ford Motors. The Watson family held somewhere between 3 and 6 per cent of the stock in IBM.[12] It will be noted from these percentages that majority ownership is not what is being counted: it is recognizable affiliation with a family in the form of some block of shares, however small. This procedure may be defended. As Canadians are aware from the data presented by both Porter and Clement,[13] companies can be effectively controlled on extremely small holdings provided no other block of shares is commanded by other groups.

More significant than the actual percentages of shares held by identifiable families was the finding that ownership and director-ships continued to overlap in those firms identified as having clear family connnections. For these Burch found that 93 per cent of the industrial firms, 97 per cent of the merchandising firms, and 80 per cent of the banking firms (private ownership of banks being possible in the United States) were actively directed or managed via executive positions by family members.

In addition to these firms in which families hold some block of shares, there still are very large corporations which are entirely family-owned and which do not trade shares publicly. Two ex-amples of complete private ownership in Canada are Eaton's and Canadian Forest Products. Ownership of 80 per cent or more of the shares are held by identifiable families in the United States for such large firms as Cargill Grain, Deering Hughes Aircraft, Bechtel Construction, Mars Candy, and the Ludwig empire which handles the largest oil tanker shipping concern in the world.

Sizable as these private and almost-private companies are,

they are not typical. Most American and Canadian corporations are formally owned by a combination of institutions – other industrial and financial corporations or governments – and private investors. It is this dispersion of stock which led Berle and Means to the conclusion that few family owners still held control. The subsequent studies, and the realization that control can be retained with relatively small holdings, re-introduce the question of how extensive is the control of a class of owning families. If nearly half of the largest American companies are still clearly identified with families and these families continue to be actively involved in the firms' affairs, it would appear at best premature to talk of a managerial revolution. What appears more likely is that between the turn of the century and mid-century, the process of stock-dispersal took place. During that time, a definite change in ownership-directorship patterns occurred, with a larger share of policy functions becoming the property of a supporting segment of, if not the owning, an executive class. While this was in process, it appeared to outsiders as a revolution: compared to the relatively small family-owned firms of the nineteenth century this was a reasonable assessment. The advantages of the dispersal of authority together with shares included extended support for property rights: a somewhat larger number of families had some stake in their preservation. The cost to the original family owners or to those who purchased controlling shares was not depreciation of ownership rights, it was merely the sharing of directorship responsibilities.

The classifications provided by Burch have been applied to 155 dominant United States corporations in 1975 by Wallace Clement. The result: 45 per cent are "probably management controlled," 23 per cent are "possibly family," and 32 per cent are "probably family." Family control was greatest in the manufacturing, resources, and trade sectors.[14]

These figures actually overestimate the extent of management control. Where Burch was unable to identify a definite family in the ownership shares or executive and directing positions, he classified the company as management-controlled. What he failed to do was examine institutional ownership patterns and the control that goes with these. Very few families in North

America are or ever have been financially capable of owning significant numbers of corporate shares. Even if all stockholders were counted as owners, which is not a very sensible means of counting because most stockholders do not own enough shares to have any voting power, the total number is very low. The most significant owners apart from identifiable families are financial institutions which trade on funds invested in the form of insurance. While the investors are frequently people who could not possibly otherwise own shares in corporations, it is the financial companies which control the funds. The small investor or pension-fund contributor only provides money.

The strongest of the financial companies are American banks. Other financial institutions are insurance and mortgage companies, investment companies, and foundations and non-profitable organizations. As reported in Chapter 1, the proportion of shares held by such institutions increases with the size of corporations, and the number of institutional investors controlling substantial proportions of stocks in the larger companies is less than that associated with medium-sized and smaller companies. The 13 major banks in 1973 held 10 per cent or more shares in a total of 30 out of the 100 largest industrials. While the Watson family controls some 5 per cent of IBM, according to Burch, 10 institutions hold 20 per cent and in all, 81 institutions hold just over 43 per cent.[15] Four of the major banks in the United States (First National City, U.S. Trust, Chase Manhattan, and Bank of America) also hold major shares in other banks and financial institutions, so that the concentration is compounded. In addition, there are some industries in which institutional ownership is both concentrated in a few financial organizations and clearly the dominating presence amongst shareholders. This is particularly true of the airlines, where 22 or fewer financial corporations hold between 33 and 56 per cent of outstanding shares.[16] Not all of these shares carry absolute or even divided voting power, and any single share by one financial institution does not usually represent controlling power, but in combination, whether through direct voting power or influence, these ownership and portfolio shares represent considerable stakes in industrial property. Such stakes, held by institutions which by their nature represent the interests of a propertied class (regardless of where the actual funds originate), do not support an argument linking dispersion of stocks to management control.

## II

There is another and somewhat different dimension to the debate on management control. This is concerned with the degree to which a specialized executive class has displaced owners as decision-makers not because stock has been dispersed but because the management of a multinational company requires an expertise beyond that of owning-class monitors. This argument is applicable only to parent companies because, as the next section indicates, subsidiaries are firmly controlled by their owning parents. But with respect to these companies, it is an argument with some evidence in its support.

Top executives in large corporations are selected by boards of directors. Such boards are legally constituted control mechanisms, held accountable under the law for the actions of corporations. Corporations must have boards, and the formal duties of the board are specified in the Corporations Act in Canada and similar legislation in the States and elsewhere. The carrying out of these duties may vary greatly from one corporation to another, but one responsibility is most unlikely to be shirked: the appointment of chief executive officers. It would be an extraordinary act of self-sacrifice for a board deliberately to select a chief officer whose interests and intentions diverged from those of the board. Indeed, the primary concern of boards in selecting officers is with how well they can serve the interests of directors: they do not consider at all candidates who would not do so.

In addition to selecting their representative, boards determine how well to pay that person. The competition for high-calibre executives, who would have to be "stolen" from other corporations if they are that good, is sufficient to guarantee high salaries. According to *Fortune* magazine, the range in 1970 began at $100,000 and soared to over $1 million.[17] In Canada, according to a study by Heidrick and Struggles in 1972, $100,000 was a starting level for top executive salaries in over three-quarters of industrial firms with sales of over $100 million.[18] In addition to high salaries – and for some firms, such as General Motors, these figures are well below executive starting salaries[19] – there are stock ownership plans, bonuses, compensations of many kinds, expense accounts far larger than most wage-earners' total incomes. Contrary to the assumption made in the Berle and Means study, these executives do have considerable property interests in the corporations. Though they may not have been born into the owning class, they grow into the part with stock options. *Fortune* recently reported that 30 per cent of the "top 800" executives in U.S. corporations owned over $1 million of their company's stock; only 10 per cent had no holdings.[20]

Such figures as these suggest the improbability that chief executive officers are independent of property interests or are members of a significantly different class than owning families. It is not their independence, then, which is involved in the argument that they have achieved some measure of control. It is, in a sense, their very existence. They have emerged as a class which, though not original owners of capital in many cases, represents owners and possibly represents them with an expertise they themselves do not possess.

Part of this argument rests on evidence that chief executives have become increasingly important and sometimes even majority members of boards of directors for their own companies, as well as members of boards for affiliated and other companies. One of the studies in this area is by Mabel Newcomer, published in the mid-1950s.[21] Unfortunately Newcomer does not distinguish between family-connected and other firms.

Newcomer examined the composition of boards for 1900, 1929, and 1949-50. She concluded that during that period there was a distinct trend toward boards dominated by "insiders," that is, employed executives of the company. Her data indicate that the proportion of members who were full-time employees increased from 14 per cent in 1900 to 39 per cent in 1949 and to 55 per cent in 1952 in the largest U.S. industrial corporations. Some very large enterprises had no directors who were not full-time employees on salary, including Standard Oil Company of New Jersey, and Bethlehem Steel Corporation. In addition, the proportion of officers on boards increased with the growth-rate of companies. That is, the faster-growing companies were more likely to be those with insider boards. Whether the insider boards brought about faster growth or were consequences of it was not known.

Newcomer noted that bankers and outside lawyers were less numerous in the 1950s than at earlier periods. This reflects the continuing trend toward insider boards: the more positions held by executive officers, the fewer positions there were for outsiders. Of the outsiders, commercial and investment bankers continued to provide about 15 per cent of the total, other businessmen another 15 per cent, insurance company officers and individual investors just under 5 per cent, lawyers 4 per cent and others unspecified between 4 and 5 per cent. There were apparently few scientists, employees without official positions, small businessmen, housekeepers, or academics except for occasional university presidents. There were no labour union representatives, or representatives of unorganized labour.

She also examined the relationship between directorships in one company and directorships in other companies. She found that the proportion of directors who held more than one directorship had declined slightly: from 17 to 13 per cent over the 1900-49 period. Of those who held more than one directorship, somewhat fewer in 1949 held large numbers of these. Some companies, Bethlehem Steel, for example, had prohibited interlocking directorships already (there are now legal limitations on interlocks in the United States). The trend stopped at chief executives. Among presidents and chairmen of large corporations, 62 per cent in 1950 held up to 9 outside directorships, and nearly 11 per cent held 10 or more; the proportion holding no outside positions had decreased to 27 per cent from 44 per cent in 1900. There is no indication in these data how many of these additional positions are on boards of subsidiary companies, how many are related to financial companies, and how many are unrelated to the original company. Representatives of the parent company are normally members of boards for subsidiaries, as the next section on Canadian subsidiaries indicates, and this could account for a large part of the directing activity of presidents and chief executives. Some of the subsidiaries are financial companies owned by parent industrial firms and playing a significant role in the financing of new ventures and extensions of continuing ones. The interlocking directorships of these officers would indicate that they, more than other members of boards, exercised a broad authority over industrial and financial activity.

These data support an argument that chief executive officers have significant controlling functions both in their own corporations and in a range of others, and that they exercise this function not only through their daily activity as salaried officials but as well through membership of boards of directors. In addition, they provide indications that this is a development over the 1900-50 period. They do not support an argument that owners have ceased to be significant in the operations of these firms, or that there is any vital difference in interests between managers and owners. The supporting members of boards continued to be representatives of the financial class.

Whether or not boards include executive members, the argument regarding their growing control of corporations finally rests on their expertise. Ultimately boards have the upper hand in the relationship because they can dismiss executives in whom they have lost trust. This does happen. MacMillan Bloedel, one of Canada's largest indigenous corporations, fired both a president and a chairman over company losses in the bleak year of 1975. Gulf Oil axed several top executives as a consequence of investigations into their political manoeuvres during the mid-1970s, following a suit against Gulf by the American Security and Exchange Commission.[22] There is little doubt that the capacity of boards to dismiss executives is a powerful sanction, but it is an extreme sanction unlikely to be used with the frequency of firings of football coaches. Frequent conflicts between a board and its executive officers would indicate to the outside investment community that the board is unable to control its properties, and would suggest to middle management that loyalty to existing officers is unnecessary. If executives are operating the company along general lines acceptable to the board, the probability is great that the executive's presentation of facts and interpretations of policy will be supported. The advantage the executive has is daily involvement in the operation, combined with both personal expertise and access to the expertise of the total organization.

One executive, interviewed by the financial magazine *Forbes* about his relationship to the board, made these comments:

What do boards do anyway? How many companies do you know that are run by their boards? . . .

I'm familiar with the law [which requires companies to be managed by a board of directors]. . . . But do you mean to tell me that if I work 100 hours a week for 4.3 weeks a month on average, so that I'm working 430 hours a month, some guy is going to come in and in three or four hours outsmart me? I mean that's crazy! No matter how smart you are, if I work 100 times harder than you on a given subject you have no way of catching me. No way.[23]

This executive just happens to be J. Peter Grace, president and chief executive officer of W.R. Grace and Company (chemicals and other products), member of the family which owns majority shares in the company. *Forbes* magazine argues that in spite of these ownership shares, the president, like any executive, came into his post on conditions established by a board. When he entered on a diversification programme, he was saved from being fired by only one vote, which he claims was cast by a non-relative who believed in supporting management whether it was right or wrong.

The case is cited here in *Forbes'* terms because it demonstrates an interesting sleight of hand that is frequently played in this debate. The question of who actually controls the organization is phrased in terms of managers and boards which differ only on specific means of attaining common goals: diversification or no diversification is the issue. Two groups may differ on their views of the profitability of such a programme. What they do not disagree on is the need to be profitable, the need to grow. An executive, whether with or without owning shares, and a board with the same or other property interests have the same objectives. The question is not whether owners and managers have become separated, but whether executives, representing owning interests, have become effective "constitutional monarchs."

If one seriously views them in this light, the boards may be understood as mini-parliaments, rather like those of an earlier, aristocratic age: they only represent one class, and their "loyal oppositions" are likely to diverge from the majority only in particulars and not overall policy objectives. Their function is to advise the king, provide outside contacts and aids where useful, and keep a moderate check on kingly excesses. They occasionally provide financial or technical expertise – in this connection,

Grace dubbed his board "cheap consultants." In sum, their function is to act as "class monitors," ensuring that this company along with others under their class purview performs its appointed tasks satisfactorily.

The main tasks of the chief executive officers are to ensure that financial policies result in the greatest annual profit possible from the viewpoint of the parent company, and to keep the company out of "trouble." Trouble may include the provision of "reasons" for investigations, lawsuits, or the nationalization and confiscation of properties on foreign soil. Creating an annual profit involves transfers of funds from one territory or plant to another, creating and maintaining an internal sales organization between subsidiaries, locating plants in territories with optimum tax regulations or suitable labour supplies, developing new products that can command guaranteed and long-term markets, and selecting the "right" sub-managers for each of the divisions and departments. All of these activities require highly specialized knowledge of accounting, engineering, national markets and politics, marketing techniques, tax laws, and production technology. Grace's observation that board members could not possibly master such intricacies and keep up with internal experts is no doubt valid: the task requires full-time experts.

The trend toward increasing specialization of management is a much more significant development than the dispersal of shares beyond the original owning group. The latter event had the effect only of extending affiliate membership in the owning class to executives and representatives of affiliated institutions. Since simultaneously the move permitted greater concentration of assets in fewer large firms, there was no overall growth in membership: small business owners lost their toehold to salaried corporate managers. But the "professionalization" of management, and particularly of financial management, has the potential of rendering a non-operational owning class unnecessary. The parallel historical development occurred during the sixteenth and seventeenth centuries when some segments of the mercantile elite moved into investments in industrial activity and property and eventually became the dominant class of industrial capitalists. Others, caught up entirely in merchant activities, lost their dominant positions as industry emerged. The emergent new class of industrial owners included those craftsmen who had gained some control over the merchant aspects of their own and other trades, often by combining forces with merchant-industrialists. In short, the precise composition and particular characteristics of the dominant class are susceptible to change as a consequence of changes in the structure of industrial production units.

One might note in this connection that the presence of a separate class of financiers is not essential to the maintenance of industrialism. Industrial corporations in capitalist countries finance their own operations from retained earnings to the extent of approximately three-quarters of all operating income and one-third of expansion funds. These institutions are not dependent on very wealthy families: their source of funds are contributions from small investors, pension-fund participants, and holders of savings accounts. These become an alternative to using taxes for the maintenance of industrial production: in either case it is public capital that is involved. The difference is in where the control rests, rather than in the ultimate source of money. In fact, the ultimate source more and more resembles taxes as corporations seek ever greater proportions of their expansion funding from public governments.

Businesses can obtain credits for exports, insurance against export risks and other loans from the Export-Import Bank in Washington, and financing for initial capital costs, feasibility surveys, and operational costs for extension into "underdeveloped" regions from the Agency for International Development. The International Bank for Reconstruction and Development (the World Bank) will not only provide funds for corporate development by financing governments which co-operate with corporations, but will as well withold such funds from recalcitrant governments, thus ensuring that only the corporate economy is able to grow. Host country governments, such as Canada's federal and provincial governments, eagerly provide extensive funds, sometimes through minority shareholdings as is the case of the Syncrude consortium, or through outright grants, incentive bonuses, favourable tax arrangements, and research funding. They do this because they have no independent options for staying within the corporate market economy.[24]

The possibility of running an industrial society through large organizational units without relying on independent owner-investors is more apparent, perhaps, when we observe that such an event is already occurring. Simultaneous with the rise of multinational corporations in the "free world," is the development of state corporations managed by a corresponding phalanx of experts in Soviet countries. These corporations are financed by taxes together with vast internal resources (profits under other names), and operate on essentially the same principles as those of the United States, Canada, and Europe.

The presence of large institutional investments by banking trust divisions and investment companies and the like may eventually reduce the prerogatives of management in capitalist countries. This could occur if finance companies, because of their own concentration of investments, were to discover themselves "locked-in" to relationships with companies which are in their view improperly managed. At the present time they are more inclined to exercise the option of withdrawing their investments, but where an investment constitutes some 5 to 10 per cent of the total, and where other institutions hold substantial shares of the remainder, the selling of shares becomes a serious problem for the investor. Shares may abruptly nose-dive where one major institution attempts to withdraw, and selling may then involve substantial losses. The alternative in such a situation would be to exercise greater control over the management of a company.

Such a case on record concerns the management of Distillers Company in Britain, in connection with the Thalidomide case discussed earlier in this book. The company took extraordinary measures against public pressure to compensate the victims of their sleeping pills. The litigation on this case lasted for a dozen years, and included a House of Commons' vote urging the company to honour its "moral responsibilities" and the repression of newspaper reports because of Distillers' prolongation of litigation. The largest shareholder of Distillers, with 5 per cent of the stock, was Prudential Assurance. In 1973, this shareholder applied pressure against Distillers for immediate settlement.[25] It should be noted in this instance that 1973 was a very late date for an investor to become concerned: public pressure had finally become sufficiently embarrassing to bring "moral" concerns into consideration of financial dealings. There are few other cases on record.

Much more common is the practice of institutional investors to concern themselves solely with financial management. A case in point of relevance to Canada is the defence by the Bank of Montreal for its investments in South Africa. Responding to public pressures against its continuing financial support for companies which benefit from Apartheid policies, one of the Bank's officials reports that in the "joint opinion" of the Board of Directors "the bank's dealings with that country and its agencies are both legally and morally correct. They feel that our company's policy is consistent in all of the countries in which we operate and that it is free from pretentiousness and hypocrisy."[26]

## III

The question most relevant to Canada is not whether owners of corporations are identifiable families, though it is an interesting exercise to identify the American families who own parent corporations which, through subsidiaries, dominate the economy. It is also possible to identify the Canadians who have controlling shares in Canadian corporations, most of whom also hold shares in American corporations and directorships in both Canadian and American-subsidiary companies in Canada. Peter Newman and Wallace Clement have drawn detailed studies of these.[27]

More crucial is the question of how American corporations exercise their ownership rights in Canada, and this involves consideration of the nature of relationships between both subsidiaries and their parents, and subsidiaries and Canadian financial institutions. It was suggested in the previous section that within the present decade the larger multinationals have developed a measure of independence from outside financiers. Traditionally, American corporations expanding into and within Canada (and other dependent countries) have relied on various forms of financing from host country sources for much of their expansion. In addition, they have used portfolio funds from the international financial community. They have not relied on their parent companies for a great deal of funding. What the parents provided rather was entry into their monopoly markets. The question is, do these companies still rely on host country funds for expansion, and if so, how is the relationship between them and their sources structured? If not, what are the implications for Canada, or more specifically for the Canadian financial class, of the growing independence of American companies?

In order to approach this subject, it is helpful to review some of the findings of contemporary researchers on the class structure in Canada. Wallace Clement, in two studies of the owning and directing class in North America, has argued that this class is manifested in Canada in the form of several fractions with distinctive functions. One of these consists of Canadians with a base in Canadian-owned companies operating mainly in the financial, transportation, and utilities sectors of the economy. This is essentially a service sector, in contrast to manufacturing and resources which are production spheres. The Canadian "fraction"may be further subdivided into those who service an international clientele, sometimes in conjunction with American corporations, and those who service only the Canadian market; and those whose corporate base is a large multinational company, contrasted with those in "middle-range," essentially national companies. Since there are relatively few Canadian-owned companies in the international category, this segment of the class is small. It is, nonetheless, extremely powerful. The larger part of the class consists of American executives representing the interests of American parent companies mainly in the resource and manufacturing spheres of the economy, and of Canadian managers of American subsidiaries. Clement uses the term "comprador" for this segment.

These elites are tied together through a series of ownership arrangements between companies (interlocking ownership) and through shared board directorships (interlocking directors); in addition they are related literally through marriage and extensive kinship networks, common backgrounds and schooling experiences, and various social ties. They are not, however, linked together in a random or shared pattern. There is a noticeable difference between the links for directors of American subsidiaries with Canadian banks, and Canadian companies and these banks.

First, a general description of the interlocking directorships between banks and other dominant corporations: Clement found that there is a high degree of overlap within the financial sector itself, to begin with. While one may not legally hold directorships in more than one bank, there is no restriction on the number of directorships open to bank directors for insurance, investment, mortgage and trust companies or on the number of directorships open to insurance company directors on bank and other financial company boards. Such investment and insurance corporations as Sun Life, Power, and Argus are strongly represented on the boards of banks and other financial companies as well as on the boards of utilities, manufacturing, resources, and trade corporations. The corporations with the highest number of interlocks overall are the Canadian Imperial Bank of Commerce (which had 90 interlocks), the Bank of Montreal (with 73), the Royal Bank (with 63), Canadian Pacific Limited (with 61), and Sun Life (with 60). All are Canadian-controlled, and all have a long history of financial control in Canadian corporations.[28]

In addition, Clement analysed the interlocks between the dominant corporations and other prominent but not dominant corporations. Some of these companies were among the dominant corporations identified twenty years earlier by John Porter,[29] and it could be assumed that their earlier dominance was still reflected in their operations. Others were middle-range corporations which have not been among the top 100 or 200, but are nonetheless very large. Some were subsidiaries of either dominant Canadian or American corporations. Clement identified 175 of these, and found that 40.6 per cent of their directorships were held by persons with directorships in the 113 dominant corporations.[30]

A further analysis revealed the phenomenon of multiple directorships for Canadians in the dominant corporations, and particularly for bank directors. Porter had discovered in 1951 that 203 individuals held between them 600 or 46 per cent of all dominant directorships.[31] Clement discovered that the pattern identified by Porter still prevailed in 1972, and that the number of multiple directorships had actually increased to 54 per cent.[32]

Michael Ornstein examined the boards of directors for a somewhat larger number of dominant corporations (248) and came to essentially the same results. The interlocks were most frequent between Canadian firms in banking and other financial companies, in transportation, communications, and other utilities, and least frequent in manufacturing, agriculture, and light industries and construction. The average number of interlocks between banks and other sectors was 53.9; between all financial companies and other sectors, 24.1; between utilities and other corporations, 19.2. The average for manufacturing corporations was 7.0, for construction, 4.8, and for agriculture and light industries, 8.4.[33]

If this were the full extent of the data, one would conclude simply that a financial elite controls other sectors of Canadian industry through its multiple directorships on their boards of directors. However, the pattern is more complex than that. A financial elite does hold an extraordinarily large number of directorships on the boards of other corporations, but its representation on the boards of American subsidiaries is considerably less dense than that on the boards of Canadian companies. Clement's data on corporate interlocks by country of control indicates that (a) Canadian financial corporations interlock extensively with all other corporations which are Canadian-owned; but (b) American-owned corporations in Canada have relatively few interlocks, fewer than the United Kingdom, for example, and far fewer than Canadian corporations. In further detailing this data, Clement notes that altogether there are seventeen out of fifty-eight Canadian firms with fewer than ten interlocking directorships, and nine are family firms. More than half of the U.S. corporations have fewer than five interlocks.[34]

Ornstein too found American firms to have fewer interlocks. He found an average of seven interlocks for American firms compared to an average of 19.6 for Canadian firms. Congruent with Newcomer's findings for the United States, he discovered a curvilinear relation between sales index and interlocks. The smaller firms (in terms of sales) and the very large firms had fewer interlocks than those in-between. Ornstein identified the three largest auto makers (all American-owned) and Massey-Ferguson, two firms in the food industry, and several distilleries and merchandising firms, Imperial Oil, Alcan Aluminum, International Utilities, and Bell Canada as corporations with small boards and few interlocks.[35]

In addition, Ornstein found that the size of boards differed by nationality of firms or parent firms if these were subsidiaries. Canadian company boards averaged 14.7 members. American subsidiaries averaged 10.1 members, British 12.0, and other foreign, 12.3. He found as well that only in the financial sector were there corporate boards numbering 25 members or more. The average size of boards for banks was 36.0, for other financial institutions, 18.8. The sample included 8 banks and 22 other financial corporations. The average size of boards in manufacturing firms was 9.5 members. In construction, wood and paper, transportation, communications, and utilities, boards averaged between 12 and 13 members.[36]

Since we know from Clement's data and many other studies of the Canadian economy that the Canadian-owned companies are mainly in the finance, transportation, communications, and other utilities sectors, this finding may be interpreted as indicating that Canadian-owned companies have much larger boards than do American-owned subsidiaries.

Not only are American subsidiaries endowed with smaller boards, their boards more frequently consist of a high proportion of "insiders," that is, executives of the subsidiary corporation. Overall, Ornstein found an average of 3 in 10 board members to be insiders, with 17 per cent of the firms having boards consisting of at least one-half executives, another 24 per cent having between one-third and one-half, and 44 per cent having between a fifth and a third. Only 15 per cent had less than 10 per cent insiders. Broken down by nation, 36 per cent of board members in American corporations were insiders compared to 26 per cent in the Canadian-controlled firms.

The differences again emerged by industry. The proportion of insiders was greatest in manufacturing, smallest in finance and utilities. Since there is a relationship between sales and industry, and also between industry and nationality, the final finding in this connection is not surprising: the 12 largest corporations in terms of sales had the largest proportion of insiders on their boards of directors.[37]

In a smaller-scale study of 28 manufacturing enterprises in southwestern Ontario which had Canadian head offices in that region, Terrance White discovered a pattern supportive of the Ornstein and Clement data. He was investigating the degree to which boards of directors were perceived by chief executive officers to have strong influence on company operations. He discovered that there were significant differences in board functions reported by companies which were subsidiaries and those which were entirely independent and self-contained. Out of 16 companies which were subsidiaries, White found 12 which said their boards were legal necessities only and had no influence on company operations. This may be compared to 3 out of 12 parent or independent firms which indicated a similar lack of influence for their boards. The differences were positively related to country of ownership. Ten out of 14 non-Canadian firms indicated that the board had no influence, compared to 5 out of 14 Canadian companies. Furthermore, firms with all insiders on their boards, which we find from the Ornstein data as well as White's to be predominantly American, were more frequently among those reporting no board influence. Fourteen out of 18 of all-insider companies compared to 2 out of 10 companies with mixed boards indicated that their boards had no influence.[38]

When all of these data are considered together, they lead to the conclusion that Canadian banks have extensive control over Canadian companies via interlocked directorships on boards that actually exercise influence on company affairs, but that American subsidiaries, with smaller and more insider-dominated boards, provide fewer opportunities for Canadian financial control. This of course does not indicate that Canadian banks and other financial companies have little financial influence over American subsidiaries, but influence and control are different dimensions. Only the latter is a significant weapon; the former depends on whether the subsidiaries expect more benefits from co-operation and voluntary affiliation than from independence.

Canadian banks are represented so heavily on the boards of Canadian companies in large part because their financial aid is essential. As partners and loan-givers the price they exact for aid is a share of directorships with clout. The question raised by their absence on many boards and low representation on others of American subsidiaries is this: do these companies have no need of Canadian financial aid?

The relationship between these parent-controlled companies and the Canadian financial institutions may become clearer if we look at the reverse situation: the number of American subsidiary directorships on the boards of Canadian banks, together with the number of Canadian companies so represented which have extensive relationships of co-ownership with American companies. Here we discover substantial representation. Indeed, it appears to be by way of accommodating these representatives that bank boards have grown to such extraordinary sizes.

Suppose we take as a generalization something along the lines of the following: American corporations in Canada are controlled by their parent corporations. Consequently they have small boards which have few functions, and a large proportion of the board members are executives. Another segment would consist of representatives from the parent corporation or other shareholding corporations. They have relatively little need for, and thus low representation from, Canadian financial or other corporate sectors. Canadian banks and financial institutions, by contrast, depend for their profits on financial investments in low-risk, high-return industries: such industries include the utilities and Canadian resource and manufacturing corporations, but more particularly include the enormous multinationals. From the beginning, they have held strong investment interests in Canadian firms, especially medium-sized firms, and thus populate their boards of directors in order to protect investments. But they have no such "legitimate" claim to American corporations and to a few Canadian giants. As the need for their services declines, their representation also declines. The only way they can attract "business" from the multinationals is to bring the directors of those corporations onto the boards of the financial institutions. In other words, the dependency is in the opposite direction to that between financial institutions and smaller Canadian-owned corporations.

The boards of all the major banks consist of representatives from the top 100 corporations. The Royal Bank, largest in Canada, includes members from Abitibi Paper, Algoma Steel, Asbestos Corporation, Canadian Pacific, B.C. Forest Products, Imperial Oil, Imasco, and Noranda. The Canadian Imperial Bank of Commerce includes representatives from Bell Canada, B.C. Telephone, Canada Cement Lafarge, Canada Packers, Crown Zellerbach, Domtar, Falconbridge Nickel, Hollinger Mines, MacMillan Bloedel, Massey-Ferguson, Noranda, Simpsons-Sears, and Trans-Canada Pipelines. The Bank of Montreal includes representatives from Alcan, B.C. Sugar Refinery, Bell Canada, Brinco, Canada Cement Lafarge, Canadian Forest Products, Canadian Pacific, T. Eaton, Seagram, International Nickel, Molson's, Rothmans, and the Steel Company of Canada. In addition, other financial corporations, Power, Argus, Brascan, the insurance companies, are well represented. Indeed, each is many-times represented, through the main holding company and then through subsidiaries. Majority representation, as this list suggests, is with Canadian companies which have a stake in the "international" market, but American firms whose main international market is Canada are still strong voices.[39]

That the reverse relationship is well understood by the participants is evident in the comments collected by Newman. The chairman of Home Oil told Newman: "Almost the sole purpose of appointing directors to banks is that they bring and retain business."[40] A former manager of the Royal Bank put it this way:

> Our directors are of considerable help to management. The product of banking is the same, so it's the personal contact that counts. If we hear of corporate business coming up, we'll look at the names of the company's directors and try to get at them through our own board and their connections. If we heard a big deal was coming up in the West, we wouldn't hesitate a minute to call up one of our Prairie directors to see if he could get us some of the action.[41]

In short, the banks provide a service to directors and thus to the companies they head. The directors' first and continuing connections are to the corporations which give them "real" economic power: the industrials operating in an international money as well as supply and distribution market.

Although Canadian banks do not exercise control over foreign companies (indeed they depend on these companies for their own continued dominance in the Canadian economy, in the Caribbean, where they maintain branches, and elsewhere such as in South Africa, where they invest in American industrial expansion), foreign corporations still use them for expansion funds. Over the post-war period a larger share of foreign company expansion funds and operating costs have come from Canadian than from foreign (parent) sources.

Foreign sources provided 22 per cent of total financing over the period 1946-67; the remainder in one form or another came from Canada.[42]

However, the various forms in which Canadian funds are generated makes a difference. The major source is retained earnings of subsidiaries. Of all *expansion* funds for foreign-controlled enterprises, retained earnings accounted for 30.7 per cent in the 1946-60 period, 37.6 per cent in the 1960-67 period. Canadian capital represented 19.4 per cent of expansion funds in the 1946-60 period, 21.3 per cent in the 1960-67 period.[43] In terms of *total financing*, foreign corporations in the asset category of $5 million or more generated 65 per cent of their funds from internal sources. Canadian corporations in the same asset category generated 67 per cent from the same sources.[44] Of the remainder, foreign-controlled firms are less dependent on long-term borrowings than Canadian firms. They borrowed 23 per cent of their total funds from external sources, compared to 28 per cent by Canadian corporations. They made up the difference by borrowing from affiliated companies. This kind of borrowing represents a transfer of funds for short-term purposes between subsidiaries of the same parent firm: a practice considerably less accessible to Canadian companies.

The difference between the two types of companies is also apparent in terms of their application of funds. Foreign corporations paid out 16 per cent of their earnings in dividends, compared to 13 per cent for Canadian corporations. They also paid out 9 per cent to affiliated companies, thus transferring their own funds for the use of sister-firms elsewhere. Only one per cent of Canadian-controlled companies' funds were applied to affiliates. There are also differences in the applications of funds for industrial purposes: foreign-owned firms spent less on the acquisition of land and depreciable assets such as buildings and equipment (51 per cent as compared to 60 per cent), and more on depletable assets in the resource sectors (10 per cent compared to 2 per cent). This reflects the different industrial concentrations for the two groups: the foreign firms in resource industries, the Canadian firms in finance and utilities. It may also represent a difference in the costs of equipment for companies in the same sectors: American equipment moving to a subsidiary firm in Canada will cost the subsidiary less than the same equipment moving to a competitive Canadian firm. This differential in costs for technology is a long-standing function of the differentials in control within the manufacturing sector.

Overall, large corporations of either foreign or Canadian origin generate some two-thirds of their funds through internal sources. In addition, foreign corporations generate funds through their affiliates, and also lend funds to affiliates. They remit higher profits via dividends to parent companies, thus ensuring the continuing dominance of the parents, and the continuing ability of such parents to finance expansion from within.

These figures for 1972 represent the capacity of multinationals to finance a very large share of their operations and expansion from retained earnings and cash-transfers, but they do not prove that the corporations have ceased to be dependent on host-country sources for expansion funds. They still obtain up to a quarter of such funds from Canadian financial sources. The same case is true elsewhere. The survey conducted by Brooke and Remmers indicated that foreign firms in Europe generated their income in the same ways: for the American-owned companies, about three-quarters of total financial resources came from internal cash flows.[45] What this would seem to indicate is that the companies are capable of sustaining themselves in the normal course of operation, but continue to use host-country financial sources for expansion.[46]

Whether they need to use such funds is debatable. As long as the funds are available and offered at attractive rates without ownership claims, they will certainly continue to use them. Borrowing is often cheaper than sinking internal cash funds into fixed assets on foreign territory. But as their growth and world integration proceed, their dependence on these funds should decrease. Moreover, as their power to make strategic decisions in head offices about the world economy, and with that, the Canadian economy, continues to increase, their alternative source of funds for expansion is not so much the Canadian financial community as the Canadian State. As the Tar Sands episode indicates, governments in dependent countries where they are unable or unwilling to resist the blackmail of monopoly-market control of their resources find themselves in the position of moneylenders. In order to stay in the capitalist economy, they provide the funds for U.S. corporate expansion.

# CONCLUSION

*At periods when Free Enterprise may not provide*
  *employment*
*We dread the thought of hungry men – it lessens*
  *our enjoyment;*
*The government must then step in, with this*
  *consideration:*
*That any public works proposed do not increase*
  *taxation.*
*Depressions, after all, my friends, much as we may*
  *deplore them,*
*Are acts of God; who ever heard of blaming*
  *business for them?*

  *CHORUS:*
*Then hail we now Free Enterprise,*
  *Extol and give it praise!*
*Of course, when profits shrink in size,*
*To lay men off is only wise;*
*We dearly love Free Enterprise –*
  *But only when it pays.*

> – "Hymn to the Glory
> of Free Enterprise,"
> J.D. Ketchum, 1944[1]

The arguments throughout this essay, and the empirical data and case studies cited, have been concerned with the Canadian economy as a segment of expanding American capitalism carried by growing multinational corporations. These arguments are that:

1. Monopoly is a characteristic form of capitalism: competition is characteristic only of the labour market.

2. Market control is more critical to national independence than possession of industrial resources.

3. National and regional governments in Canada are con-

256

strained in their exercise of political power by their limited economic power relative to multinational corporations.

4. Such governments, however, have not attempted to move beyond apparent constraints and have, historically, performed functions supportive of the growth of both highly concentrated economic power and foreign ownership of Canadian industry.

5. Multinational corporations do not operate in the interests of the world or national society, but in their own interests. These are not coincident.

6. Multinational corporations are becoming more, not less, centralized in decision-making power.

7. Technology is harnessed by multinational corporations and directed to their ends by virtue of their capacities to purchase knowledge rather than because of their technical advantages.

8. A continuing effort by multinational corporations is directed toward reduction or elimination of dependence on labour for production; there is no compensating effort directed toward alternative means by which workers may benefit from production increases. Workers continue to be managed and manipulated by essentially coercive organizations.

9. Management workers are co-opted by appearances of participative democracy in the office as well as by high incomes, prestige, and shares in authority at the plant level. Current theories of organizational behaviour contribute to an ideology which omits reference to the authority structure and economic realities of large corporations. They also contribute to organizational failures to shoulder responsibility for the social consequences of corporate behaviour.

10. Corporate capitalism is directed by an owning and policy-making class. In Canada this class is divided into a foreign segment directing subsidiaries of multinational corporations, and a national elite connected mainly to the financial and utilities sectors.

All of these arguments pertain to the situation of a dependent nation within an expansionary phase of capitalism. What is the situation for the same dependent nation when the economy loses its expansionary momentum?

It is appropriate to consider that situation, because there is every indication that American capitalism has moved into a non-expansionary phase, especially with respect to the established industrial countries and Canada (which, as we have noted, is neither an established industrial country nor an underdeveloped one in the more usual senses of that term). In spite of their extensive efforts to eliminate risks through mergers, monopoly of markets, manipulation of governments, containment of technology, systematic management and rationalization of production processes, and control of capital, large industrial corporations exist in an unstable environment in the 1970s. They have not encountered such a situation since the 1930s. The actions of both corporations and governments during the depression together with indications of responses by both powers in the past few years are subject to study in this final chapter because they add another and crucial dimension to our understanding of the corporate economy.

I

Consider first why the environment is unstable. In large part it is because corporations have been so successful in eliminating competitive risks. They face glutted markets in the "developed" countries, brought about by overproduction of consumer goods. These coincide with declining numbers of new consumers in the age group born after the 1950 s, although the "baby-boom" postwar generation continues to require new products. However, high unemployment rates in the "baby-boom" post-war group reduce its purchasing power. Such unemployment is at least partly due to technological developments which have successfully reduced the need for labour, though how much of this unemployment is due to such developments cannot be assessed (and from the point of view of the corporations this is a fortunate incapacity in our technical skills). It cannot be assessed because so much of it is in "contingent" areas, where jobs are eliminated on the fringes of technological development rather than at the centre of corporate production.

Coincident with unemployment is a rising rate of inflation, due in large part to the effects of monopoly control over world markets by resource and manufacturing companies, and their capacity to transfer profits around the world. Inflation is engendered as well by the costs of technological development, passed on to consumers, of whom governments become ever more prominent, and by the costs of maintaining the vast service functions of government in the form of schools, welfare programmes, judicial systems, medical systems, roads, railways, pipelines, air transportation systems, trade commissions abroad, export service agencies, immigration controls, income tax departments, and so forth. Much more obvious to the general population, but not more significant as a cause of inflation, are the wage demands of that small proportion of workers who are unionized and employed in the corporate bodies of both private and public corporations.

Restriction on supplies of currently necessary fuels, particularly oil, is another factor contributing to insecurity. This, as we have seen, is overrated as a problem, in part because it can so easily be blamed on Third World countries which have begun to resist the continued exploitation of their resources. The discovery that the central capitalist countries are not self-sustaining in oil, that other countries can restrict oil supplies or offer them at much higher prices, and that further oil resource extraction will be more costly than in the past (though apparently not from Canada) is what is implied in the "crisis" over oil. Oil has always been depletable: the difference between our view of it in the 1970s and in the 1950s is that it is now a social issue rather than simply a technical one.

Added to these conditions is the "problem" of technological development. Each major change in technology involves for corporate participants an investment in plant and equipment and further investment in the training of a specialized labour force which ties up their capital. Such fixed assets make sense only if there is reason to suppose that no further technological development will render these plants and specialties obsolete before their production has "paid off." If such plants fail to generate immediate profits, and particularly if they continue to fail in this objective over any period of time, they create a serious problem for a company even where it has very high "book value" assets, because these assets cannot be transformed into fluid cash. In the normal course of an expanding economy, such as that of North America over the better part of the past century – except for the decade prior to the large-scale war of the 1940s – investment in industrial plants pays off handsomely. But in an economy that fails to expand, such investments are capable of turning corporations (and the labour force dependent on them, as the INCO case illustrates) into casualties. The corporation can withdraw to safer investments, losing fixed assets in the process; the labour force, of course, loses everything.

In the present environment, there is every reason to suppose that investment in existing technology would be risky. The incentive to "discover" new energy sources is very great, and any such development would affect the way in which industry is organized. Plants dependent on an existing fuel source and on markets dependent on that fuel source would encounter, for a time, genuine competition from plants built on the basis of any new technology in energy supplies.

These industries look to public sources of funds for retooling of antiquated plants, using threats of withdrawal and claims that they can no longer be "competitive" if not supported. As this is being written an executive of the privately owned Canadian Forest Products (which in turn owns Cornet Industries and its many subsidiaries) has informed the press that the forestry industry in British Columbia will be unable to expand without government aid in retooling existing industries.[2] This industry is in trouble on many fronts from excessive capacity in Canada, out-classed technology in many of its mills, and declining world markets for construction wood and newsprint. Private owners of capital choose not to sink further funds in it, turning its accumulated profits instead to more lucrative ends. Thus it becomes a "government responsibility" in a province with a third of the labour force dependent on it. In manufacturing industries, and particularly those associated with defence industries, public funding is a commonplace means of "overcoming" the costs of technological development. And in 1978, the Royal Commission on Corporate Concentration, headed by business representatives, has recommended that public funding in the form of less onerous tax laws be advanced to highly concentrated businesses. Their rationale for this is that it would increase the accumulation of savings for investment – and as we have noted, this is one of the primary functions of democratic governments. Yet at the same time, as we have also noted, a large portion of accumulated savings by private corporations is delivered to foreign corporations, because such investments are less risky than investments in Canadian development.

Meanwhile U.S. corporations seek both new markets and new production territories where they will have lower tax loads, lower labour costs, or less vociferous nationalist protests. Latin American, Asian, and African countries become strategically important, and for that reason, also become battlegrounds between the corporate extensions of both the East and West industrial societies. The viability of the West's corporate extensions into Eastern Europe appears to rest with the outcomes of these variously cold and hot battles. War, as one means of overcoming depression, is a possibility. For the moment, the alternative is new markets in the Soviet sphere, based on stable labour supplies and guaranteed, if less than astronomical, investment returns. If these corporations are experiencing obstacles to expansion in Canada, and are saddled with Canadian labour costs and instability into the bargain, they need little more incentive to withdraw from this country and re-establish themselves on more stable territory. The cold war comes full circle.

Putting all these factors together, we might expect the Canadian economy (together with that of most industrial nations, though the process would be uneven) to lose its expansionary momentum. In fact, this is already occurring, and the closures of some operations by companies such as INCO and prolonged lay-offs in manufacturing as well as resource industries attest to it.

The most obvious consequence is a reduction in employment. Direct employees of withdrawing corporations are disemployed, but no alternative employment is available as a substitute. Employees of service companies and the owners of these are also disemployed. As they move out of regions without industry, the entire region suffers increasing unemployment. This process particularly affects the young who are entering the labour force for the first time and who are already affected by technological changes which reduce employment opportunities. It also affects particularly those whose skills are least essential to corporate activity and whose marketability is low even in good times. But finally it affects many others. It affects unskilled workers whose competitive cohort is increased by entrants who would, in more affluent times, compete in other markets. It affects managerial workers and technical specialists whose competitive marketability is reduced, no longer enhanced, by their specialization. It affects a large portion of the middle class for whom, in an expanding economy, there were always new positions opening up in middle management, professional, technical, and clerical work; their mobility, like that of labourers, is restricted. Unlike labourers, they cherish expectations unattainable within those restrictions. Class barriers to upward mobility are suddenly apparent.

Another consequence is an increase in, but also a shift in the location of, regional disparities. In a non-expanding economy, parent corporations would be acting in their interests by withdrawing from hinterland operations and concentrating economic activity in home plants. They would do this particularly in manufacturing industries where relatively little is to be gained from production in subsidiaries which have neither independent markets nor cheaper labour costs. In the resource industries, a somewhat different situation pertains: in order to maintain the home industries, foreign resources remain essential. With home resources running low or still higher priced than Canadian resources, the United States has considerable incentive to reduce all risks of resource depletion from Canada. "Continentalism" is the name of the policy of risk-reduction: it means full integration of Canadian resources into the American economy through full ownership and/or controlling rights of both resources and transmission lines. The policy is backed up by the sovereign authority of the U.S. government, through an integrated military force and an integrated defence production industry. Those regions containing valuable resources – Alberta and Northern Canada – become new centres of economic activity. While ultimately their local elites lose control of their region, in the short run they gain a great deal of private wealth, a vigorous bargaining position vis-à-vis their traditional rulers in Central Canada, and a realignment in their favour of the national balance of power.

These consequences exert pressure on a federal government to remedy the situation, and they do this because the population at large has been taught to think of the state, rather than of the corporations, as the agency with ultimate power to change society or its economy. Yet the state has neither the power nor the financial resources to remedy the situation. A dependent state, such as that in Canada, cannot control the causes of inflation, unemployment, or technological insecurity. It is called upon to do more at a time when it can only do less for its citizens, and this gulf between demands and capacities creates doubts about the legitimacy of the state's claims to represent the collective interest. Like the French monarchy in the eighteenth century, the national government holds political office but no real economic power. Since its utility to those who do hold economic power rests with its legitimating function, it is obliged to seek alternative means to maintain its political sovereignty.

## II

In an expanding economy, growing corporations demand less government interference in their internal affairs. This has never meant less financial support, less use of force in times of unrest or labour strife, or less public involvement in the development of an infrastructure for industry. But it has meant less restriction on appetites for profit, less social welfare legislation unless this is perceived as necessary to the legitimation of government, and fewer trade restrictions except where trade restrictions are seen as beneficial by that dominant class fragment which is strongest.

In a non-expanding or contracting economy, the government is called upon to interfere more forcefully, and to interfere in a way that will "restore balance to the economy," or "restrain inflationary pressures," or "maintain Canada's competitive position in world markets." What these phrases mean when translated into concrete action which national or provincial governments could actually take, appears to be the financial support on a greater scale of established industry, the curbing of wage increases, reduction of corporate taxes, and a redesign of the welfare system so that more workers will have employment of some kind while the overall cost of maintaining them may be reduced.

In particular, it is valuable to consider the contradictions of wage controls. These were implemented together with price controls, but, as was obvious beforehand and eventually acknowledged by government spokesmen, it was not possible to exert price controls in an economy dominated by foreign subsidiaries. Since a large part of international trade in Canada consists of sales between subsidiaries and their parent companies, price controls could be ignored through arbitrary repricing of internally exchanged goods and services. Imported goods, in any case, could not be subjected to controls. In effect, then, wage and price controls became simply wage controls. The question is, why was government expected to legislate on wages? Wages in a "free enterprise" market system are supposed to be subject to market controls, and corporations have been zealous in their defence of market controls for all other aspects of their operations. Clearly when the interests of the corporations involved an unpopular measure, the responsibility was shifted to government. Even more interesting than corporate shifting of responsibility is the acceptance of this by the population. Though anger was sufficient to mount a one-day general strike against wage controls, the anger was not directed at the shift in responsibility from the wage payers to government. There was a widespread acceptance of the "right" of government to enact legislation pertaining to wages, and the question asked publicly was rather whether the government was acting wisely. It would appear that the ideology of the independent and sovereign government remains strongly fixed in Canadian thinking, even when large groups within the population disagree with government actions.

In order to carry out such actions, the state maintains a continuing effort to legitimate not only its own legislation but as well other features of the structure of power. The "free enterprise" ideology was particularly viable between the late 1940s and the late 1960s. During the depression of the 1930s, however, and again in the second half of the present decade, one hears a redefinition of the status quo. It is a redefinition which legitimates wage controls, public financing for private enterprise, state "interference" in the economy, and the existence of (though laundered for moral imperfections) giant corporations. Consider this remark from a Trudeau speech, widely quoted, of 1976: "The fact is that for over a hundred years, since the government stimulated the building of the Canadian Pacific Railway by giving it Crown land, we have not had a free market economy in Canada."[4] He continued with his redefinition of the Canadian situation, making these arguments:

1. We have a "mixed economy – a mixture of private enterprise and public enterprise." This mixture is responsible for "the prosperity we have enjoyed."

2. Private enterprise is divided into two sectors. One of these is monopolistic, and the other, competitive. The monopolistic sector does not depend on consumer choice. It depends on cornering a market. It has deprived consumers of a meaningful choice, and in some instances, has undermined the choice of consumers through "fraudulent advertising." It also consists of unions "which achieve monopoly control over the price of labour." The competitive sector consists of small businesses which are associated with "self-reliant men and women" and with identifiable communities.

3. Government intervention has always been a feature of the economy. Government has intervened as business partner, business financier, regulatory agency, and as provider of services to the public.

4. The most serious problem facing the country is inflation.

5. In addition, there are limited reserves of oil and gas. As Canadian reserves dwindle, dependence on foreign suppliers will increase.

6. As well, there are problems of pollution which are expensive not only in dollars but as well in human health and environmental damage.

7. And finally, conflicts between labour and management in industry are causing an enormous loss of productivity.

This is not the liberal version of society throughout the post-war era. It recognizes, as post-war liberal spokesmen have not done, that society consists of large corporate entities as well as individuals; that these entities have interests, and such interests are not necessarily coincident with the population's interests, and that government has always been involved as a partner with these large entities.

On the basis of this version of Canadian society, Trudeau proposed solutions which include:

1. More government intervention at all levels except with respect to the competitive sector; intervention to include "encouragement" for a reduction in industrial consumption of

energy, which might include "producing longer-lasting consumer goods, so that we will use less energy and materials to replace or repair the things we buy." It would also include greater power to impose pollution controls.

2. More control over monopolies (both industry and unions) "to ensure that their power is used in the public interest and is directed toward the achievement of national goals."

3. Possibly a tripartite system of continuing consultation between corporations, labour, and government. This suggestion is not made explicit in the speech quoted above, but became part of the Trudeau proposals in ensuing debates.

While the protestations throughout this speech are many and eloquent, it is apparent that these solutions could be achieved only with considerably more "state control." But what does more "state control" mean, if the state has, all along, been one of the major players in the game? In fact, if one studies the BNA Act and constitutional amendments, one is struck by the fact that constitutionally, the Canadian government has an enviable degree of power. If there are monopolies which cause problems of inflation, unemployment, pollution, energy waste, and other events contrary to the public interest, these have developed behind the shield of the same government which now regards them as problems. It is not, then, a constitutional change which Trudeau seeks in his call for greater control by the state.

The answer is buried in yet another statement in the speech: "Every reasonable person now recognizes the duty of the federal government to manage the country's economy in the interests of all its people and all its regions."

The federal government, traditionally representing the interests of a central Canadian financial class combined with a continentalist class based in United States, was asserting its dominance over regional governments and regional financiers and at the same time preparing the way for the co-optation of labour in a tripartite power structure. It was providing the initial stages of legitimation for a redefinition (though not a restructuring) of the existing power arrangements, and in so doing was preparing the population for a period in which high expectations of mobility for the middle class, corporate acceptance of wage demands by labourers, and the general affluence that attends growth would not be appropriate.

A widespread belief in free enterprise and all that that implies – no government intervention, open markets, competition, bargaining, individual freedom, upward mobility, apparent social change – is an impediment to control where no structural equivalents are available. Expectations of better jobs for each generation, ever-higher wages, a steadily increasing standard of material wealth – these are incongruous with the demand that wages be frozen, with increasing levels of unemployment, and with an open alliance between government, multinational business, and international labour unions. A government which has successfully induced the population to believe that CPR and Imperial Oil are components of a free-enterprise economy is faced with the task of "de-programming." Free enterprise must "cease to exist" and the most persuasive element in the official turnabout is the argument that, after all, it never existed in the first place.

The central focus of liberalism as ideology has been the individual: individual happiness, individual consumer choice, individual mobility. These have displaced a focus on the growth of corporate organizations, and placed the burden of personal success in life on the private person. Those who established the rules were not identified as a ruling class; their central organizations were not perceived as ruling institutions. Government was viewed as a mediator, and society as a pluralistic arrangement.

Two alternatives to this at both an ideological and structural level are focused on collectivities. One of these is socialism, which at an ideological level proposes the establishment of a society in which the needs of society-at-large take precedence over individuals but with continual participation in decision-making by all individuals. As a utopian solution, socialism has been perceived in the "free world" as a Marxist programme. In fact, Marx had a great deal more to say about the evils of capitalism than about the means of transcending it. In any event, this almost Rousseauian proposal has been approached in practice in China, Cuba, and, with so far less startling results, elsewhere. It has involved repression and destruction of property owners and strong dissidents. This may be viewed as the other side of the same coin represented during the industrial revolution (since all of these societies are still undergoing initial phases of industrialism), where the repression and destruction was of peasants, workers, and dissidents of the "left." Since this type of society has nowhere been attempted in fully industrial situations, one can go no further in assessing it in the context of industrialism.

The second alternative, while also focusing on collectivities, is intended to achieve entirely different results. This is fascism, for which the corresponding ideology is variously labelled fascist and corporatist. At an ideological level, corporatism consists of statements about the world which are consonant with stability and centralized planning. Its guiding principles are faith in law and order, limitations on individual appetites, a recognition that corporate groups take precedence over private persons, and the legitimacy of a ruling class. The state has a definite role and that is actively and openly to co-ordinate the interests of other dominant economic groups in the society; to act, in fact and in ideology, as the central planning commission for the ruling groups. This involves a much larger proportion of public business being conducted outside Parliament and between government agencies and private business. The shift in ideology introduced by the Trudeau speech in 1976 and maintained since that time has been labelled corporatism by political commentators in Canada.

The shift is not one that basically alters the prevailing order as far as the larger body of the population is concerned, though it may be connected to slight alterations in relative power for dominant groups. Basically it is a shift in definition of what that prevailing order is like, and it is intended to provide the basis for control of the order during a time of crisis and contraction. In considering the same speech, political economist J.T. MacLeod has characterized corporatism as "an ideology or a conception of society seeing the community as composed of economic or functional groups rather than an amalgam of atomistic individuals."[5] He argues that:

The essence of corporatism is private or capitalist ownership coupled with state control. The characteristic objective of the corporate state is to avoid – as much as possible – adversarial confrontation between business and labour, or business and government. Private ownership is left undisturbed. . . . In place of market competition, corporatism would substitute state control.

Historian Kenneth McNaught, in the same issue of *Canadian Forum* which contains MacLeod's interpretation of the Trudeau speech, compares its postulates with those uttered by R.B. Bennett during the depression of the 1930s. Both, he argues, are attempts to "save the special interest groups from themselves." Says McNaught: "The 'debate' never has been about free enterprise and an unregulated market system. It has always been and still is about who benefits most and who pays most within a very complex set of relationships amongst government, business, labour and farmers."[6] Corporatism and liberalism, then, become simply alternative ways of persuading the population to accept a basically non-egalitarian social structure, one in which dominant interest groups use various methods according to need for maintaining their prerogatives.

Fascism as a political condition is associated, historically, with extremely repressive states. Fascist states, maintaining the prerogatives of private capital and corporate structures for its development, were established in Italy and Germany in the 1930s and 1940s. These emerged within the confines of economic depression, class struggles, and general disbelief in the legitimacy of liberal democratic states. State force was used to maintain a ruthless suppression of workers and to prevent the development of political opposition. Corporatism dressed in Catholicism played a similar, though less open role in Quebec prior to World War II. While force was not used in the same degree nor against such a large proportion of the population of English-speaking Canada, the Western regions of this country experienced some early thrusts of fascism during the same depression era. It became evident to the unemployed workers who travelled the rails in search of work and ended up in military camps on the Pacific Coast that political rebellion would not be met with the liberal response. Within a framework of liberal democracy, lip service to private freedom, even if mainly a means of legitimating private greed, involves certain civil liberties for individuals. Within that of corporatism, the legitimated greed of corporate bodies obliterates even these individual freedoms. Lord Acton's dictum might be rephrasable. Power corrupts, but absolute power renders deceit unnecessary. It can be exercised with naked honesty.

Whether the ideology of corporatism will lead to forms of fascism in Canada and the United States if depression succeeds recession is open to debate, but not to dismissal. As the Syncrude deal makes clear, the Canadian state has unequivocally joined American capitalism, using public money for the purpose, to exploit Canadian resources in the interests of a dominant class. What is interesting about this particular expression of a more general relationship is that it accepts the dominant class as a foreign one. The national financial class which historically aided this end result has become indistinguishable, and as a group has lost its identifiable role. In its place, but without its power yet, is a rising regional bourgeoisie whose power is exercised in a regional government as shareholder in the project.[7] This group, though regionally based and defined in regional terms vis-à-vis the national leaders, has been nurtured in the continentalist ideology of an oil economy. There is no strong national power centre capable of opposing the form of state capitalism that the "politics of oil," to use Pratt's phrase, demands.

In addition, given declining revenues from other sources, there is increasing pressure on the central government to decrease its expenditures on welfare. If wages are controlled and in any event decline, if unemployment rises, and if welfare alternatives are reduced, one might reasonably expect a reaction from the working class – which, without mobility, would include ideologically as well as factually a larger proportion of the middle classes than is the case in times of affluence. If rebellion takes the form of widespread labour militancy and political protest, the state, in order to maintain its defence of private capitalism and even at the expense of its legitimation function, would be obliged to resort to force.

The historical alternative has been war, and one cannot dismiss the continuing stockpiling of armaments, the growing expenditures on defence. In spite of all evidence to the effect that a war between superpowers, or even a more conventional war beginning between smaller powers, is likely to incur massive or total destruction of life, the preparations for war continue. And with reason of a mad variety: such preparations and conventional war itself constitute highly profitable business.

### III

It will be recalled that corporations are defined as persons; endowed, as we have noted, with the rights and privileges of natural persons. At the same time, they are composed of large numbers of private individuals whose private and class interests motivate their actions though these actions are taken on behalf of the corporation and continue to be valid after the death of the actors. This double-edged reality creates for any society a dilemma that few societies have managed even to articulate. A mediaeval Pope is reported to have declared that corporations, not being human, could not sin. The statement might be treated as a silly and at best premature judgement; it may also be a gloss over the errors and not infrequent greed of the corporate Church; it may, however, be a profound insight into the nature of the dilemma societies encounter in their dealings with corporate organizations and the changing themes of corporate ideology.

At one level there can be little doubt that only human agents can make decisions: at that level corporations as such do not actually exist. They are, and they should be dealt with as, legal fictions. In that event the decision-makers as individuals should be held accountable for their private actions, though such actions are formally taken by corporate groups. The director, the executive, the owner, of course; but as well the scientist, the lab technician, the secretary; the foreman, the production worker, the janitor, the troops. All and each may reasonably be called to account for whatever actions each has taken which contributes to any corporate undertaking ultimately harmful to the society at large – assuming the society were ever able to identify such action and such harm.

At another level it becomes evident that there is something in the nature of large-scale organizations which induces individuals to act without regard for ultimate social consequences. This may consist of several and perhaps contradictory forces. Private ambitions no doubt play a part, and where all rewards in a society are attached to corporate position there is little incentive to promote the interests of a national or regional society. Accumulated layers of ignorance about the larger society and its situation, a long history of colonialism; these must also contribute to the inability of corporate members to recognize conflicts of interest between their organization and a national society. Beyond these explanations, however, there is an energy in human beings which is bridled by organized institutions in such a way that the participants experience a sense of importance. For this importance, this sharing in power even if the sense is largely illusory, people are willing to give generously of their energies toward some cause, any cause, larger than personal survival. This may be the same capacity that saves societies from annihilation when attacked, the same capacity that underlies the prodigious range of artistic creations people have produced; the same capacity that encourages actors in a drama to respond to the audience and the theatre so that their presentation becomes "larger than life." It is a capacity which can be used toward any end, since in itself it has no moral imperatives.

Those who command corporate instruments have the means to harness this energy. Corporations do emerge, die, undergo transformations; and they do this because human actors decree that they should be so moved. They know, though others may not, that corporations are only legal fictions; fictions designed to legitimate whatever actions their directors deem necessary and in their private interests. But the play can be enacted day after day, year after year, civilization after civilization, only because when large numbers of actors are brought together in the same theatre and given roles in an apparently meaningful drama, they form a company. The company takes on its own character, its own mystique, its own vitality. The play is written and choreographed by the director, but rewarded actors become willing participants who respond to their cues.

This turning of energies toward corporate rather than larger social ends is possible in the absence of a societal framework that calls forth the same energies and rewards them. There are, in Canada, few expectations that people could act altruistically on behalf of the public good, and the current level of cynicism about people who claim to do so is no doubt deserved. People who claim to act on social principles typically look to corporate and class sources for their rewards: the society has few other means to reward them. There are even penalties for altruism, since jobs, income, and social status are tied to corporate positions. It is naive to suppose that people would continue to maintain a clear vision of society independent of these groups in such circumstances.

Our study of corporations would suggest that the society acts in this self-defeating manner because corporate organizations hold such a disproportionate degree of social power. The society, moulded in the interests of corporations and their leading interest groups, has been unable to create an alternative framework for the exercise of power. Ideology plays a cementing role in creating an inability and sustaining an unwillingness of participants to identify their situation and consider alternatives. Yet a time of "forced change" at the ideological level may be an occasion for public reassessments. Asked to erase freedom from their historical interpretation, people might reasonably ask how much else of their stock of beliefs has been based on false information or answers that obliterate questions. The emergence over the past five years of a strongly critical social science indicates that such skepticism does arise when ideological change is in process. A rewriting of Canadian history, political development, sociology, and economics is clearly occurring, and the themes go beyond the reinterpretation presented at an official level. The skeptics are still a minority in colonial universities, but they form a new spearhead of opposition to the status quo which did not previously exist in Canada.

However, much more than a spearhead of opposition would be required before social change could be brought about. What we have learned in studying the development of technology, markets, systematic management techniques, the labour force, and ownership arrangements is that fundamental social change is not in the interests of corporate organizations. Changes in ideology rather than structure, in consumer habits rather than control of technology, and in labour force characteristics rather than labour's role in production processes are means of supporting, not altering, the existing system. To go beyond these, Canadians would have to identify their own distinctive interests and learn how to act on them.

# NOTES

## Introduction

1. Prime Minister P.E. Trudeau, speech to the Canadian Clubs of Ottawa, as published in text in *The Vancouver Sun*, January 20, 1976.
2. Elliott Leyton, *Dying Hard*, Toronto: McClelland and Stewart, 1975.
3. Andrew Hacker, *The Corporation Take-Over*, New York: Harper and Row, 1964, p. 10.
4. Dodge v. Ford Motor Co., 204 Mich. 259, 170 N.W. 668 (1919) cited in Phillip I. Blumberg, *The Megacorporation in American Society: The Scope of Corporate Power*, Englewood Cliffs, N. J.: Prentice-Hall, 1975, p. 6.
5. George Grant, *Technology and Empire*, Toronto: House of Anansi, 1969, p. 116.
6. Lucien Karpik, "Technological Capitalism," in Stewart Clegg and David Dunkerley (eds.), *Critical Issues in Organizations*, London: Routledge and Kegan Paul, 1977, pp. 41-71, at p. 57.

## Chapter 1: Legal Fictions

1. *Canada Business Corporations Act*, C. 33, 1974-75, Part III, article 15 (1), p. 12.
2. Sir Henry Sumner Maine, *Ancient Law*, London: George Routledge and Sons, 1905, pp. 152-53.
3. *Canada Business Corporations Act*, C. 33, 1974-75, Part I, Article 2 (1), pp. 3-4.
4. U.S. Chief Justice Marshall, with reference to Dartmouth College in 1819, as quoted in Scott Buchanan, "The Corporations and the Republic," in Andrew Hacker, *The Corporation Take-Over*, New York: Harper and Row, 1964.
5. Werner Sombart, *Encyclopaedia of the Social Sciences*, New York: Macmillan, 1930, vol. III, p. 200.
6. The term "world system" is used by Immanuel Wallerstein in *The Modern World System*, New York: Academic Press, 1976.
7. For a general description and a list of such strictures see S. B. Clough and C. W. Cole, *Economic History of Europe*, Boston: D. C. Heath, 1946, pp. 18-19 and 66-71.
8. Maurice Dobb, *Studies in the Development of Capitalism*, New York: International Publishers, revised edition, 1963, p. 88.
9. *Ibid.*, p. 102.
10. The table given here does not do justice to the range of information

provided in the 1974 *CALURA Report*, which provides much detail on foreign ownership and control.

11. *Financial Post*, "The Financial Post 300," Summer, 1977.

12. Centre for Development Planning, Projections and Policies of the Department of Economic and Social Affairs of the United Nations Secretariat. A partial reporting of this data is given in Blumberg, *op.cit.*, Table 2-11 and accompanying text, p. 35.

13. Wallace Clement, *The Canadian Corporate Elite* and *Continental Corporate Power*, Toronto: McClelland and Stewart, 1975 and 1977 respectively.

14. *Ibid.*, 1977, Tables 6 and 17.

15. *Ibid.*, 1975, Appendix VII.

16. Blumberg, citing 1973 *Statistical Abstract*, Table 777; *Survey of Current Business*, July, 1973, Tables 6.4, 6.15, 6.19; NYSE 1973 *Fact Book*, and *Economic Report of the President* (U.S.), Table C-75; pp. 30-31.

17. *Institutional Investor Study, Report, 1971*, Securities and Exchange Commission, U.S., reported in Blumberg, *op.cit.*, pp. 97-98.

18. *Ibid.*, p. 100.

19. Statistics Canada, *Manufacturing Industries of Canada: Geographical Distribution, 1970*. Ottawa: Information Canada, 1974, (cat. no 31-209).

20. Antoni Kaminski, discussion paper for Polish-Canadian seminar held in Poland, May 14-21, 1977 (unpublished).

21. *Ibid.*

22. Jean Jacques Rousseau, *The Social Contract*, trans. G. D. H. Cole, London: J. M. Dent, 1958 edition.

23. Adam Smith, *An Inquiry into the Nature and Causes of the Wealth of Nations*, Oxford: Oxford University Press, 1976 edition.

24. For a review of the history see C. B. MacPherson, *The Real World of Democracy*, Toronto: University of Toronto Press, Chs. 1 and 2.

25. See Leo Panitch, "The Role and Nature of the Canadian State," in Panitch (ed.) *The Canadian State*, Toronto, University of Toronto Press, 1978, and other essays in this volume for application of the debate to Canada. Major contributors to the more general debate are Ralph Miliband, *The State in Capitalist Society*, London: Weidenfeld and Nicolson, 1969, and Nicos Poulantzas, *Les Classes sociales dans le capitalisme aujourd'hui*, Paris: Editions du Seuil, 1974. For a review of the terms of the debate see "The Problem of the Capitalist State," in R. Blackburn (ed.) *Ideology in Social Science*, London: Fontana, 1972.

26. Hugh Armstrong, "The Labour Force and State Workers in Canada," in Panitch, *op.cit.*

27. I am indebted for this understanding to researchers in the "Marginal Work Worlds" project at the Institute of Public Affairs, Dalhousie, Halifax; in particular to unpublished papers by Fred Wien, Donald Clairmont, Martha MacDonald.

28. *Corporations and Labour Unions Returns Act, Report for 1974, Part II, Labour Unions;* Part IA, pp. 8-15, and Part IC, pp. 20-23; see also *Labour Organizations in Canada* (annual), Ottawa: Labour Canada.

29. *Ibid.,* Part IC, pp. 26-27.

30. For further reading on trade unions in Canada, see Robert Laxer, *Canada's Unions,* Toronto: James Lorimer, 1976. A short essay on the implications of women and public service workers being unionized is given in Patricia Marchak, "Les femmes, le travail, et le syndicalisme," *Sociologie et Sociétés,* vol. 6:1 (May 1974), 35-53, reprinted in English in *International Journal of Sociology,* vol. 1:4 (Winter 1975-76).

31. See particularly, David J. Bercuson, *Fools and Wise Men: The Rise and Fall of the One Big Union,* Toronto: McGraw-Hill Ryerson, 1978, and *Confrontation at Winnipeg,* Montreal: McGill-Queen's University Press, 1974; Paul Phillips, *No Power Greater: A Century of Labour in B.C.,* Vancouver: B.C. Federation of Labour Boag Foundation, 1967; and Stuart M. Jamieson, *Times of Trouble: Labour Unrest and Industrial Conflict in Canada 1900-66,* Task Force on Labour Relations Study No. 22, Ottawa: Information Canada, 1971.

## Chapter 2: "Technology and Empire"

1. George Grant, *Technology and Empire,* Toronto: Anansi, 1969, p. 137.

2. Robert M. Pirsig, *Zen and the Art of Motorcycle Maintenance,* Toronto: Bantam, 1974, p. 16.

3. Fernand Braudel, *Capitalism and Material Life 1400-1800,* New York: Harper and Row, 1967, p. 245.

4. Abbott Payson Usher, "The Textile Industry, 1750-1830," in *Technology in Western Civilizations,* edited by Melvin Kranzberg and Carroll W. Pursell, Jr., New York: Oxford University Press, 1967, vol. I, p. 230.

5. S. B. Clough and C. W. Cole, *Economic History of Europe,* revised edition, Boston: D. C. Heath and Company, 1946, pp. 183-84.

6. Maurice Dobb, *Studies in the Development of Capitalism,* New York: International Publishers, revised edition, 1963, p. 147.

7. G. E. Fussell, "The Agricultural Revolution, 1600-1850," in Kranzberg and Pursell, *op.cit.,* vol. I, p. 130.

8. W. G. Phillips, *The Agricultural Implement Industry in Canada*, Toronto: University of Toronto Press, 1956, provides data on previous harvesters and the early history of implements companies in both the U.S. and Canada.

9. *Ibid.*, p. 12, citing statistics from U.S. Census of Manufacturers (Washington, 1900).

10. *Ibid.*, Ch. 2.

11. *Ibid.*, pp. 38 and 39.

12. R. T. Naylor, *The History of Canadian Business 1867-1914*, 2 vols., Toronto: James Lorimer, 1975, vol. II, p. 42.

13. Wayne Rasmussen, "Scientific Agriculture," in Kranzberg and Pursell, vol. II, p. 338.

14. Don Mitchell, *The Politics of Food*, Toronto: James Lorimer, 1975, p. 34.

15. Vernon Fowke, *The National Policy and the Wheat Economy*, Toronto: University of Toronto Press, 1957.

16. Employment figures and discussion of the mergers and effect of tariff removal are provided in Christopher J. Maule, *Productivity in the Farm Machinery Industry*, Study no. 3, Royal Commission on Farm Machinery, Ottawa, 1969, ch. 3. Rasmussen, *op. cit.*, p. 337, states that the ratio of farm workers to farm products needed was 1:14 in 1946, 1:37 in 1966, and that farm output per man hour, using 1957-58 as 100, increased from an index of 49 in 1946 to 153 in 1965. Maule estimates the Canadian ratio to vary around 80 per cent of the American figures for the post-war period through to 1966.

17. A detailed description of the peach-canning industry is provided by Wallace Clement and Anna Janzen, in "Just Peachy: The Demise of Tender Fruit Farmers," in *This Magazine*, vol. 12:2 (1978) pp. 22-26.

18. Mitchell, *op.cit.*, especially Chs. 2 and 3.

19. For further readings on the agricultural industry, see Federal Task Force on Agriculture, *Canadian Agriculture in the Seventies*, Ottawa: Queen's Printer, 1970.

20. Clough and Cole, *op.cit.*, pp. 409-15.

21. Bruce C. Netshert, "Developing the Energy Inheritance," in Kranzberg and Pursell, vol. II, p. 238.

22. *Ibid.*, p. 238.

23. *Ibid.*, p. 239.

24. Anthony Sampson, *The Seven Sisters*, London: Hodder and Stoughton, 1975, p. 41.

25. *Ibid.*, p. 41, with quotes from Allan Nevins, *John D. Rockefeller*, New York, 1940, vol. I, p. 304.

26. *Ibid.*, p. 42, original quote contained in Ida M. Tarbell, *The History of the Standard Oil Company*, New York, 1904, vol. II, p. 157.

27. *Ibid.*, p. 43.

28. Netshert, *op.cit.*, p. 243.

29. Thomas Jefferson, quoted in C. W. Wright, *Economic History of the United States*, 1941, and cited in W. G. Phillips, *op.cit.*, p. 5.

30. Raymond Vernon, *Manager in the International Economy*, 2nd edition, Englewood Cliffs, N.J.: Prentice-Hall, 1972, pp. 206-8.

31. Mira Wilkins, *The Emergence of Multinational Enterprise: American Business Abroad from the Colonial Era to 1914*, Cambridge, Mass.: Harvard University Press, 1970, provides case data on Singer and Colt manufacturing adventures abroad. See also Vernon, *op.cit.*, pp. 202-3.

32. Wilkins, *op.cit.*, pp. 37-45.

33. *Ibid.*, pp. 42-43.

34. Braudel, *op.cit.*, p. 249.

35. John H. Dunning, "Technology, United States Investment, and European Economic Growth," in *The International Corporation, A Symposium*, edited by Charles P. Kindleberger, Cambridge, Mass: The MIT Press, 1970, pp. 141-76, citing Organization for Economic Cooperation and Development, "Technological Gaps: Their Nature, Causes, Effects," OECD *Observer*, no. 33 (April 1968), pp. 18-28; and *The Level and Structure of Europe's Research and Development Effort*, Paris: OECD, 1968.

36. Willart F. Mueller, "Origins of DuPont's Major Innovations, 1920-1950," in James R. Bright (ed.), *Research Development and Technological Innovation*, Homewood, Ill.: Richard D. Irwin, 1964, pp. 383-400.

37. This is reported in Pierre Bourgault, *Innovation and the Structure of Canadian Industry*, Science Council of Canada, Ottawa: October, 1972, pp. 37-39. The OECD report is entitled: *Gaps in Technology between Member Countries: Analytical Report*, OECD, Paris, 1969.

38. *Ibid.*, p. 42.

39. *Ibid.*, p. 50.

40. See also M. P. Bachynski, "Science Policy in Canada: Study and Debate Must Now Be Replaced by Action," *Science Forum*, 31 (February 1973), pp. 19-27.

41. Bourgault, *op.cit.*, p. 64.

42. *Ibid.*, p. 68. Note: the word "popular" in this context is used by Bourgault.

43. *Ibid.*, p. 70.

44. *Ibid.*, p. 73.

45. Joseph Schumpeter, *Business Cycles*, New York: McGraw-Hill,

1939, and *The Theory of Economic Development*, Cambridge: Harvard University Press, 1935.

46. John Kenneth Galbraith, *American Capitalism*, New York: Houghton-Mifflin, 1952, and *The New Industrial State*, New York: New American Library, second edition, revised, 1971.

47. John Jewkes, David Sawers, and Richard Stillerman, *The Sources of Invention*, London: Macmillan, 1969.

48. Jacob Schmookler, *Invention and Economic Growth*, Cambridge, Mass., Harvard University Press, 1966. See also F. M. Scherer, *Industrial Market Structure and Economic Performance*, Chicago: Rand McNally, 1970, and *The Economics of Multi-Plant Operation: An International Comparisons Study*, Cambridge, Mass: Harvard University Press, 1975.

49. E. Mansfield, *Research and Innovation in the Modern Corporation*, New York: W. W. Norton, 1972, and *The Economics of Technological Change*, New York: W. W. Norton, 1968, p. 217.

50. J. W. Markham, "Market Structure, Business Conduct and Innovation," *American Economic Review*, vol. 51:2 (May 1965), p. 327.

51. Almarin Phillips, *Technology and Market Structure*, Lexington, Mass: Heath Lexington, 1971, p. 9. Phillips' arguments rest finally on his very detailed analysis of technical development in the aircraft industry.

52. Arthur D. Little, "Patterns and Problems of Technical Innovation in American Industry," *The Role and Effect of Technology in the Nation's Economy*, Hearings before a Subcommittee of the Select Committee on Small Business, United States Senate, 88th Congress, First Session, discussed in Mansfield, 1968, *op.cit.*, p. 111.

53. Thomas Kuhn, *The Structure of Scientific Revolutions*, Chicago: University of Chicago Press, 1962.

## Chapter 3: Resources, Markets, and the State

1. Prime Minister P. E. Trudeau, speech to the Canadian Clubs of Ottawa, as published in text in the *Vancouver Sun*, January 20, 1976.

2. Bruce Willson, cited in Walter Stewart, "Bulldozers Inc.," *Maclean's*, June 28, 1976, p. 28.

3. "Slocan Valley Community Forest Management Project, Report," Slocan: Local Initiatives Programme. Feasibility project on forestry utilization alternatives, 1975, pp. 2-43. Mimeo.

4. One of the leading proponents of this position is Walter W. Rostow, *Stages of Growth, A Non-Communist Manifesto*, Cambridge, Mass: Harvard University Press, 1960.

5. Within Canada, economists are generally agreed that some form of "dependency theory" is required to explain the country's failure to

develop as an industrial economy. Views differ as to whether the dependency on staples production for American markets constitutes the colonial counterpart of imperialism. The "staples theory" approach of H. A. Innis, V. Fowke, G. Britnell, and A. F. W. Plumptre provided the basis for a theory of imperialism but was not phrased in these terms until adapted by M. H. Watkins, K. Levitt, D. Drache, W. Clement, and R. T. Naylor. A particularly important contribution to the argument is by T. W. Acheson, "The National Policy and the Industrialization of the Maritimes, 1880-1910," *Acadiensis*, vol. 1:2 (Spring 1972), 3-28. This examines the process of "de-industrialization" in the Atlantic region.

6. A few of the current publications in sociology which explore this case are: Ralph Matthews, "The Biases, Weaknesses and Failure of Canada's Regional Development Strategy: A Dependency Theory Perspective," in *Plan Canada*, Toronto: Town Planning Institute of Canada, vol. 19, June 1977: and "The Significance and Explanation of Regional Divisions in Canadian Society," prepared for presentation to the Poland-Canada Exchange Seminar, Warsaw, Poland, May 1977; Henry C. Veltmeyer, "The Methodology of Dependency Analysis: An Outline for a Strategy of Research on Regional Underdevelopment;" Brian Gibbon, "Internal Dependency in Canada: A Theoretical Model for the Prairie Case"; John Baker, "Canadian Banking and the Under-Development of Atlantic Canada: 1867-1920"; all of these delivered at meetings of the CSAA, May 1977. See also D. Bercuson (ed.), *Canada and the Burden of Unity*, Toronto: Macmillan, 1977.

7. See, for examples, John Galtung, "A Structural Theory of Imperialism," *Journal of Peace Research*, vol. 8 (1971), 81-117; Sivert Langholm, "On the Concepts of Center and Periphery," *Journal of Peace Research*, vol. 8 (1971), 273-79; Anibal Quijarro Obregon, "The Marginal Pole of the Economy and the Marginalised Labour Force," *Economy and Society*, vol. 3 (1974), 393-428; and Anibal Pinto and Jan Knakal, "The Centre-Periphery System, Twenty Years Later," *Social and Economic Studies*, vol. 22:1, 34-89.

8. Hugh G. J. Aitken, "Government and Business in Canada: An Interpretation," from John J. Deutsch *et al.* (eds.), *The Canadian Economy*, revised edition, Toronto: Macmillan, 1965, pp. 493-512, at pp. 494-95. Reprinted by permission of the Macmillan Company of Canada Limited.

9. Gustavus Myers, *The History of Canadian Wealth*, Toronto: James, Lewis and Samuel, 1972 (original, 1913), pp. 161-62. See also E. P. Neufeld, *The Financial System of Canada: Its Growth and Development*, New York: St. Martin's Press, 1972; Bray Ham-

mond, "Banking in Canada before Confederation, 1772-1867," in W. T. Easterbrook and M. Watkins, eds., *Approaches to Canadian Economic History*, Toronto: McClelland and Stewart, 1967; and Tom Naylor, *The History of Canadian Business 1867-1914*, vol. I, *The Banks and Finance Capital*, Toronto: James Lorimer, 1975.

10. Many recent publications list these members and their financial interests in much greater detail. Among these are Myers, *op.cit.*, pp. 150-217; Wallace Clement, *The Canadian Corporate Elite*, Toronto: McClelland Stewart, 1975, pp. 56-59; Stanley Ryerson, *Unequal Union*, Toronto: Progress, 1968; G. Tulchinsky, "The Montreal Business Community, 1837-1853," in D. MacMillan (ed.), *Canadian Business History: Selected Studies 1497-1971*, Toronto: McClelland and Stewart, 1972; Hammond, *op.cit.*, pp. 127-68; Easterbrook and Watkins, *op.cit.*, pp. 450-52; T. W. Acheson, "The Nature and Structure of York Commerce in the 1820's," *Canadian Historical Review*, December 1969, p. 423; R. T. Naylor, "The Rise and Fall of the Third Commercial Empire of the St. Lawrence," in G. Teeple, *Capitalism and the National Question*, Toronto: University of Toronto Press, 1972, pp. 1-42.

11. Frank Underhill, *Image of Confederation*, Massey Lectures, Third Series, Toronto, 1964, pp. 24-25.

12. For a history of American multinational expansion see Mira Wilkins, *The Emergence of Multinational Enterprise: American Business Abroad from the Colonial Era to 1914*, Cambridge, Mass.: Harvard University Press, 1970.

13. *Ibid.*, pp. 16-20.

14. *Ibid.*, pp. 135-48.

15. *Ibid.*, pp. 141-42.

16. Royal Commission on Canada's Economic Prospects: *Final Report, 1957*, Ottawa, Queen's Printer: pp. 75-92.

17. *Ibid.*, pp. 76-88.

18. *Ibid.*, p. 91.

19. *Ibid.*, p. 92.

20. Department of Defence Production, *Production Sharing Handbook*, Ottawa: Queen's Printer, 1967, pp. 1-3, A1-A5.

21. Canadian government funds between 1959 and 1967 for 306 projects under the Defence Production Sharing Agreements amounted to 48.5 per cent of the total. The Defence Industrial Research Programme stipulates that companies (including American subsidiaries) may obtain up to 50 per cent of their research costs without repayment obligations. With respect to the effect of these agreements and the research expenditures in terms of the loss of national sovereignty over the Canadian military establishment, see John W. Warnock,

*Partner to Behemoth, The Military Policy of a Satellite Canada*, Toronto: New Press, 1970.

22. Article 1 (c), Agreement Concerning Automotive Products between the Government of Canada and the Government of the United States of America, 1965.

23. I. A. Litvak, *et al.*, *Dual Loyalty*, Toronto: McGraw-Hill, 1962.

24. As quoted in Bryce Richardson, *James Bay*, Toronto: Sierra Club in association with Clarke, Irwin, 1972, p. 13.

25. Hon. J. E. Perrault, cited in Leslie Roberts, *Noranda*, Toronto: Clarke, Irwin, 1956, at p. 67.

26. Eric Kierans, Foreword to Tom Naylor, *The History of Canadian Business 1867-1914*, 2 vols., Toronto: James Lorimer, 1975, p. xiv.

27. *New York Times*, October 1, 1972, reported in Irving Louis Horowitz, "Capitalism, Communism, and Multinationalism," in Abdul A. Said and Luiz R. Simmons (eds.), *The New Sovereigns, Multinational Corporations as World Powers*, Englewood Cliffs, N.J.: Prentice-Hall, 1975, pp. 120-38.

28. Horowitz, *op.cit.*, provides details on a number of these.

29. Mira Wilkins, "The Oil Companies in Perspective," in Raymond Vernon (ed.), *The Oil Crisis*, New York: W. W. Norton, 1976. For further background see also other essays in the same volume and Christopher Tugendhat, *Oil, The Biggest Business*, London: Eyre and Spottiswoode, 1968, and Anthony Sampson, *The Seven Sisters*, London: Hodder and Stoughton, 1976.

30. *Report of the Select Committee of the Senate*, appointed to enquire into the resources of the Great Mackenzie Basin, session of 1888.

31. Before 1970 British and American authors say very little about the oil reserves in Canada. Canada is sometimes treated even by authors opposed to the oil companies as an extension of American domestic reserves. The dates for these Alberta wells may be found in William Kilbourn, *Pipeline, TransCanada and the Great Debate. A History of Business and Politics*, Toronto: Clarke, Irwin, 1970, Chs. 1 and 2. This also provides, as its title suggests, a study of one of the major pipeline constructions.

32. René Fumoleau, *As Long as This Land Shall Last*, Toronto: Mc-Clelland and Stewart, 1974, especially Ch. 4.

33. James Wah-Shee, Northwest Territories, 1921, quoted in René Fumoleau, *op.cit.*, p. 157.

34. The "Schultz Report," *The Oil Import Question*, a report on the relationship of oil imports to the national security, by the Cabinet Task Force on oil import control, Washington, February 1970, pp. 98, 362. Also the "Paley Report," *Resource for Freedom: The Outlook for Energy Sources*, Washington, 1952.

35. Robert C. Fitzsimmons, "The Truth about Alberta Tar Sands,

quoted in Larry Pratt, *The Tar Sands, Syncrude and the Politics of Oil*, Edmonton: Hurtig, 1976, p. 31.

36. *Ibid.*

37. Zuhayr Mikdashi, "The OPEC Process," in Vernon, *op.cit.*, pp. 203-16. Also George Lenczowski, "The Oil-Producing Countries," in same volume.

38. Mr. Manucher Farman Farmaian, Ambassador of Iran to Venezuela, Speech to the Inter-American Press Association Conference, Caracas, Venezuela, October 1974. The ambassador mentions such problems as disappearing briefcases, bugged hotel rooms, the need for clandestine meetings.

39. Minister of Energy, Mines and Resources, J. J. Greene, December 1969, quoted in James Laxer, *The Energy Poker Game*, Toronto: New Press, 1970, p. 1.

40. Walter J. Levy Consultants Corporation, "Emerging North American Oil Balances: Considerations Relevant to a Tar Sands Development Policy," p. vii, cited in Pratt, p. 63.

41. For extended discussions of these events see Vernon, Sampson, and Tugendhat, all listed above.

42. Pratt, pp. 127-28.

43. J. D. House, "The Social Organization of Multinational Corporations, Canadian Subsidiaries in the Oil Industry," *Canadian Review of Sociology and Anthropology*, vol. 14:1 (February 1977), 4.

44. *Ibid.*

45. *Ibid.*, p. 5.

46. Pratt, p. 123.

47. *Ibid.*, p. 125.

48. House, pp. 6-7.

49. *Ibid.*, p. 11.

50. Pratt, p. 139.

51. *Ibid.*, p. 178.

52. *Minutes of Proceedings and Evidence*, Standing Committee on Indian Affairs and Northern Development, Issue #3, March 28, 1972, quoted in *Whiteout: The Mackenzie Valley Pipeline Proposal*, edited and produced by anthropology honours students at Carleton University, Ottawa, 1975, pp. 3-5. Previous statements by Hon. Jean Chrétien are also given in this publication, including policy statements made in Dallas, Texas, March 9, 1971, to the 1971 Symposium on Petroleum Economics and Evaluation in a speech entitled "Northern Development and Northern Pipelines." The 1974 reiteration of this position is contained in a speech on the occasion of the opening of the 51st session of the Council of the Northwest Territories, Yellowknife, January 18, 1974, *Ibid.*, p. 13.

53. John Helliwell, Peter H. Pearse, Chris Sanderson, and Anthony

Scott, "Where does Canada's National Interest Lie? – A Quantitative Appraisal," in Peter H. Pearse (ed.), *The Mackenzie Pipeline, Arctic Gas and Canadian Energy Policy*, Toronto: McClelland and Stewart, 1974, p. 212; see also John Helliwell, "Policy Alternative for Arctic Gas," in Gas from the Mackenzie Delta; Now or Later?" in *Canadian Arctic Resources Committee*, vol. 2:5, 1974.

54. T.R. Berger (Commissioner), *Northern Frontier Northern Homeland, The Report of the Mackenzie Valley Pipeline Inquiry* (2 vols.), Ottawa: Supply and Services, Canada, 1977. Reproduced by permission of the Minister of Supply and Services Canada and James Lorimer and Company Publisher.

55. National Energy Board, *Reasons for Decision, Northern Pipelines*, 3 vols., Ottawa, June 1977. See also Pipeline Application Assessment Group, *Mackenzie Valley Pipeline Assessment: Environmental and Socio-Economic Effects of the Proposed Canadian Arctic Gas Pipeline on the Northwest Territories and Yukon*, Ottawa: Issued Under the Authority of the Minister of Indian Affairs and Northern Development, November 1974.

56. Andrew Thompson (Commissioner), Royal Commission to Investigate the Kitimat Pipeline Proposal, *Report*, February 1978.

57. *Financial Post*, March 4, 1978. See also *Financial Post* series of articles on energy, January 28 to February 25, 1978. The Alaska Highway Route financing is covered in the issue of February 25, 1978.

58. Reported in *Financial Post*, February 25, 1978.

59. See, for example, T. L. Powrie, *The Contribution of Foreign Capital to Canadian Economic Growth*, Edmonton: Hurtig, 1978.

60. Earle McLaughlin, speech to the Canadian Club, June 2, 1978, as quoted in the *Vancouver Sun*, June 3, 1978.

61. See for detailed description, Dennis Olsen, "The State Elites," in Leo Panitch (ed.), *The Canadian State*, Toronto: University of Toronto Press, 1978; also Leo Panitch, "Role and Nature of the State," *ibid.*

62. Eric Kierans, quoted at note 26.

## Chapter 4: Systems for Management

1. Alfred Krupp, quoted in F. J. Nussbaum, *A History of Economic Institutions of Modern Europe*, 1933, p. 379, as cited in Alvin Gouldner, *Patterns of Industrial Bureaucracy*, New York: Free Press, 1954, pp. 179-80.

2. Mira Wilkins, *The Emergence of Multinational Enterprise*, Cambridge, Mass: Harvard University Press, 1970.

3. H.H. Gerth and C. Wright Mills (eds.), *From Max Weber: Essays in Sociology*, New York: Oxford University Press, 1958, p. 214.

4. Adam Smith, *Wealth of Nations*, Bk. I, Ch. 1, contains the basic argument on relationships between differentiation and market demand.

5. M. Piore, "On the Technological Foundations of Economic Dualism," *mimeo*. Cambridge, Mass.: Massachusetts Institute of Technology, n.d.

6. For accounts of Canadian entrepreneurs, see Alexander Ross, *The Risk Takers. The Dreamers Who Build a Business from an Idea*. Toronto: Maclean-Hunter, 1975.

7. Alfred Chandler, *Strategy and Structure*, Boston, Mass.: Massachusetts Institute of Technology Press, 1962.

8. *Ibid.*, p. 70.

9. Gerard Colby Zilg, *DuPont – Behind the Nylon Curtain*, Englewood Cliffs, N.J.: Prentice-Hall, 1974.

10. Chandler, *op.cit.*, p. 79.

11. This account is based on Mira Wilkins and Frank Ernest Hill, *American Business Abroad: Ford on Six Continents*. Detroit: Wayne State University Press, 1964.

12. *Ibid.*, p. 8.

13. *Ibid.*, p. 10.

14. *Ibid.*, pp. 99-100.

15. Nancy Foy, *The IBM World*, London: Eyre Methuen, 1974.

16. Vincent Massey, *What's Past is Prologue*, p. 79. as quoted in E. P. Neufeld, *A Global Corporation: A History of the International Development of Massey-Ferguson Ltd.*, Toronto: University of Toronto Press, 1969, p. 33.

17. *Ibid.*, pp. 76-77.

18. *Ibid.*, p. 161.

19. *Ibid.*, discussed through Ch. 7.

20. *Ibid.*, p. 201.

21. *Ibid.*, p. 218.

22. One detailed description of these grants is given in Gustavus Myers, *A History of Canadian Wealth*, Toronto: James Lorimer, reprint (original 1939), 1971.

23. The ownership structure is obtained by studying data in Statistics Canada, 1972 *Inter-Corporate Ownership Directory*, Ottawa: Queen's Printer, 1972, and annual reports of the company.

24. Fortune, *The Fortune Double 500 Directory*, 1973, provides current statistics (updated annually). The more general description here is based on information on IBM in Louis Turner, *Invisible Empires*, London: Hamish Hamilton, 1970; Christopher Tugendhat, *The Multinationals*, London: Eyre and Spottiswoode, 1971. See also, John E. Brent, "Case Study: IBM, World Trade Corporation:

History, Policy and Organization," *International Management Association Special Report*, no. 1-3 New York, 1957, and Nancy Foy, *op.cit.*

25. Michael Z. Brooke and H. Lee Remmers, *The Strategy of Multinational Enterprise, Organization and Finance*, London: Longman Group, 1970, p. 71; see also F. G. Conner, *The World-Wide Industrial Enterprise*, New York: McGraw-Hill, 1967, pp. 35-36.

26. Turner, *op.cit.*, p. 16. Quotation from a speech in Britain in 1966, original source not given.

27. Tugendhat, *op.cit.*, p. 118.

28. Alcan Smelters and Chemicals Ltd., *Alcan in British Columbia*, Vancouver: Evergreen Press, January 1977; and *Alcan in Canada*, no publisher or date given. These are brochures distributed by Alcan at Kitimat for public information on the smelting process.

29. Tughendhat, pp. 202-3.

30. J. B. Flavin and G. R. Parisot, "The IBM World Trade Planning System," in *Multinational Corporate Planning*, edited by George A. Steiner and Warren M. Cannon, New York: Macmillan Company, 1966, pp. 82-83.

31. Michael Z. Brooke and H. Lee Remmers, *op.cit.*, 1970, pp. 18-19 and Ch. 12. Brooke and Remmers have also published a study of European firms, *The Multinational Company in Europe: Some Key Problems*, same publisher, 1972.

32. A study of relationships between control and technologies and other factors is given in Robert J. Alsegg, *Control Relationships between American Corporations and Their European Subsidiaries*, New York: American Management Association, 1971.

33. Richard Robinson, "Nationalism and Centralized Control," in H. R. Hahlo, J. G. Smith, and R. W. Wright, *Nationalism and the Multinational Enterprise*, New York: N.Y. Oceana Publications, 1973, pp. 207-13, at p. 209.

34. T. J. Gilbert, "Functions of the Financial Office in International Operations," *Applying Financial Controls in Foreign Operations*, New York: International Management Association, 1957, as cited in Brooke and Remmers, *op.cit.*, 1970, pp. 94-95.

35. Brooke and Remmers, 1970, pp. 192-95.

36. As the Tar Sands case demonstrates, see Larry Pratt, *The Tar Sands*, Edmonton: Hurtig, 1976.

### Chapter 5: The Management of Labour

1. Emile Durkheim, *Division of Labour in Society*, translated by George Simpson, New York: Free Press, 1933 (original, 1893), p. 371.

2. Leonard R. Sayles, *Behavior of Industrial Work Groups: Prediction and Control*, New York: John Wiley, 1958, p. 3.

3. The agricultural labour force in Canada in the mid-1970's is approximately 7 per cent of all workers.

4. Harry Jerome, *Mechanization in Industry*, New York: National Bureau of Economic Research, 1934, p. 63. This survey covered a large number of different industries during the years 1880 and 1930, and is an excellent source of detailed information on the technological changes and their consequences for the first part of this century.

5. James R. Bright, *Automation and Management*, Boston: Division of Research, Graduate School of Business Administration, Harvard University Press, 1958. Bright provided one of the most distinguished surveys of automation up to the late 1950s, including detailed descriptions of processes in eleven different industries, and their effects on employment rates and types of work. For the 1950s, his argument that automation in the long run appears to reduce skill requirements although in the short run it may increase them was not in keeping with conventional wisdom. In the 1950s the full effects of mechanization were still being analysed: the effects of automation were yet to be discovered.

6. Ratios in a study of 100 plants with different technical systems are given in Joan Woodward, *Industrial Organization: Theory and Practice*, London: Oxford University Press, 1964. Especially discussion in chapter 4, pp. 50-69.

7. *Ibid.*, The following section summarizes these arguments.

8. Martin Meissner, *Technology and the Worker*, San Francisco: California: Chandler Publishing Company, 1969, p. 239.

9. *Ibid.*

10. Woodward, *op.cit.*, p. 55.

11. Charles R. Walker, *Steeltown: an Industrial Case History of the Conflict between Progress and Security*, New York: Harper and Brothers, 1950; *Toward the Automatic Factory*, New Haven: Yale University Press, 1957.

12. Robert Blauner, *Alienation and Freedom: The Factory Worker and His Industry*, Chicago: University of Chicago Press, 1964.

13. For reviews of Taylor and his methods see Milton J. Nadworny, *Scientific Management and the Unions, 1900-1932*, Cambridge, Mass.: Harvard University Press, 1955; Hugh G. J. Aitken, *Taylorism at Watertown Arsenal, Scientific Management in Action, 1903-1915*, Cambridge, Mass.: Harvard University Press, 1960. The "historical" sections of most textbooks on organizations provide a description of the main theories as well.

14. *Encyclopedia Britannica*, vol. XV, 14th ed., as cited in Charles R.

Walker and Robert H. Guest, *The Man on the Assembly Line*, Cambridge, Mass.: Harvard University Press, 1952, p. 10. See also *The Foreman on the Assembly Line*, same publisher, 1956.

15. Andrew Ure, *The Philosophy of Manufacturers*, London: H. G. Bohn, 1861 (originally published 1835), pp. 15-16, as quoted in Reinhard Bendix, *Work and Authority in Industry*, New York: Harper and Row, 1956.

16. C. S. Myers, *Mind and Work*, p. 23, quoted in Georges Friedman, in *Industrial Society*, London: Free Press of Glencoe, 1955, p. 58.

17. Fritz J. Roethlisberger and W. J. Dickson, *Management and the Worker*, Cambridge, Mass.: Harvard University Press, 1939. See also, Thomas N. Whitehead, *Leadership in a Free Society*, 1936; *The Industrial Worker*, 1938; and Fritz Roethlisberger, *Management and Morale*, 1941, all published by Harvard University Press.

18. Elton Mayo, *The Human Problems of an Industrial Civilization*, New York: Macmillan, 1933; *Teamwork and Labor Turnover in the Aircraft Industry of Southern California*, Boston, Mass.: Division of Research, Graduate School of Business Administration, Harvard University, 1944; *The Social Problems of an Industrial Civilization*, Boston, Mass.: Harvard University, 1947.

19. Lloyd H. Fisher and Ruth Deutsch, "Plant Sociology: The Elite and the Aborigines," in Clark Kerr (ed.), *Labor and Management in industrial Society*, New York: Anchor Books, Doubleday, 1964 p. 44.

20. Herbert Simon, Donald Smithburg, and Victor Thompson, *Public Administration*, New York: Alfred Knopf, 1950, pp. 113-14.

21. A. Zalesnik, C. R. Christensen, and F. J. Roethlisberger, *The Motivation, Productivity, and Satisfaction of Workers: A Prediction Study*, Boston: Harvard University Graduate School of Business Administration, 1958.

22. Leonard Sayles, *op.cit.*

23. Stanley E. Seashore, *Group Cohesiveness in the Industrial Work Group*, Ann Arbor: University of Michigan, 1954.

24. A. Zalesnik, *Worker Satisfaction and Development*, Boston: Harvard University Press, 1956, p. i.

25. *Ibid.*, p. iii.

26. Sayles, p. 2.

27. Zalesnik, *et al.*, 1958.

28. John R. P. French, Jr. and Alvin Zander, "The Group Dynamics Approach," in *Psychology of Labor Management Relations*, edited by Arthur Kornhauser, Champaign, Illinois: Industrial Relations Research Association, 1949, discuss some of the problems for managers.

29. For examples see Robert Bales, *Interaction Process Analysis*, Cam-

bridge, Mass.: Addison, Wesley Press, 1950; and A. Paul Hare, Edgar F. Bogota, and Robert F. Bales (ed.), *Small Group Studies in Social Interaction*, New York: Alfred A. Knopf, 1966.

30. William Foote Whyte, *Organizational Behavior, Theory and Application*, Homewood, Ill.: Richard D. Irwin, and the Dorsey Press, 1969, p. 166.

31. Harrison Trice, "Night Watchmen: A Study of an Isolated Occupation," *ILR Research*, vol. 10:2 (1960), 3-9, reported in Whyte, p. 99.

32. Allen M. Schwartzbaum, "Lateral Interaction and Effectiveness in Vertical Organizations," unpublished Ph.D. thesis, Cornell University, 1968, p. 55, cited in Whyte, p. 107.

33. Michel Crozier, *The Bureaucratic Phenomenon*, Chicago: University of Chicago Press, 1964, p. 28.

34. Elliott D. Chapple, "The Standard Experimental (Stress) Interview as used in Interaction Chronograph Investigations," *Human Organization*, vol. 12:2 (Summer, 1953), 23-32; and Chapple, *et al.*, "Behavioral Definition of Personality and Temperament Characteristics," *Human Organization*, vol. 13:4 (Winter 1955), 34-39.

35. A useful critique is given in George Strauss, "Some Notes on Power-Equalization," *Social Science of Organizations*, edited by Harold J. Leavitt, Englewood Cliffs, N.J.: Prentice-Hall, 1963, pp. 41-84.

36. Among the proponents of theories in this general direction are Chris Argyris (*Interpersonal Competence and Organizational Effectiveness*, Homewood, Ill.: Richard D. Irwin, and the Dorsey Press, 1962); Peter Blau (*Exchange and Power in Social Life*, New York: John Wiley, 1964); George C. Homans (*The Human Group*, New York: Harcourt Brace, 1950); R. Likert (*New Patterns of Management*, New York: McGraw-Hill, 1961); A. H. Mazlow (*Motivation and Personality*, New York: Harper and Brothers, 1954); and Frederick Herzberg, B. Maussner, and B. Snyderman (*The Motivation to Work*, New York: John Wiley, 1959).

37. Chris Argyris, "The Individual and Organization: An Empirical Test," *Administrative Science Quarterly*, 4 (1959-60), 145-67.

38. *Ibid.*, p. 167.

39. George B. Strother, "Problems in the Development of a Social Science of Organization," in *The Social Science of Organizations*, edited by Harold J. Leavitt, Englewood Cliffs, N.J.: Prentice-Hall, 1963, p. 14.

40. Job design consultant at Case Western Reserve University cited in *New York Times*, April 2, 1972, as quoted in Harry Braverman, *Labor and Monopoly Capital*, New York: Monthly Review Press, 1974, p. 35.

41. Woodward, *op.cit.*, pp. 62-63.

42. Walker, Charles R. and Robert Guest, *The Man on the Assembly Line*, Cambridge, Mass.: Harvard University Press, 1952, pp. 91, 116-22. The findings are supported by U.S. Bureau of Labor Statistics for automobile assembly plants.

43. R. D. Algar *et al.*, "Report of the Task Force on Hourly Employee Turnover," 1973, for Alcan at Kitimat, mimeo.

44. Unpublished data compiled by M. P. Marchak in connection with study of forestry towns in British Columbia during 1974-77.

45. J. A. MacMillan, J. R. Tulloch, D. O'Brien, M. A. Ahmad, *Determinants of Labor Turnover in Canadian Mining Communities*, Series 2:19, Winnipeg, Man.: Center for Settlement Studies, University of Manitoba, 1974.

46. See, for reviews of the literature and new studies, series published by Center for Settlement Studies, University of Manitoba, including L. B. Siemens, *Single-Enterprise Community Studies in Northern Canada*, series 5:7, 1973; John S. Matthiasson and James N. Kerri, *Two Studies on Fort McMurray*, Series 2:6, 1971; and P. H. Wichern, G. Kunka, and D. Waddell, *The Production and Testing of a Model of Political Development in Resource Frontier Communities*, Series 2:4, 1971.

47. Algar, *op.cit.* See also Don Bryant, Cal Hoyt, and Bert Painter, *Labour Instability in the Skeena Manpower Area*, Vancouver: The B.C. Research Council, 1978; and Don Bryant and Bert Painter, *Action Research at Mackenzie*, Report no. 1, prepared for B.C. Forest Products Ltd., Woods Products (Mackenzie division), project #76-5460, Vancouver: The B.C. Research Council, August 1976.

48. This observation and others following are based on my own research on forestry communities in B.C. Data not yet published.

49. Rex Lucas, *Minetown, Milltown, Railtown: Life in Canadian Communities of Single Industry*, Toronto: University of Toronto Press, 1971, esp. pp. 140-41.

50. A study of this experiment was conducted by a team of researchers at the Tavistock Institute, and is reported in Eliott Jaques, *The Changing Culture of a Factory*, London: Tavistock Publications, 1951. The impact of the research is the subject of a later book by the managing director of the firm, Wilfred Brown, *Exploration in Management*, New York: John Wiley, 1960.

51. Jaques, *op.cit.*, p. 64.

52. West Germany Trade Union Federation (DGB), "Co-Determination in the Federal Republic of Germany," reprinted in Gerry Hunnius, G. David Garson, and John Case (eds.) *Workers' Control. A Reader on Labor and Social Change*, New York: Vintage Books, 1973 pp. 194-210, at p. 198. This reader also contains discussion of advances

in workers' control in Yugoslavia and Israel, and of isolated examples elsewhere.

53. See for example, Helmut Schauer, "Critique of Co-determination," in Hunnius, *et al.*, *op.cit.*, pp. 210-24.

54. Peter H. Pearse, *Timber Rights and Forest Policy in British Columbia*, Victoria: Queen's Printer, 1976, vol. I, p. 61.

55. Based on interviews with both small business owners and workers, and large business managers and workers throughout B.C. in my own study, cited above.

56. Philip Mathias, *Forced Growth*, Toronto: James Lewis & Samuel, 1971.

57. Elliott Leyton, *Dying Hard, The Ravages of Industrial Carnage*, Toronto: McClelland and Stewart, 1975.

58. The Institute of Social and Economic Research, Memorial University, St. John's, Newfoundland, publishes a series entitled Newfoundland Social and Economic Studies. Among these are David Alexander, *The Decay of Trade, An Economic History of the Newfoundland Saltfish Trade, 1935-1965*, Study no. 19, 1977; Tom Philbrook, *Fisherman, Logger, Merchant, Miner: Social Change and Industrialism in Three Newfoundland Communities*, Study no. 1, 1966; Ottar Brox, *Newfoundland Fishermen in the Age of Industry*, Study no. 9, 1972; Cato Wadel, *Now, Whose Fault is That?*, Study no. 11, 1972; and Noel Iverson and D. Ralph Matthews, *Communities In Decline*, Study no. 6, 1968.

59. The band at Aiyansh, B.C., now has the local school on its reserve, and provides staff for the teaching of the Nishga language. In addition this band organized the fishermen amongst its members into what has now become a major union in the fishing industry.

60. S. Ostry and M. A. Zaidi, *Labour Economics in Canada*, Toronto: Macmillan, 1972, Table 54, p. 266.

61. *Ibid.*, p. 283.

62. Women's Bureau, Labour Canada, *Women in the Labour Force: 1971 Facts and Figures*, Ottawa: Information Canada, 1972, Table 14. In 1971, 72 per cent of all clerical workers were women; 36.5 per cent of all women held paid jobs.

63. Patricia Marchak, "Bargaining Strategies of White-Collar Workers in B.C.," unpublished Ph.D. thesis, University of British Columbia, 1970. Several papers have been based on the data and current information on labour force participation. These include: Marchak, "Les femmes, le travail, et le syndicalisme," *Sociologie et Sociétés*, vol. 6:1 (May 1974), 35-53, reprinted in English as "Women, Work and Unions," in *International Journal of Sociology*, vol. 5:4 (Winter 1975-76).

64. Jenny R. Podoluk, *Incomes of Canadians*, Dominion Bureau of Statistics, Ottawa: Queen's Printer, 1968. Table 4.8, based on *1961 Census of Canada*, Occupations by Sex, Showing Age, Marital Status and Schooling, Table 17 (cat. no. 94-509).

65. Several studies have been conducted on this relationship, including particularly, Byron G. Spencer and Dennis C. Featherstone, *Married Female Labour Force Participation: A Micro Study*, Ottawa: Dominion Bureau of Statistics, 1970. The subject is re-examined with even stronger conclusions by M. Patricia Connelly in "The Economic Context of Women's Labour Force Participation in Canada," in Patricia Marchak (ed.), *The Working Sexes*, Institute of Industrial Relations, UBC, 1977.

66. Leo A. Johnson, *Incomes, Disparity and Impoverishment in Canada since World War II*, Toronto: New Hogtown Press, 1973, pp. 17-20.

67. For well-documented examples from a large sample survey, see: Elisabeth Humphreys, "Role Bargaining: A Means of Adaptation to Strain within Dual Work Families," unpublished MA thesis, UBC, 1974. Also, Martin Meissner, Elisabeth W. Humphreys, Scott M. Meis, and William J. Scheu, "No Exit for Wives: Sexual Division of Labour and the Cumulation of Household Demands," *Canadian Review of Sociology and Anthropology*, vol. 12:4 (Part 1 [1975]), 424-39. The theme is further expanded in Martin Meissner, "Sexual Division of Labour and Inequality: Labour and Leisure," in M. Stephenson (ed.), *Women in Canada*, 2nd revised edition, Don Mills, Ont.: General Publishing, 1977.

68. For one interpretation of this position see Dorothy Smith, "Women, the Family and Corporate Capitalism," in M. Stephenson (ed.), *Women in Canada*, Toronto: New Press, 1973. This article is quoted in Ch. 8.

69. Harold J. Leavitt and Thomas L. Shisler, "Management in the 1980's," *Harvard Business Review*, November-December 1958, pp. 41-49; Ida Russakoff Hoos, *Automation in the Office*, Washington, D.C., Public Affairs Press, 1961.

70. Leavitt and Shisler, *ibid.*

71. Marchak, *op.cit.*, 1970.

72. Analysis of trends in unemployment statistics as they affect women are contained in Morley Gunderson, "Work Patterns," in Gail Cook (ed.), *Opportunities for Choice: A Goal for Women in Canada*, Ottawa: Statistics Canada and C. D. Howe Institute, 1976, Ch. 6; Beth Niemi, "Geographic Immobility and Labour Force Mobility: A Study of Female Unemployment," in Cynthia B. Lloyd, *Sex, Discrimination and the Division of Labour*, New York: Columbia University Press, 1975, pp. 61-81; and Lorna Marsden, "Unemploy-

ment among Canadian Women: Some Sociological Problems Raised by its Increase," in Marchak (ed.), *op.cit.*, 1977.

73. For an extended and detailed argument to this effect see Harry Braverman, *Labor and Monopoly Capital*, New York: Monthly Review Press, 1974.

## Chapter 6: The Management of Management

1. George Konrad, *The Case Worker*, translated from Hungarian by Paul Aston, Toronto: Bantam, 1976, pp. 176-77, reprinted by permission of Harcourt Brace Jovanovich, Inc.

2. This is a paraphrase of Emile Durkheim, *The Division of Labor in Society*, translated by George Simpson, New York: Free Press, 1933 (1893 original), especially p. 267. The theory is discussed below.

3. Michel Crozier, *The Bureaucratic Phenomenon*, Chicago: University of Chicago Press, 1964, pp. 145-46.

4. Talcott Parsons (ed.), *Max Weber: The Theory of Social and Economic Organization*, New York: Free Press, 1947, pp. 145-46.

5. H. H. Gerth and C. Wright Mills, eds., *From Max Weber: Essays in Sociology*, New York: Oxford University Press, 1958, p. 215.

6. *Ibid.*, p. 214.

7. Indeed, the "dysfunctions of overconformity" or "working to the rule" have been the subject of worried attention by organizations theorists. A particularly stimulating essay on the subject is by Robert K. Merton, "Bureaucratic Structure and Personality," in Merton, *Social Theory and Social Structure*, London: Free Press of Glencoe, 1949.

8. George Strauss, "Tactics of Lateral Relationship: The Purchasing Agent," *Administrative Science Quarterly*, vol. 7:2 (September 1962), 160-86.

9. *Ibid.*, pp. 175-76.

10. Terrance Hanold, chairman of the executive committee, Pillsbury Company of Minneapolis, in Richard A. Jackson (ed.), *The Multinational Corporation and Social Policy. Special Reference to General Motors in South Africa*, New York: Praeger, 1974, p. 5.

11. *Ibid.*, p. 5.

12. *Ibid.*, p. 7.

13. Durkheim, *op.cit.*, p. 267.

14. J. G. March and Herbert A. Simon, *Organizations*, New York: John Wiley, 1964; R. M. Cyert and J. G. March, *A Behavioral Theory of the Firm*, Englewood Cliffs, N.J.: Prentice-Hall, 1963; Herbert Simon, *Administrative Behavior*, New York: Macmillan, 1955; and H. Simon, D. W. Smithburg and V. A. Thompson, *Public Administration*, New York: Alfred A. Knopf, 1966.

15. Simon *et al.*, *op.cit.*, p. 382.

16. Cyert and March, *op.cit.*, p. 43.
17. For an example of influence as contrasted with formal authority, see M. Dalton, *Men Who Manage*, New York: John Wiley, 1964.
18. Tom Burns and G. M. Stalker, *Management of Innovation*, London: Tavistock, 1968.
19. *Ibid.*, pp. 5-6.
20. *Ibid.*, Chs. 1,5, and 6. Detailed specification of the characteristics of organic as compared with mechanistic systems is given in Ch. 6.
21. *Ibid.*, pp. 121-22.
22. *Ibid.*, p. 122.
23. The study involved a fairly detailed examination of several Scottish firms, then a less detailed study of eight English firms. The general attributes of these firms are discussed at various points in the book, and an overall description of the sample is given in Ch. 1. This does not give an indication of the frequencies of the characteristics cited. The fact that the firms differed in their positions within larger corporate bodies is mentioned rather than examined.
24. Brian Campbell, "The Social Production of News," unpublished MA thesis, Department of Anthropology and Sociology, UBC, 1977.
25. Sonja Sinclair, "ITT Canada: An Inconspicuous Giant," *Canadian Business*, March, 1974, pp. 6-13.
26. *Forbes, The Forbes 500s Annual Directory Issue*, May 15, 1977.
27. Anthony Sampson, *The Sovereign State of ITT*, Greenwich, Conn.: Fawcett, 1973.
28. Sinclair, *op.cit.* All quotations are from this article.
29. Dr. M. Gloor, "Policies and Practices of Nestlé Alimentana SA," in British Institute of Management, conference on Multinational Companies, July 1968, pp. 2, 3, 12-13; as cited in I. A. Litvak and C. J. Maule, "Foreign Subsidiaries as an Instrument of Host Government Policy," in *Nationalism and the Multinational Enterprise*, H. R. Hahlo, J. Graham Smith, Richard W. Wright (eds.), New York: Oceana Publications, 1973, p. 201.
30. Hanold, *op.cit.*, p. 11.
31. Anthony W. Connole, administrative assistant to vice-president, United Auto Workers, in Jackson, *op.cit.*, pp. 15-16.
32. Ernie Regehr, *Making a Killing: Canada's Arms Industry*, Toronto: McClelland and Stewart, 1975, p. 34.
33. Bruce Page, Phillip Knightey, Elaine Potter, Antony Terry, "Behind the Thalidomide Tragedy," *Sunday Times of London*, June 27, 1976, reprinted in *Atlas World Press Review*, September 1976, pp. 15-20. All quotations are from this reprint.
34. Ellis N. Brandt, "Napalm – Public Relations Storm Center," *Public Relations Journal*, July 1968, pp. 12-13, is quoted in S. Prakash

Sethi, *Up against the Corporate Wall*, Englewood Cliffs, N.J.: Prentice-Hall, 1971, p. 265.

35. *Ibid.*, p. 255, based on interview by Sethi with public relations department executive.

36. Merton, *op.cit.*, p. 197.

37. Thornton V. Greenhill, quoted in "Life on the Assembly Line," by David Lewis Stein, *Weekend Magazine*, September 24, 1977, p. 12.

38. Lawrence J. Lasser, "Dow Chemical Company," case study for classes at the Harvard Business School, 1968, pp. 27-32, cited in Sethi, *op.cit.*, p. 251.

39. Walter Ullmann, *The Growth of Papal Government in the Middle Ages*, London: Methuen, 1955, p. 3.

40. Anon. *The Seneschaucy*, from Walter of Henley and Other Treatises on Estate Management and Accounting, Dorothea Oschinsky (ed.), London: Oxford University Press, 1971, pp. 265-95.

## Chapter 7: Ownership and Control

1. Joseph Schumpeter, *Social Classes and Imperialism*, two essays translated by Heinz Norden, Cleveland: World Publishing Company, 1955, p. 137.

2. *Ibid.*, p. 151.

3. Adolf A. Berle, Jr. and Gardiner C. Means, *The Modern Corporation and Private Property*, New York: Macmillan, 1932. See also an updated version of this in A. Berle Jr., *Power without Property*, New York: Harcourt, Brace and World, 1959. The term "managerial revolution" was made popular by James Burnham, in *The Managerial Revolution*, New York: John Day, 1941.

4. United States Temporary National Economic Committee, *The Distribution of Ownership in the 200 Largest Nonfinancial Corporations*, Monograph No. 29, Washington, 1940.

5. Much the same argument is apparent in, for example, John Kenneth Galbraith, *The New Industrial State*, Boston: Houghton Mifflin, 1967.

6. Robert J. Larner, "Ownership and Control in the 200 Largest Nonfinancial Corporations: 1929 and 1963," *American Economic Review*, vol. 56:4 (September 1966), pp. 777-87.

7. Robert J. Larner, *Management Control and the Large Corporation*, New York: Dunellen Publishing, 1970.

8. Robert Sheehan, "Proprietors in the World of Big Business," *Fortune*, vol. 74:1 (June 15, 1967), pp. 178-83.

9. Philip H. Burch, Jr., *The Managerial Revolution Reassessed*, Lexington, Mass.: Lexington Books, 1972.

10. *Ibid.*, Ch. 2 outlines sampling methods.
11. *Ibid.*, p. 18.
12. *Ibid.*, Table A-1.
13. John Porter, *The Vertical Mosaic*, Toronto: University of Toronto Press, 1956; Wallace Clement, *Canadian Corporate Elite*, Toronto: McClelland and Stewart, 1975.
14. Clement, 1975, pp. 340-48.
15. Wallace Clement, *Continental Corporate Power*, Toronto: Mc-Clelland and Stewart, 1977, Appendix XIII, Table XII-2.
16. U.S. Securities and Exchange Commission, 1969 ("Institutional Investors Study"), reported and analysed in Robert M. Soldofsky, *Institutional Holdings of Common Stock, 1900-2000: History Projection, Interpretation*, Michigan Business Studies 18, no. 3, Ann Arbor, Mich.: Bureau of Business Research, University of Michigan, 1971; and in Phillip I. Blumberg, *The Megacorporation in American Society: The Scope of Corporate Power*, Ch. 5.
17. Civil Aeronautics Board Report, *Thirty Largest Stockholders of U.S. Certified Air Carriers and Summary of Stock Holdings of Financial Institutions* (1974), as reported in Blumberg, *op.cit.*, pp. 100-1.
18. *Fortune*, vol. 89:4 (January 1974), p. 54.
19. Heidrick and Struggles, Inc., *Profile of the Board of Directors*, Chicago: Heidrick and Struggles, 1971.
20. Robert T. Averitt, *The Dual Economy*: The Dynamics of American Industry Structure. New York: W. W. Norton, 1968. Salaries of various executives for dominant corporations are given in Clement, *op.cit.*, 1977, Appendix XIII.
21. Mabel Newcomber, *The Big Business Executive: The Factors That Made Him, 1900-1950*, New York: Columbia University Press, 1955. Data on board memberships given in Ch. 3. All of the figures cited below are from this source.
22. For a detailed account of the Gulf transactions, see John J. McCloy, *The Great Oil Spill*, New York: Chelsea House Publishers, 1976.
23. *Forbes*, May 15, 1976, p. 76, quoting J. Peter Grace, president and chief executive officer of W. R. Grace and Company, p. 76.
24. There is a voluminous literature designed to inform managers about government sources for funds. Among these are John S. Ewing and Frank Meissner, *International Business Management*, Belmont, Calif.: Wadsworth Publishing Co., 1964, which includes an article by Business International, "Financing Foreign Operations," pp. 210-37; another by Raymond F. Mikesell, "The World Bank in a Changing World," pp. 203-10. These provide an indication of the extent of government aid to "developing corporations."
25. As reported in Phillip Burch, *op.cit.*, pp. 134-35.

26. Stuart Clark, branch manager, Bank of Montreal, letter to the editor, *The Ubyssey*, student newspaper at University of British Columbia, November 10, 1977.

27. Peter Newman, *The Canadian Establishment*, vol. I, Toronto: McClelland and Stewart, 1975; Clement, 1977.

28. Clement, 1975, p. 163.

29. Porter, *op.cit.*

30. Clement, 1975, pp. 164-66, and Appendix X.

31. Porter, p. 589.

32. Clement, 1975, pp. 166-68.

33. Michael Ornstein, "The Size, Composition, and Interlocks among the Directorates and Executives of the Largest Canadian Corporations," presented to the session on Canadian Corporations at the meetings of the Canadian Sociology and Anthropology Association, Edmonton, May 1975, p. 19.

34. Clement, 1975, pp. 163-64.

35. Ornstein, pp. 18-19.

36. *Ibid.*, pp. 11-15.

37. *Ibid.*, pp. 15-17.

38. Terrence White, "Some Methodological Problems in the Study of Corporate Boards of Directors," presented to the session on Canadian Corporations at the meetings of the CSAA, Edmonton, May 1975. Data are reported in Tables 1 to 4, appendices to the paper.

39. Newman, *op.cit.*, from lists on pp. 91-94 for 1975.

40. *Ibid.*, p. 113.

41. *Ibid.*, pp. 110-11.

42. Government of Canada, *Foreign Direct Investment in Canada*, Ottawa: Queen's Printer, 1972, Tables 9 and 10, and pp. 24-26.

43. *Ibid.*

44. This and subsequent figures are reported in CALURA, 1972, statement 11, and pp. 27 and 28.

45. Michael Z. Brooke and H. Lee Remmers, *The Strategy of Multinational Enterprise, Organization and Finance*, Bristol: Longman, 1970, p. 157.

46. Given the availability of Canadian funds and the eagerness of the financial community to supply these, it is difficult to advance the argument on the basis of financial evidence. It should be recalled, however, that the argument is about sources of economic power, not sources of influence.

### Conclusion

1. J. D. Ketchum, "Hymn to the Glory of Free Enterprise," first published in *The Nation*, New York, March 18, 1944, republished in F. R. Scott and A. J. M. Smith, *The Blasted Pine*, Toronto: Mac-

millan, 1957. According to Scott and Smith, the poem was set to music for the Toronto revue, *Spring Thaw*, in 1954. The solo parts, by various presidents of business enterprises, were careful paraphrases of speeches by prominent Canadians during World War II.

2. Ron Longstaffe, quoted in the *Vancouver Sun*, November 15, 1977.

3. For an argument to the effect that the state in United States faces a financial crisis, see James O'Connor, *The Fiscal Crisis of the State*, New York: St. Martin's Press, 1973.

4. Pierre Eliott Trudeau, speech to the Canadian Clubs of Ottawa, as published in text in the *Vancouver Sun*, January 20, 1976. Subsequent quotations are from this speech.

5. J. T. McLeod, "The Free Enterprise Dodo is No Phoenix," in *Canadian Forum*, August 1976, pp. 6-13.

6. K. W. McNaught, "Plus ça change," *Canadian Forum*, August 1976, pp. 10-11.

7. See, for examination of these changes, Reg Whitaker, "Images of the State in Canada," in Leo Panitch (ed.), *The Canadian State*, Toronto: University of Toronto Press, 1978.

# SUGGESTED FURTHER READING

### I. Canadian Political Economy and Class Structure

Alexander, David. *The Decay of Trade: An Economic History of the Newfoundland Saltfish Trade, 1935-1965.* Newfoundland Social and Economic Studies No. 19. St. John's Nfld: Institute of Social and Economic Research, Memorial University, 1977.

Armstrong, Pat and Hugh Armstrong. *The Double Ghetto: Canadian Women and Their Segregated Work.* Toronto: McClelland and Stewart, 1978.

Bercuson, David J. *Fools and Wise Men. The Rise and Fall of the One Big Union.* Toronto: McGraw-Hill Ryerson, 1978.

Bercuson, David J. (ed.). *Canada and the Burden of Unity.* Toronto: Macmillan of Canada, 1978.

Bliss, Michael. *A Living Profit. Studies in the Social History of Canadian Business, 1883-1911.* Toronto: McClelland and Stewart, 1974.

Bourgault, Pierre. *Innovation and the Structure of Canadian Industry.* Ottawa: Science Council of Canada, 1972.

Brox, Ottar. *Newfoundland Fishermen in an Age of Industry: A Study of Economic Dualism.* St. John's, Nfld.: Institute for Social and Economic Research, Memorial University, 1972.

Clement, Wallace. *The Canadian Corporate Elite.* Toronto: McClelland and Stewart, 1975.

Clement, Wallace. *Continental Corporate Power.* Toronto: McClelland and Stewart, 1975.

Deverell, John and the Latin American Working Group. *Falconbridge: Portrait of a Canadian Mining Multinational.* Toronto: James Lorimer, 1975.

Easterbrook, W. T. and Hugh G. J. Aitken. *Canadian Economic History.* Toronto: Macmillan, Canada, 1956.

Easterbrook, W. T. and M. Watkins (eds.). *Approaches to Canadian Economic History.* Toronto: McClelland and Stewart, 1967.

Government of Canada. *Foreign Direct Investment in Canada.* Ottawa: Information Canada, 1972.

Grant, George. *Lament for a Nation.* Toronto: McClelland and Stewart, 1965.

Grant, George. *Technology and Empire.* Toronto: Anansi, 1969.

Innis, H. A., *Essays in Canadian Economic History.* Toronto: University of Toronto Press, 1956.

Innis, H. A. *The Fur Trade in Canada: An Introduction to Canadian*

*Economic History.* Toronto: University of Toronto Press, 1956.

Jamieson, Stuart M. *Times of Trouble: Labour Unrest and Industrial Conflict in Canada, 1900-66.* Ottawa: Information Canada, 1972.

Kilbourn, William. *The Elements Combined. A History of the Steel Company of Canada.* Toronto: Clarke, Irwin, 1960.

Laxer, R. M. (ed.). *(Canada) Ltd.* Toronto: McClelland and Stewart, 1973.

Laxer, Robert. *Canada's Unions.* Toronto: James Lorimer, 1976.

Levitt, Kari. *Silent Surrender: The Multinational Corporation in Canada.* Toronto: Macmillan of Canada, 1971.

Litvak, I. A., C. J. Maule, and R. D. Robinson. *Dual Loyalty. Canadian-U.S. Business Arrangements.* Toronto: McGraw-Hill, 1971.

Lucas, Rex. *Minetown, Milltown, Railtown.* Toronto: University of Toronto Press, 1971.

MacMillan, D. (ed.). *Canadian Business History, Selected Studies, 1490-1971.* Toronto: McClelland and Stewart, Toronto, 1972.

Macpherson, C. B. *Democracy in Alberta.* Toronto: University of Toronto Press, 1962.

Macpherson, C. B. *The Real World of Democracy.* Oxford: Clarendon Press, 1966.

Marchak, M. Patricia. *Ideological Perspectives on Canada.* Toronto: McGraw-Hill, 1975.

Mathias, Philip. *Forced Growth: 5 Studies of Government Involvement in the Development of Canada.* Toronto: James Lewis & Samuel, 1971.

Myers, Gustavus. *The History of Canadian Wealth.* Toronto: James Lewis & Samuel, 1972 (original publication, 1913).

Naylor, Tom. *The History of Canadian Business, 1867-1914.* Vol. 1: *The Banks and Finance Capital.* Vol. 2: *Industrial Development.* Toronto: James Lorimer, 1975.

Neufeld, E. P. *A Global Corporation. A History of the International Development of Massey-Ferguson Ltd.* Toronto: University of Toronto Press, 1969.

Neufeld, E. P. (ed.). *Money and Banking in Canada.* Toronto: McClelland and Stewart, 1964.

Newman, Peter C. *The Canadian Establishment.* Toronto: McClelland and Stewart, 1975.

Panitch, Leo (ed.). *The Canadian State. Political Economy and Political Power.* Toronto: University of Toronto Press, 1978.

Pearse, Peter H. (ed.). *The Mackenzie Pipeline, Arctic Gas and Canadian Energy Policy.* Toronto: McClelland and Stewart, 1974.

Pentland, H. C. "The Development of a Capitalistic Labour Market in Canada," *Canadian Journal of Economic and Political Science,* 25 (1959), 450-61.

Phillips, W. G. *The Agricultural Implement Industry in Canada, a Study of Competition.* Toronto: University of Toronto Press, 1956.

Porter, John. *The Vertical Mosaic.* Toronto: University of Toronto Press, 1965.

Pratt, Larry. *The Tar Sands, Syncrude and the Politics of Oil.* Edmonton: Hurtig, 1976.

Rae, K. J. *The Political Economy of the Canadian North.* Toronto: University of Toronto Press, 1968.

Ryerson, Stanley. *Unequal Union.* Toronto: Progress Books, 1968.

Teeple, Gary (ed.). *Capitalism and the National Question in Canada.* Toronto: University of Toronto Press, 1973.

Warnock, John W. *Partner to Behemoth. The Military Policy of a Satellite Canada.* Toronto: New Press, 1970.

Watkins, M. H. "The Staple Theory Revisited," *Journal of Canadian Studies,* vol. 12:5 (Winter 1977).

Whitaker, Reg. *The Government Party: Organizing and Financing the Liberal Party of Canada, 1930-1958.* Toronto: University of Toronto Press, 1970.

## II. General Studies of Multinational Corporations and Technology

Averitt, Robert T. *The Dual Economy: The Dynamics of American Industry Structure.* New York: W. W. Norton, 1964.

Baker, Elizabeth Faulkner. *Technology and Woman's Work.* New York: Columbia University Press, 1968.

Barnet, Richard J. and Ronald E. Muller. *Global Reach, The Power of the Multinational Corporations.* New York: Simon and Schuster, 1974.

Berle, Adolf A., Jr. *Power without Property.* New York: Harcourt, Brace and World, 1959.

Berle, Adolf A., Jr., and Gardiner Means. *The Modern Corporation and Private Property.* New York: Macmillan, 1948 (originally published 1932).

Blauner, R. *Alienation and Freedom: The Factory Worker and His Industry.* Chicago: University of Chicago Press, 1964.

Blumberg, Philip I. *The Megacorporation in American Society: The Scope of Corporation Power.* Englewood Cliffs, N.J.: Prentice-Hall, 1975.

Bright, James R. *Automation and Management.* Boston: Division of Research, Graduate School of Business Administration, Harvard University, 1958.

Brooke, Michael A. and Lee H. Remmers. *The Strategy of Multinational Enterprise.* New York: Longman, 1970.

Brown, Courtney (ed.). *World Business.* New York: Macmillan, 1970.

Burch, Philip H. *The Managerial Revolution Reassessed: Family Con-*

*trol in America's Largest Corporations.* Lexington, Mass.: D. C. Heath, Lexington Books, 1972.

Faunce, William A. *Problems of an Industrial Society.* New York: McGraw-Hill, 1968.

Galbraith, John Kenneth. *The New Industrial State.* New York: New American Library, revised edition 1971.

Hanlo, H. R., J. Graham Smith, and Richard W. Wright (eds.). *Nationalism and the Multinational Enterprise.* New York: Oceana Publications, 1973.

Heilbroner, Robert L. *et al. In the Name of Profit: Profiles in Corporate Irresponsibility.* Garden City, N.Y.: Doubleday, 1972.

Hoos, Ida Russakoff. *Automation in the Office.* Washington, D.C.: Public Affairs Press, 1961.

Jewkes, J., D. Sawers, and R. Stillerman. *The Sources of Invention.* New York: W. W. Norton, 1970.

Kaplan, A. D. H. *Big Enterprise in a Competitive System.* Washington, D.C.: Brookings Institute, 1964.

Kindleberger, Charles P. *American Business Abroad.* New Haven: Yale University Press, 1969.

Kindleberger, Charles P. *The International Corporation: A Symposium.* Cambridge, Mass.: MIT Press, 1970.

Kranzberg, Melvin and Carroll W. Pusell, Jr. (eds.). *Technology in Western Civilization.* New York: Oxford University Press, 1967. 2 volumes.

Larner, Robert J. *Management Control and the Large Corporation.* New York: Dunellen Publishing Co., 1970.

Mansfield, Edwin. *Technological Change.* New York: W. W. Norton, 1971.

Mansfield, Edwin (ed.). *Monopoly Power and Economic Performance: The Problem of Industrial Concentration.* New York: W. W. Norton, 1974.

Mansfield, Edwin, J. Rapoport, J. Schnee, S. Wagner, and M. Hamburger. *Research and Innovation in the Modern Corporation.* New York: W. W. Norton, 1972.

Meissner, Martin. *Technology and the Worker. Technical Demands and Social Processes in Industry.* San Francisco, Calif.: Chandler, 1969.

Phillips, Almarin. *Technology and Market Structure, A Study of the Aircraft Industry.* Lexington, Mass.: Heath Lexington, 1971.

Rowthorn, Robert and Stephen Hymer. *International Big Business.* New York: Cambridge University Press, 1971.

Sampson, Anthony. *The Seven Sisters.* London: Hodder and Stoughton, 1975.

Sampson, Anthony. *The Sovereign State of ITT.* Greenwich, Conn: Fawcett, 1974.

Sherer, F. M. *The Economics of Multi-Plant Operation: An International Comparisons Study.* Cambridge, Mass.: Harvard University Press, 1975.

Schmookler, J. *Invention and Economic Growth.* Cambridge, Mass.: Harvard University Press, 1966.

Sethi, S. Prakish and Richard H. Holton (eds.). *Management of the Multinationals. Policies, Operations, and Research.* New York: Free Press, 1974.

Tugendhat, Christopher. *The Multinationals.* London: Eyre and Spottiswoode, 1971.

Turner, Louis. *Multinational Companies and the Third World.* New York: Hill and Wang, 1973.

Vernon, Raymond (ed.). *The Oil Crisis.* New York: W. W. Norton, 1976.

Wilkins, Mira. *The Emergence of Multinational Enterprise: American Business Abroad from the Colonial Era to 1914.* Cambridge, Mass.: Harvard University Press, 1970.

Wilkins, Mira. *The Maturing of Multinational Enterprise.* Cambridge, Mass., Harvard University Press, 1974.

# INDEX

,58, 256, 264, 267; and
government intervention,
267; "Hymn" to, 256
"free labour force," 8, 162;
*see also* labour
"free market," 9, 96, 99, 264
"free world," 8, 14, 15, 27,
150, 184, 245, 267
French government
organization, 203
fuel and energy industries,
76-80; 107-9, 113-22,
124-37, 158-59


**G**
Galbraith, John Kenneth,
89-92
Galt, A.T., 103
Galtung, John, 101
General Electric, 44
General Motors, 43, 44, 47
84, 106, 135, 141, 151, 238
general strike, 264
"general will," 54
Genstar, 43
Germany, 223, 229; West,
185
"good management," 172
Goodyear Tire and
Rubber, 106
Government of Canada,
*see* Canada; *see also*
province names
Grace, J. Peter, 242, 243
Grant, George, 14, 60
Great Canadian Oil Sands,
116, 117
Great Slave Lake, NWT, 114
Green Joe, 116
Grünenthal, 223
Guest, Robert, 181
Gulf Oil, 43, 46, 47, 79, 87,
113, 117, 121, 122, 241

**H**
Hamilton, Ontario, 48,
50-51
Hawthorne works, 175-76;
- paradox, 181
Heidrick and Struggles,
Inc., 238
Hertz Rent-A-Car, 112
hierarchical bureaucracy,
202-12
Hincks, Sir Francis, 104
Holland, 28
Hollerith, Herman, 144
Hollinger Mines, 43, 149,
252
Home Oil, 253
"horizontal" level of
bureaucracy, 206
House, Douglas, 118, 119
Hudson's Bay Company, 31,
104, 228
Hughes Aircraft, 235
"human relations"
management school,
175-79, 182
Hutterites, 187
hydro-electricity, Canada,
109-10
Hydro Quebec, 109
"Hymn to the Glory of Free
Enterprise," 256

**I**
ideology, 8, 9; capitalist, 53;
continentalist, 270; in
coalition theory, 227-28;
corporatist, 8-9, 14, 17,
268-71; early capitalist, 29;
fascist, 268-70; "free
enterprise," 9, 17, 54, 58,
256, 264; "free world,"
8, 14, 15, 27, 150, 184,
245, 267; of the "human
relations" school, 175-76;

research a: ·l development,
83-87; *see also* technical
development
resource industries labour
force, 163, 167, 182-84
Ricardo, David, 212
Richard II, 31
risk-taking, 157-59
Robin Hood Multifoods, 76
Rockefeller, John D., 78-79;
family, 235
Rothman's, 253
Rousseau, Jean Jacques, 53,
54, 267
Royal Bank of Canada, 248,
252-53
Royal Commission on
Canada's Economic
Prospects (1957), 107
Royal Commission on
Corporate Concentration
(1978), 44, 126, 260
Royal Commission on
Forest Resources (BC,
1976), 186
Russia, 48, 112

**S**
Sampson, Anthony, 79, 219
Saudi Arabia, 116
Savage, Tom, 219
Sayles, Leonard R., 160
Schultz Report (U.S., 1970),
109, 115, 116
Schumpeter, Joseph, 89, 91,
231
science, and ethics, 222-25;
and technical innovation,
61, 78, 82-95
Science Council of Canada,
85
scientific management, 64,
172-75
Seagram, 43, 253

Sheehan, Robert, 234
Shell Oil, 79, 113, 126
Simon, Herbert A., 202
Simpsons-Sears, 252
Sinclair, Sonja, 219
Singer sewing machines, 81,
82
SKF (Akteibolaget Kullager-
Fabriken), 152, 155
*Slocan Valley Report* (1975),
96, 97
small business owners, 57-58
small groups laboratories,
178
Smith, Adam, 53, 133, 212
Smith, Donald, 104
Social Contract, 53
socialism, 267
social science, 62, 273
Sombart, Werner, 23
South Africa, 246
Soviet industrial system, 25,
52
Soviet Union, 49
Spanish company, 31
spinning-jenny, 65
St. Lawrence Corporation,
Nfld., 11
Stalker, G.M., 202,
215-17, 228
Standard Broadcasting, 43
Standard Oil, 78-79; of New
Jersey, 44, 84, 101, 113,
235, 239; *see also*
Exxon and Imperial; of
California (SOCAL), 113
state (government): role of,
8-9, 31-32, 53-56, 96-102,
110-11, 158-59, 224, 255,
256-57, 263-71; in Canada,
85-87, 102-11, 114-17,
121-27, 255, 262, 271; and
United States, 98, 107-9,
115-17, 122, 224, 241, 262;